Contributions to Finance and

The book series 'Contributions to Finance and Accounting' features the latest research from research areas like financial management, investment, capital markets, financial institutions, FinTech and financial innovation, accounting methods and standards, reporting, and corporate governance, among others. Books published in this series are primarily monographs and edited volumes that present new research results, both theoretical and empirical, on a clearly defined topic. All books are published in print and digital formats and disseminated globally. This book series is indexed in Scopus.

Nordine Abidi • Bruno Buchetti •
Samuele Crosetti • Ixart Miquel-Flores

Why Do Banks Fail and What to Do About It

The Role of Risk Management, Governance, Accounting, and More

Nordine Abidi
International Monetary Fund
Bethesda, MD, USA

Bruno Buchetti
University of Padua and Toulouse Business School
Padua, Italy

Samuele Crosetti
Single Resolution Board
Brussels, Belgium

Ixart Miquel-Flores
European Central Bank
Frankfurt am Main, Germany

ISSN 2730-6038 ISSN 2730-6046 (electronic)
Contributions to Finance and Accounting
ISBN 978-3-031-52313-7 ISBN 978-3-031-52311-3 (eBook)
https://doi.org/10.1007/978-3-031-52311-3

This Springer imprint is published by the registered company Springer Nature Switzerland AG
The registered company address is: Gewerbestrasse 11, 6330 Cham, Switzerland

Authors' Comment

The authors' knowledge on the subject does not derive uniquely from academic background but also from the professional experience on the subject on primary institutions such as Credit Suisse AG, European Central Bank (ECB), Single Resolution Board (SRB), and International Monetary Fund (IMF).

This book should not be reported as representing the views of these institutions. The views expressed are those of the authors and do not necessarily reflect those of these organizations.

Disclaimer

This paper should not be reported as representing the views of the European Central Bank (ECB), the International Monetary Fund (IMF), or the Single Resolution Board (SRB). The views expressed are those of the authors and do not necessarily reflect those of the ECB, the IMF or the SRB. We thank Francesca Colombo for her valuable research assistance. The datasets employed in this book contain confidential statistical information. Its use for the purpose of the analysis described in the text has been approved by the relevant ECB decision making bodies. All the necessary measures have been taken during the preparation of the analysis to ensure the physical and logical protection of the information.

Introduction

Banking crises are not new. Countries all over the world continue to experience banking failures. These catastrophic events are generally considered of utmost importance because of the essential role banks play in the economy. Banking failures are mainly caused by major risk management deficiencies, creative accounting, inadequate internal control systems, and above all, greedy executive directors. However, questions arise, such as: Why do banks fail? What are the main drivers of these banking failures? Can we avoid a banking crisis? What happens when a bank fails?

Chapter 1 delves into the pivotal roles and functions of banks within the economic ecosystem. It highlights banks as essential intermediaries that facilitate liquidity provision, manage payments, transform assets, and oversee borrowers. Emphasizing their dual function of accepting deposits and granting loans, the chapter underscores the importance of banks in managing and mitigating various types of risks. The narrative further examines the emergent challenges in the banking sector, such as cyber threats, climate change implications, and geopolitical instabilities. Lastly, the chapter underscores the crucial role banks play in the transmission of monetary policy.

Banks are susceptible to a range of risks, and Chap. 2 investigates these risks and how they may trigger banking failures. These include liquidity risk (a bank's ability to meet its cash and collateral obligations), credit risk (the risk that a bank borrower will fail to meet its obligations), market risk (a bank's risk of losses in off and on-balance sheet positions arising from adverse movements in market prices), interest rate risk (the risk that a rise in interest rates could force the bank to pay relatively more on its deposits than it receives on its loans), and new risks (e.g. IT risk and environmental risks).

Chapter 3 describes and compares the financial statements of commercial and investment banks, explaining how they differ from those of non-financial companies. Moreover, it delves into the consequences of creative accounting and how these have played a major role in the most recent banking failures.

Chapter 4 outlines how governance issues can trigger banking failures, specifically how directors' insufficient risk monitoring through the board has played a vital role during the recent financial crisis.

Finally, Chap. 5 illustrates the functioning of resolution, detailing how resolution authorities have, over time, operationalized the resolvability of banks.

This book aims to explain why banks are important in today's economy, how they differ from other companies, the major risks they face in their day-to-day operations, and what happens when they fail (or are at risk of failing). All in all, this book makes a threefold contribution: for researchers, it describes the main drivers of banking failures; for regulators, it offers suggestions on how to improve banks' regulation; and for practitioners, it explains real cases of banking failures and how to manage them.

Contents

About the Authors

Dr. Nordine Abidi was an Economist in the Monetary Policy Department at the European Central Bank (ECB). He was responsible for monitoring, analysing, and conducting studies on the non-bank transmission of monetary policy and on cyclical and structural developments in the financial markets that have an impact on the euro area from a monetary policy perspective. He was also in charge of the evaluation of the ECB's corporate asset purchase programme. Since September 2019, he joined the International Monetary Fund (IMF) and worked on a variety of analytical and policy endeavours (e.g. monetary and capital market issues, policy response to the COVID-19 crisis, regional economic outlook). He obtained a PhD in Economics from Toulouse School of Economics, France in 2016.

Dr. Bruno Buchetti is an Assistant Professor of Financial Accounting at the University of Padua, Italy. He also serves as an Adjunct Professor at Toulouse Business School (TBS), where he teaches International Corporate Governance. Previously, he worked at the European Central Bank in Frankfurt am Main, Germany, as a Supervision Analyst in the 'COI – Centralized On-Site Inspections' division of the Single Supervisory Mechanism (SSM). He has also been employed at Credit Suisse AG in Zurich, Switzerland, as a bank inspector. Dr. Buchetti earned his PhD in Management and Innovation from UCSC University in Milan, Italy. He has a BSc in Economics and Business Administration and an MSc in Banking and Finance (earned with summa cum laude distinction). During his MSc studies, he was awarded a scholarship for academic merit and participated in an exchange program at Stanford University in California, USA. He is the author of *Corporate Governance and Firm Value in Italy: How Directors and Board Members Matter* and *Corporate Governance in the Banking Sector: Theory, Supervision, ESG, and Real Banking Failures*, both published by Springer Nature in 2021 and 2022, respectively. His primary research interests centre on corporate governance, financial accounting, and banking.

Samuele Crosetti is a Bank Resolution Expert at the Single Resolution Board (SRB), where he carries the ongoing tasks of resolution planning and resolvability assessment for the banks in its portfolio. Before joining the Single Resolution Board, he worked as Supervision Analyst in the European Central Bank, as part of the Joint Supervisory Team of a G-SIB and member of the ECB Brexit Task Force. Alongside his main professional activity, Samuele Crosetti is a PhD candidate at Maastricht University, where he is conducting research on the impact of resolution regimes and their operationalisation on financial and non-financial crisis resilience of banks. Since 2017, he has been pro bono teaching assistant of Public Economic Law at LUISS University in Rome.

Ixart Miquel-Flores is a doctoral candidate in the Finance Department at Frankfurt School of Finance & Management. He has as well been a visiting PhD student to the finance departments in The University of Virginia Darden School of Business, as well as The University of Chicago Booth School of Business.

He uses modern applied econometric methods to understand the effects and consequences of monetary policy, financial regulation and new technologies on the banking sector and other macro-financial stability issues, and he is focused on producing policy-relevant studies. His research has been the focus of articles in reputable newspapers such as the *Financial Times* and *Les Échos*, as well as blogs such as Quantpedia and the Oxford University Business Law Blog. Ixart works at the European Central Bank (ECB), where he has acquired experience in different fields such as Monetary Policy and Banking Supervision (Crisis Management, Market Risk and Valuation Banking Inspections, Quantitative Risk Analysis in the context of Market Risk Stress Testing as well as Banking Cyber Resilience Stress Testing). You can visit his website at: www.ixartmiquel.com.

Chapter 1
The Role of Banking

1 Banks Are at the Heart of the Financial System

They connect borrowers to savers and allocate available funds throughout the economy.[1] However, banking is also an inherently risky business. Banks lend money and make investments, and they can lose money if borrowers default on their loans or if investments go sour. According to the Federal Deposit Insurance Corporation (FDIC):'*A bank failure is the closing of a bank by a federal or state banking regulatory agency. Generally, a bank is closed when it is unable to meet its obligations to depositors and others.*'[2] Therefore, bank failures occur when a bank is unable to meet its obligations to depositors and other creditors. This can happen due to insolvency, when the value of the bank's assets is lower than the value of its liabilities, or because of illiquidity, when the bank is unable to meet its short-term obligations. Although the concepts of illiquidity and insolvency may seem close at first glance, distinguishing between them can be difficult during crisis times (Bernanke, 2013).

A sound understanding of a bank's balance sheet, which comprises its assets, liabilities, and capital (equity), is essential for the analysis of a large set of banking issues. Loans and securities are the primary assets on a bank's balance sheet. To obtain the capital necessary to make loans and acquire assets, banks also rely on liabilities and equity. Customer deposits (e.g. checking and savings accounts) and any debt the bank owes (e.g. bonds or short-term interbank loans) are the primary liabilities.[3] By law, the bank is obligated to repay these funds to its customers and lenders. From an accounting viewpoint, the bank's equity is simply computed

[1] In this chapter, the terms *'bank'* and *'commercial bank'* are used synonymously to refer as (1) a depository institution overseen and insured by a regulatory authority or (2) the holding company.

[2] https://www.fdic.gov/consumers/banking/facts/.

[3] See Box 'Case Study Bank of America'.

N. Abidi et al., *Why Do Banks Fail and What to Do About It*, Contributions to Finance and Accounting, https://doi.org/10.1007/978-3-031-52311-3_1

as the difference between its assets and liabilities. Equity represents therefore the shareholders' ownership. Mathematically, the bank's equity can be expressed as follows:

$$\text{Equity} = \text{Assets} - \text{Liabilities} \tag{1.1}$$

Case Study: Bank of America (BoA)
Assets:

- Total loans and leases: $1,051 billion. This is the largest asset category, and it represents the amount of money that the BoA has lent to its clients (e.g. households, non-financial firms).
- Cash and cash equivalents: $374 billion. This includes the most liquid assets that BoA has in its vaults and on deposit with other financial institutions.
- Investment securities: $756 billion. This represents, *inter alia*, treasuries, bonds, and other debt instruments.

Liabilities:

- Total deposits: $1,877 billion. Customers' deposit is the largest liability category.
- Long-term debt: $286 billion. This represents the securities and loans that BoA has issued on the market.
- Global Liquidity Sources (average): $867 billion. This represents other type of funding.

Equity:

- Common shareholders' equity: $255 billion. If all assets are liquidated and liabilities are repaid, the common equity will be split across equityholders.

As a financial intermediary, BoA provides important financial services to firms, households, and government entities. The bank offers loans to businesses for investment and it provides checking and savings accounts. BoA also plays a role in financial markets, by trading securities and derivatives. As of 2023, it is the second-largest US banking institution, after JPMorgan Chase, and the second-largest bank in the world by market capitalisation.[a] Given the BoA's size, the bank is also classified as a Global Systemically Important Bank (G-SIB), which means that its failure could have a significant impact on

[a]In December 2022, the FDIC reported that there were 4,715 US banks. The average total domestic deposits across the top 250 banks listed were about $65 billion. The top five banks by total domestic deposits were: JPMorgan Chase Bank: $2 trillion, Bank of America: $1.9 trillion, Wells Fargo Bank: $1.4 trillion Citigroup: $777 million.

(continued)

the global financial system. G-SIBs are viewed as *'too big to fail'* and subject to stricter regulation. For instance, all US G-SIBs are not only required to comply with some stricter capital ratio requirements but also required to submit an emergency Resolution Plan each year to the US regulator, i.e. the Federal Reserve.

Balance Sheet for Bank of America (BoA), Q2-2023

Item	Amount (in billion USD)
Assets	
Total loans and leases	1,051
Cash and cash equivalents	374
Investment securities	756
Liabilities	
Total deposits	1,877
Long-term debt	286
GLS—Global Liquidity Sources (average)	867[b]
Equity	
Common shareholders' equity	255

[b] GLS includes cash and high-quality, liquid, unencumbered securities, such as US government and agency securities, non-US government and supranational securities, and other investment-grade securities. It excludes Federal Reserve Discount Window or Federal Home Loan Bank borrowing capacity

In the event of a failure, the bank may attempt to meet its obligations by looking for financing from other solvent counterparties, selling its assets at *"fire sale"* prices or by borrowing from the central bank (i.e. lender of last resort). If solvent banks are unwilling or unable to provide liquidity (e.g. due to frozen interbank markets or counterparty risk), depositors may become worried and withdraw their funds, which can lead to a banking panic. In the past, this took the form of depositors *'running'* on a bank, when a large number of depositors withdraw their deposits because they believe the bank is insolvent or may become insolvent.[4] Today, given the technology and the role of wholesale short-term funding (e.g. repos, collateralized loans, commercial papers), runs can be more rapid and invisible (Gorton, 2010). In

[4] The movie "*It's a Wonderful Life* shows a classic example of a bank run: https://www.youtube.com/watch?v=iPkJH6BT7dM.

Fig. 1.1 The 2007 run on Northern Rock

Fig. 1.2 A bank run during the US Great Depression, February 1933

general, panics can further strain the bank's liquidity and make it more difficult to meet its debt-related obligations (Kindleberger et al., 2005) (Figs. 1.1 and 1.2).

Why Banks Are So Special? The short answer is that the collapse of a bank can have a more significant impact than the collapse of other firms. Unlike other businesses, banks can fail but their failure can have broader externalities—affecting depositors, other financial institutions and the market as a whole. For instance, customer deposits can be frozen, loan relationships can break down, and lines of credit that firms draw on to make payrolls or pay suppliers may not be renewed. In addition, one bank failure can lead to other bank failures, even if those institutions are financially sound. This is because depositors may withdraw their money from these institutions in fear of losing their savings. This contagion effect or negative externalities can magnify across the banking and financial system, amplifying the overall economic impact of such bank failures.[5] Economists typically refer to this as bank interconnectedness (Roncoroni et al., 2021; Jackson and Pernoud, 2021). Empirical studies have also shown that the market value of non-financial companies that are linked to a defaulting bank can be adversely affected (Brewer III et al., 2003).

The importance of bank stability has led to the implementation of stringent regulatory measures around the world,[6] particularly post-2008 Global Financial Crisis (GFC). These reforms which include *inter alia* new liquidity requirements, resolution planning, new stress tests, updated risk management standards, stronger capital requirements, and specific large bank supervisory processes aim at protecting depositors and preventing bank collapses from causing a systemic event or a significant economic recession (Borio et al., 2020; Dobler et al., 2021).

Nonetheless, the recent collapses of Silicon Valley Bank (SVB), Silvergate Bank, and Signature Bank have revived the debate on the priorities of reform and the fault lines in the global financial system. These collapses, and their international impact, particularly in Europe with Credit Suisse, which was later bought by its competitor UBS Group AG, have raised questions about whether post-GFC regulatory and supervisory frameworks are sufficient to protect the financial system as a whole from systemic risk. Indeed, these failures demonstrate that, *a priori*, even well-capitalised and regulated banks can be vulnerable to typical shocks such as interest rate and liquidity risks.[7] The debate on reform priorities is likely to continue, as regulators are looking for ways to improve the resilience of the financial system and mitigate the risk of future crises. Some of the main reform priorities that are being currently discussed include: (i) Strengthening and updating capital and liquidity requirements for banks, (ii) Increasing the oversight of shadow banking activities, (iii) Improving the resolution framework for failing banks, and (iv) Addressing the "too-big-to-fail" problem.

---

[5] This is why after the global financial crisis of 2008, the European Union (EU) has created the European Systemic Risk Board or ESRB and its mission is to be responsible for the macroprudential oversight of the EU financial system and the prevention and mitigation of systemic risk. The ESRB therefore has a broad remit, covering banks, insurers, asset managers, shadow banks, financial market infrastructures, and other financial institutions and markets. In pursuit of its macroprudential mandate, the ESRB monitors and assesses systemic risks and, where appropriate, issues warnings and recommendations.

[6] https://www.imf.org/en/Publications/GFSR/Issues/2018/09/25/Global-Financial-Stability-Report-October-2018.

[7] For more details, see Chap. 2.

2 What Are Banks, What Do They Do and Why Do We Need Them?

While the scope of banking activities can be broad, a simple definition considers a bank as *'an institution primarily engaged in extending loans and accepting public deposits'*. This operational distinction serves as a guiding principle for regulators to determine which financial intermediaries fall under the purview of existing banks' prudential norms.[8] This definition highlights the two core functions of banks: (1) *facilitating deposits* and (2) *extending loans*. Several aspects of this definition warrant some attention:

- The term *'primarily'* emphasises the distinction, as many non-financial firms may engage in lending or borrowing activities on an intermittent basis.
- The simultaneous activity of both lending and borrowing highlights the unique character of commercial banks. By funding a significant portion of their loans with public deposits, banks inherently assume specific risks.[9] This interaction forms the *kernel* of banks' vulnerability, shedding light on the need for regulatory oversight.
- The word *'public'* emphasises the bank's role in supplying unique financial services, such as liquidity provision and payment systems, to the general public. However, unlike professional investors, the *quidam* may also not be adequately equipped to assess banks' soundness and resilience. Given this context, in which a public utility (i.e. payment system) is provided by private entities (i.e. commercial banks), there is a dual rationale for public oversight in banking: (1) *ensuring depositor protection*—by requiring banks to hold sufficient capital and liquidity to withstand shocks, and (2) *maintaining the integrity and efficiency of the payment system*—by making sure that banks have sound procedures to process payments efficiently.

From a theoretical viewpoint, banks play a key role in the efficient allocation of funds in the economy. Banks are financial intermediaries that collect deposits from savers and lend to borrowers (Adrian & Shin, 2010). In contrast with direct finance, this process of intermediation allows banks to pool risks and allocate capital to its most productive uses (Fig. 1.3).[10] As Merton (1993) noted, an efficient financial system helps to smooth household consumption over time. This is because banks can provide loans to households that need capital to finance their investments or current expenses. In turn, this can help households to smooth out their consumption

[8] For instance, within the European Union (EU) framework, *'credit institutions'* are defined in Article 4(1)(1) of Regulation (EU) No 575/2013 as entities that accept deposits or other repayable funds from the public and extend credits on their own behalf.

[9] See also Chap. 2.

[10] Figure 1.3 is adapted from Mishkin and Eakins (2006).

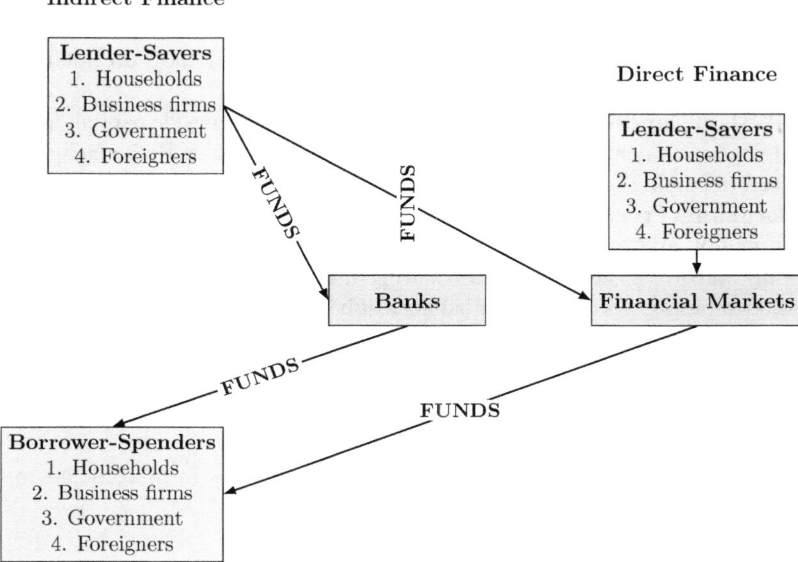

Fig. 1.3 Banks and financial intermediation

and avoid having to dip into their savings during times of need. Also, bankers have the expertise and resources to assess the creditworthiness of borrowers, hence the existence of indirect finance and financial intermediation (Fig. 1.3). This allows banks to lend money to borrowers who are likely to use it productively, which can help allocate capital efficiently and promote economic growth.[11]

To understand the role of banks in improving capital allocation, it is central to examine the specific functions banks perform. Using the most recent banking literature, we categorise these functions into four main areas:

1. **Liquidity Provision and Payment Facilitation**: Banks provide liquidity to the economy by accepting deposits and making loans. They also facilitate payments by operating clearing and settlement systems.[12]

[11] Historically, banks have been the primary providers of essential financial services. However, since the 1980s, there has been a significant expansion of financial markets and a proliferation of financial innovations. As a result, many of the services that were once the exclusive domain of banks are now available through other channels. For example, non-financial firms can now use futures markets to hedge against currency fluctuations, bypassing traditional bank contracts. Some of these firms have become major players in an area that was once dominated by banks.

[12] Clearing involves network operators routing messages and other information among financial institutions to facilitate payments between payers and payees. Interbank settlement is the discharge of obligations that arise in connection with faster payments either in real-time or on a deferred schedule.

2. **Asset Transformation**: Transforming illiquid assets (e.g. loans) into more liquid assets (e.g. sight deposits) is the core business of banks. This function allows firms and households to access credit markets even if they do not have the liquidity on hand to do so.
3. **Risk Management**: Diversifying their portfolios, setting aside capital, and using hedging instruments are the ways banks manage their risks. Risk management is therefore helping banks to protect their depositors and investors from losses.
4. **Information Processing and Borrower Oversight**: Bankers collect and process information about borrowers, which allows them to assess lending risks. Monitoring borrowers' activities and ensuring that they are using the funds for the intended purpose is also part of bankers' job.
5. **Transmission of Monetary Policy**: Commercial banks play an important role in the effective implementation of monetary policy, which is a key tool that central banks use to promote financial stability, sustainable economic growth, and low inflation.[13]

The following sections explore each of these functions in more detail to help clarify the role of banks in our modern financial system.

1. **Liquidity Provision and Payment Facilitation**
   In a frictionless environment (Arrow & Debreu, 1954), without transaction costs, there would be no need for money. However, in the real world, transaction costs exist, and using money as an intermediary for the exchange of goods and services is more efficient than barter.[14] Over time, the nature of money has evolved from being commodity-based, where the medium of exchange has intrinsic value, to a fiat system, where the value is not intrinsic but is guaranteed by an institution (private or public), The legal tender is also guarantee by such

[13] See Box: Monetary Policy Pass Through Banks.

[14] In early August 2021, Chinese archaeologists from the State University of Zhengzhou announced the discovery of the world's oldest known, securely dated coin minting site in Guanzhuang, Henan Province, China. The site, which is dated to around 640 BCE, contains evidence of the production of spade coins, one of the earliest forms of standardised metal coinage: https://www.cambridge.org/core/journals/antiquity/article/abs/radiocarbondating-an-early-minting-site-the-emergence-of-standardised-coinage-in-china/178ECC2B245A017BF684BE1EFC732BD1.

institution,[15] making it an accepted medium of exchange.[16] In this context, banks have played a dual role in the management of fiat money: (1) *facilitating currency exchanges between different issuing entities* and (2) *providing payment services*. These services not only involve managing deposit accounts but also ensuring the settlement of payments. In essence, banks guarantee the successful settlement of the payer's debt to the recipient through the secure transfer of funds.

Some History of Banking

From Coin Weighing to Depository Functions

The evolution of banking can be traced back to its origins as a money-changing service (Gilbart, 1866). The Greek word for bank, *'trapeza'*, refers to the balance used by ancient money changers to weigh coins and evaluate their value. The Italian word *'banco'* refers to the counter or bench where these changers displayed their coins.[a] Banks played a significant part in European trade during the later part of the Middle Ages.

In terms of deposit management, banks developed quite naturally from their role as money changers. This transition was initially rudimentary, often requiring the physical presence of both the payer and payee, as well as a notary, for verification. In many cases, these early deposits did not earn any interest or even resulted in losses or opportunity costs, as they were simply stored rather than invested. The main appeal of converting coins into a less liquid asset was the security it offered, particularly in terms of reducing theft's risk. This early banking model was based on the public's

[a]Many scholars attribute the historical origins of the modern banking system to medieval and Renaissance Italy, particularly the wealthy cities of Florence, Venice, and Genoa. The Bardi and Peruzzi families were prominent banking dynasties in fourteenth-century Florence, with branches throughout Europe (Hoggson, 1926).

(continued)

[15] For example, within the euro area, only the euro has the status of legal tender. Article 128 (1) TFEU (Treaty on the Functioning of the European Union) lays down the legal tender status of euro banknotes, and article 11 of Regulation EC/974/98 does so with regard to euro coins. According to the Commission recommendation on the scope and effects of legal tender of euro cash (2010/191/EU) and as confirmed in a judgment by the European Court of Justice in January 2021, legal tender entails, in principle, the mandatory acceptance of cash, at full face value, with the power to discharge from a payment obligation. This means that the creditor is obliged, in principle, to accept a payment made in euro which subsequently discharges the debtor from his payment obligation. There can be exceptions to this principle of mandatory acceptance, for instance where the parties to a contract agree on another means of payment, or where a refusal of cash is made in good faith. Limits to cash payments are also possible for example to combat tax evasion and money laundering.

[16] The Chinese began using paper money around 700 CE. By the time Marco Polo visited China in approximately 1271 CE, the emperor of China had a sophisticated system for managing the money supply, including a variety of denominations (Prasad, 2017).

assurance that deposits would be kept safe, which gave bankers a reputation for risk aversion.

In addition to safekeeping, the quality and consistency of coins were also important concerns. Due to the heterogeneous composition of precious metals in coins and the ensuing standards imposed by governing authorities, banks were under pressure to ensure that their transactions involved top-quality currency. As Kindleberger (1993) explained, this led to a premium being placed on bank money, especially when compared to regular currency. However, as coins became more standardised in terms of their quality, this value's premium declined. It is important however to note that the standardised coinage was inherently appealing due to its consistent value but the absence of deposit insurance meant that this efficiency did not necessarily extend to deposits. This distinction became increasingly important, particularly in the context of the free banking episodes.[b]

On Payment: The Clearing and Settling Functions

Historically, the use of tangible currency, or species, posed challenges for large-scale transactions due to logistical constraints and hazards. For example, merchants at commercial fairs would often end up with significant monetary imbalances, that they needed to transport back to their headquarters. This issue of transporting and protecting the large amounts of cash was very risky and time-consuming to settle. Recognising the need for a more efficient system to settle payments, private banks began to facilitate the process. By the late nineteenth century, this had evolved into the complex payment systems that we rely on today. These systems enable fund transfers among diverse bank accounts, regardless of their location.[c]

[b]Free banking is a monetary system in which banks are free to issue their own paper currency (banknotes) without government regulation. For example, in the United States from 1837 to 1862, there was a period of *'free banking'*. During this time, only state-chartered banks were allowed to operate, and they were free to issue banknotes that were backed by specie (i.e. gold and silver coins). The states heavily regulated these banks, by setting *inter alia*, reserve requirements, interest rates, and capital ratios.

[c]Today, electronic funds transfers (EFTs) are known by different names in different countries. In the United States, they are often called electronic checks. In the UK, they are called 'BACS Payments'. In Canada, they are called 'e-transfers'. And in several other European countries, they are called 'giro transfers'.

(continued)

One of the most important milestones in the evolution of payment systems was the establishment of the New York Clearing House in 1853 (Gibbons, 1859). The Clearing House brought together the banks of New York City to settle checks on a daily basis. The centralisation effect significantly reduced the time and effort required for settlement, and it also helped to improve efficiency as well as to reduce errors. The Clearing House model was soon adopted by other financial centres, and it remains an essential part of the global payment system today.[d] Other important developments in the evolution of payment systems include the introduction of credit cards and debit cards in the 1950s and 1960s, and the rise of electronic payments in the 1990s.

The increasing complexity and interconnectedness of payment systems has made them a critical part of our modern global financial system. As a result, regulators and central banks have placed a growing emphasis on ensuring the robustness and efficiency of these systems.[e] Recently, there have been a number of initiatives to improve the resilience of payment systems. These include, *inter alia*, the introduction of central bank digital currencies (CBDCs), instant payments (e.g. TIPS in Europe), and the development of new risk management frameworks.[f]

?

---

[d]For example, LCH (originally London Clearing House) is a British clearing house group that provides clearing services to major international exchanges and over-the-counter (OTC) markets. LCH provides clearing services for a large set of asset classes such as commodities, securities, interest rate swaps, credit default swaps, and exchange traded derivatives. Like other central counterparty (CCP), LCH acts as a buyer to every seller and a seller to every buyer of cleared contracts.

[e]For instance, in Europe, TARGET2 is a real-time gross settlement (RTGS) system operated by the Eurosystem for central and commercial banks. It settles payments for monetary policy operations, interbank, and commercial transactions, with a value nearly equivalent to the euro area GDP processed every five days. TARGET2 directly involves over 1,000 banks, but its current reach, in 2023, extends to approximately 52,000 global banking entities and their clientele.

[f]https://www.federalreserve.gov/paymentsystems.htm.

2. **Asset Transformation**

   Commercial banks have traditionally played a vital role in asset transformation, implementing three separate functions:

   (a) *Convenience of denomination*: Bankers adjust the size of their financial products, whether deposits or loans, to meet the needs of their clients. Gurley et al. (1960) argued that banks bridge the gap between the financial instruments that firms want to issue and those that investors prefer. In turn, this allows banks to pool together small deposits to finance large-scale loans.

(b) *Quality transformation*: Through this function, banks enable depositors to achieve better adjusted risk-return portfolios than they could through direct investments. Quality transformation occurs when there is indivisibility or information asymmetry, making banks better informed than individual depositors.[17]

(c) *Maturity transformation*: Modern banking involves converting short-term deposits into long-term loan securities. This function carries risks, primarily due to the illiquidity of assets (i.e. loans) relative to depositors' claims. However, these risks can be mitigated through several mechanisms such as interbank lending and derivatives, although these can, on their own, introduce additional vulnerabilities.

3. **Risk Management**

Typically, bank management textbooks define three main sources of risk that correspond to different lines on a bank's balance sheet:

(a) *Credit risk*: Borrowers could default on their loans. Credit risk is primarily associated with the loan portfolio.

(b) *Interest rate risk*: Changes in interest rates can have an asymmetric impact on the value of bank's assets and liabilities. Interest rate risk is primarily associated with the interest-sensitive assets and liabilities

(c) *Liquidity risk*: The risk that a bank will not be able to meet its obligations to its depositors or other creditors. Liquidity risk is usually associated with the cash and near-cash assets.

Other risks exist. For instance, off-balance-sheet (OBS) activities, which have grown significantly can also pose significant risks to banks (King and Tarbert, 2011). OBS activities include derivative contracts, letters of credit, securitization products, and other contingent liabilities.[18] These activities can be difficult to value and manage and can therefore lead to significant losses for banks.[19]

---

[17] In general, information asymmetry refers to the situation where one party to a transaction has more information than the other party. In the case of loans, borrowers typically have more information about their own financial situation than lenders. This can lead to problems, as borrowers may have an incentive to withhold negative information from lenders. Banks can overcome these problems by pooling the deposits of many individuals and using this information to assess the quality of loans. This allows banks to offer loans to borrowers and it also helps to reduce the risk of lending.

[18] https://www.bis.org/publ/bcbs18.htm.

[19] The Basel Committee on Banking Supervision (BCBS) has issued guidelines on the management of OBS activities. These guidelines aim to ensure that banks have a comprehensive understanding of their OBS activities and that they are adequately managing the associated risks. Supervisory and prudential authorities round the world have also issued and adopted guidance on the management of OBS activities. The idea is to focus on the risks associated with specific types of OBS activities, such as derivative contracts and securitization products.

In recent years, new risks have emerged that challenge the traditional risk management frameworks of banks.[20] The main ones include:

(a) *Cyber risk*: The increasing use of digital technologies by banks has made them more vulnerable to cyberattacks. These attacks can disrupt operations, steal data, or even cause financial losses.[21]
(b) *Climate change risk*: Climate change is a long-term risk that could have a significant impact on banks' operations and financial performance. For example, banks may face losses due to extreme weather events, or they may have to invest in new technologies to reduce their carbon footprint.
(c) *Regulatory risk*: The regulatory environment for banks is constantly changing, and this can create uncertainty and make it difficult for banks to comply with all the relevant rules.
(d) *Geopolitical risk*: Geopolitical instability can pose a risk to banks' operations, especially in countries with weak governance. For example, banks may be nationalised or expropriated by the government, or they may face restrictions on their activities.[22]

The next chapter of the book will provide a comprehensive overview of the management of these old and new risks.

Informed Intermediaries and Information Asymmetry—The Holmström-Tirole Model
The Basic Model:
Introduction

In this box, we present a simplified version of the Holmstrom and Tirole (1997) framework. This model is based on the idea that borrowers (agents) have private information that is not known to the lenders (principals), and that the principal cannot directly observe the agent's effort. The model considers the trade-offs between providing incentives for effort and protecting the agent from bearing excessive risk. With very few assumptions, the model predicts that borrowers with more net worth can rely on cheaper, less information-

(continued)

[20] For more details, see Chap. 2.

[21] The Financial Stability Board (FSB) warned in April 2020 that a major cyber incident, if not properly contained, could have serious implications for financial stability. Such an incident could disrupt financial systems, including critical financial infrastructure and have significant economic costs and damage public trust and confidence.

[22] Recently and in response to the Russian invasion of Ukraine, many governments have imposed a range of financial sanctions on Russia, including asset freezes and the exclusion of Russian banks from the Society for Worldwide Interbank Financial Telecommunication (SWIFT). These sanctions aim to disrupt Russia's financial system and economy and to pressure the government to end the war.

intensive financing channels, while borrowers with less net worth must pay higher interest rates and may have difficulty obtaining loans. The model also suggests that a decline in supervisory capital can push borrowers with low capital to face challenges, and that credit constraints can widen the gap between intermediated and direct market funding.

Assumptions

(a) Three types of agents exist: firms (or entrepreneurs), intermediaries (like banks), and investors.
(b) Two time periods exist with returns only realised at $t = 2$.
(c) All agents are risk-neutral and protected by limited liability.
(d) Different firms have different initial endowments A (interpreted as cash).
(e) The distribution of A across firms follows a cumulative distribution function $G(A)$.
(f) Firms cannot monitor other firms, and excess cash in firms earns an exogenous return γ.

The Real Sector (Firms or Entrepreneurs):

Aggregate capital outlay by firms is given by:

$$K_f = \int AdG(A)$$

The firm's project at $t = 1$ requires an investment I greater than 0, leading to an initial funding requirement of $I - A$ if $A < I$.

Return on Investment:

- 0 if the project fails.
- R if the project succeeds.

Without incentives or monitoring, entrepreneurs can diminish the project's success probability to p_L, yielding them a private benefit B.

The Financial Sector:

Monitoring costs are $C > 0$, but it prevents the larger private benefit B, reducing it to $b < B$. All projects financed by intermediaries are perfectly correlated.

Investors:

We assume that investors are uninformed relative to the intermediaries. They demand an expected return γ, which is exogenous, which implies infinite opportunities on the open markets.

(continued)

Direct Financing (Two-Party Contract):
For a firm to prefer diligence:

$$p_H R_f \geq p_L R_f + B \tag{1.2}$$

Defining pledgeable income:

$$R_U = R - \frac{B}{\Delta p} \tag{1.3}$$

Given that the opportunity cost of funds supplied by investors is $\gamma(I - A)$, a necessary condition for direct finance:

$$\gamma(I - A) \leq p_H \left(R - \frac{B}{\Delta p}\right) \tag{1.4}$$

From which we derive that only firms above a threshold can invest using direct finance:

$$\bar{A}(\gamma) = I - \frac{p_H}{\gamma}\left(R - \frac{B}{\Delta p}\right) \tag{1.5}$$

Indirect Financing:
If R_m is the return due to the intermediaries, and their monitoring eliminates B, then returns allocation can be written as:

$$R_m + R_U + R_f = R \tag{1.6}$$

Modified firm's incentive:

$$R_f \geq \frac{b}{\Delta p}$$

For the intermediary to monitor, with a cost C, and ensure a positive return, the following must hold with strict inequality:

$$\frac{R_m - C}{\Delta p} > 0 \tag{1.7}$$

The maximum pledgeable expected income to investors is:

$$p_H \left(R - \frac{b + C}{\Delta p}\right) \tag{1.8}$$

(continued)

Using Eq. (1.8), we get the minimum contribution an intermediary can make to a project that it monitors is:

$$\beta = \frac{p_H R_m}{I} \tag{1.9}$$

From (1.8), the minimum intermediary contribution is:

$$I_M(\beta) = \frac{p_H C}{\Delta p \beta} \tag{1.10}$$

The endowment level A so that a firm can be financed with uninformed capital must be above the following cutoff:

$$\bar{A}(\gamma, \beta) = I - I_M(\beta) - \frac{p_H}{\gamma}\left(R - \frac{b+C}{\Delta p}\right) \tag{1.11}$$

The minimum acceptable β is defined by:

$$\beta_{min} = \frac{p_H}{p_L}\gamma > \gamma \tag{1.12}$$

Condition for social benefit from monitoring:

$$p_H(\beta - b) > C\Delta p \tag{1.13}$$

Key Results:

(a) For $A > \bar{A}(\gamma)$, the firm gets direct finance.
(b) For $A < \bar{A}(\gamma, \beta_{min})$, the firm does not receive funding.
(c) For $\bar{A}(\gamma, \beta_{min}) \leq A < \bar{A}(\gamma)$, the firm uses mixed finance and requires monitoring.

In other words, the size of the intermediary's stake in a firm is a signal of the firm's ex-post behaviour. This means that the larger the intermediary's stake, the more likely it is that the firm will behave in a way that is beneficial to the intermediary. This, in turn, will encourage uninformed investors to commit capital to the firm. This is known as the *'free rider'* problem of intermediated finance. This is because uninformed investors do not have to bear the full cost of monitoring the firm, as the intermediary does. Therefore, they are willing to put or commit capital to the firm even if they do not have full information about the business's prospects.

4. **Information Management, Oversight, and Monitoring**

As we have seen, banks play a vital role in addressing the challenges posed by information asymmetry between borrowers and lenders. In the era of big data and artificial intelligence, banks can now for the first time in the world's history, leverage advanced technological tools to carefully evaluate loan applicants and continuously monitor their financial performance. The seminal paper of Mayer (1988) found that this close oversight can help to build lasting relationships between businesses and banks, which can mitigate the risk of moral hazard.[23]

This approach distinguishes traditional bank lending from securities issuance in capital markets. While bond valuations are based on price-driven information, the value of a bank loan is largely rooted in the long-standing bank-client relationship. Loans value is difficult to assess and often opaque to both the broader market and regulatory authorities. As Merton (1993) put it, bank loans are inherently *'opaque'*.

From a macroeconomic perspective, banks play also an important role in shaping the allocation of capital, the dispersion of risk, and very likely the overall trajectory of economic growth. This concept was first emphasised by Hellwig (1990). Before that, Gerschenkron (2015) showed that the banking sector was instrumental in the economic development of some countries. The view that banks contribute significantly to economic growth is an old debate among scholars, as noted by Edwards and Ogilvie (1996) or more recently by Levine (2021).

Likewise, theories of *'scarcity of funds'*, while difficult to reconcile with a general equilibrium framework, offer valuable insights into development economics. Economies with underdeveloped financial intermediation and illiquid financial markets may struggle to allocate savings efficiently. This could make it difficult to finance important developmental projects, such as infrastructure investments, which often have high risk premiums.[24] Few decades ago already, Greenwood and Jovanovic (1990) presented a theoretical framework for understanding the relationship between financial markets and economic development.

The rapid growth of bank-centred economies, such as Japan and Germany in the 1980s, has also led to further research on the macroeconomic role of banks. Allen and Gale (1997) compared the financial systems of Germany and the

[23] Generally, moral hazard occurs when one party to a contract has an incentive to behave in a way that is not in the best interests of the other party, because the first party is not fully exposed to the consequences of its actions. This can happen in a variety of contexts, including financial markets. For example, a borrower may be more likely to take on excessive risk if he knows he will be bailed out in case of default. To mitigate moral hazard risks, contemporary banking literature suggests that policymakers need to put in place appropriate regulations and monitoring mechanisms.

[24] We define risk premium as the additional return that investors demand for bearing the risk of an investment. Mathematically, it is computed as the difference between the expected return on an investment and the risk-free rate of return. Put simply, the risk premium is compensation for the possibility that the investment's return could be lower than expected, or that the investor could lose money altogether.

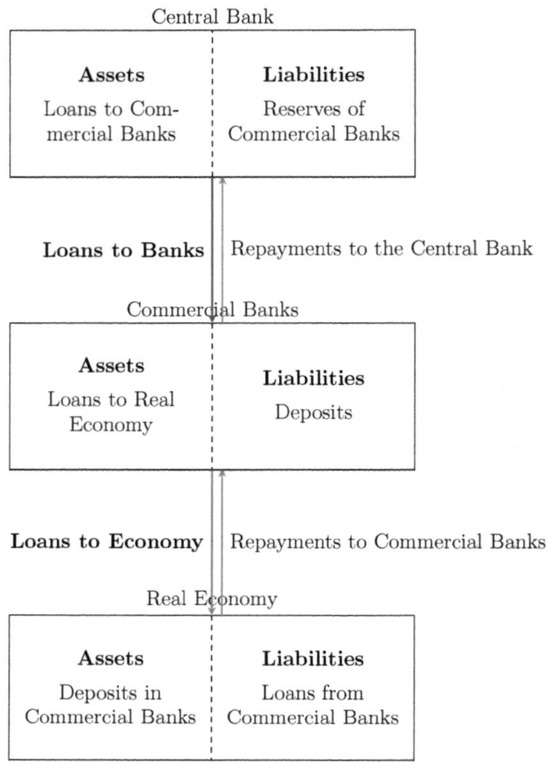

Fig. 1.4 The pivotal role of banks

United States. They argued that market-based economies may have difficulties in mitigating non-diversifiable risks.[25] For example, households in the United States and the UK tend to invest heavily in equities, while households in bank-dominated economies such as Japan and Germany tend to invest in 'safer' securities.

5. **Monetary Policy Transmission**

   Commercial banks are at the heart of the monetary policy transmission mechanism (Rostagno et al., 2021). They circulate money and provide loans to households and firms, which ultimately affects aggregate output (Fig. 1.4).

   Mainstream macroeconomic textbooks incorrectly explain how the modern central bank implements monetary policy (Ihrig et al., 2021). As of today and for most of the advanced and emerging market economies, central bankers do not directly control the money supply but rather influence it through changes in

[25] Generally, non-diversifiable risks are those risks that cannot be eliminated through portfolio diversification. These risks include for example market risk—which reflects systemic fluctuations in asset prices, or geopolitical risk, which is the risk that events such as wars, natural disasters, or political instability.

administered interest rates also called policy rates. In practice, when a central bank expands the monetary base, it typically does so by buying government securities or other financial assets from banks.[26] The concept of the *'money multiplier'* is often used to explain this relationship, but it is an outdated and inaccurate model.[27] Using policy rates and its other policy implementation tools (e.g. quantitative easing, refinancing operations), the central bank ensures that any change in the policy rate transmits effectively and efficiently through the economy. For example, when the central bank raises its policy rate (e.g. interest on reserve balances rate in the United States), banks earn more on the funds they place in their reserve accounts at their central bank (Fig. 1.4). This sets a higher reservation rate for banks' investment and operational decisions and banks generally will not accept a lower rate of return than this new policy rate on any investment. Then, through *arbitrage*, similar market interest rates are also increased, including the interbank rates.

Therefore, the central bank's changes in its policy rates affect not only the short-term interest rates at which banks borrow and lend but also transmit to other interest rates in the economy and to financial market conditions more broadly.[28] For example, as noted above, changes in the policy rate influence how much banks charge households and businesses for loans. The changes also help anchor where various short-term market interest rates settle and thereby influence the levels of longer-term market interest rates. In addition, changes in the general level of interest rates affect the prices—or valuations—of financial assets, such as stocks, bonds as well as some non-financial assets, like houses. Such changes in overall financial conditions influence consumers' and firms' interest-sensitive spending and investment decisions. For example, higher interest rates in the economy might dissuade an entrepreneur from taking a bank loan. Also, a sustained rise in the value of a household's assets might cause it to feel wealthier and encourage additional spending.

As households and firms make their various saving and expenditure decisions, the overall demand for supply of goods and services are affected. Put simply,

---

[26] Open market operations (OMOs) are a tool used by central banks to manage the money supply and interest rates. OMOs involve the purchase or sale of government securities in the open market. When a central bank buys securities, it injects money into the economy, which can lead to lower interest rates. When a central bank sells securities, it withdraws money from the economy, which can lead to higher interest rates. OMOs can be used to achieve a variety of policy goals, such as stimulating economic growth, controlling inflation, or stabilising the exchange rate. The effectiveness of OMOs depends on a number of factors, including the size of the purchase or sale, the interest rate environment, and the expectations of market participants.

[27] Traditional banking theories hold that private banks must have prior reserves in order to issue credit. This is known as the *'money multiplier'* view. However, recent research has challenged this approach, arguing that banks can create money through credit issuance without the need for prior reserves. When a bank provides a loan, it creates a deposit in the borrower's account. In other words. instead of being limited by the amount of reserves they have, banks can create money through credit issuance.

[28] *Box: Monetary Policy Pass Through Banks.*

as aggregate demand and supply shift, so does the need for labour and other inputs to produce those goods and services. And of course, shifts in demand and supply also affect the prices of these goods and services. Therefore, changes in the central bank's monetary policy stance ultimately move the economy with the typical objectives of sustainable economic growth and low inflation.

Introduction to Monetary Policy and the Role of Banks

Monetary Policy 101

The central bank maintains an exclusive control over the issuance of banknotes and bank reserves, giving it a monopoly on the creation of the monetary base.[a] Through this monopoly, the central bank has the power to influence money market conditions and steer short-term interest rates.[b] While monetary policy is a powerful tool, often been referred as the *'Only Game in Town'* (El-Erian, 2017), it is important to keep in mind its limitations and boundaries. There are many things that central bankers simply cannot do.

In the short term, when the central bank adjusts administered interest rates,[c] it sets off a chain reaction in the whole economy, ultimately impacting macroeconomic variables like output and inflation. This process, known as the *'monetary policy transmission mechanism'*, is dynamic and multidimensional. While its main features are easily understandable, there is no universally accepted understanding of all its elements (Bindseil, 2014).

A typical example is the well-known idea of *'money neutrality'*. Roughly speaking, this concept suggests that in the long term, after all economic adjustments have played out, an increase in the money supply, *ceteris paribus*, leads to an increase in the general price level, without causing lasting changes in real variables such as actual output or employment (Friedman & Schwartz, 1963; Walsh, 2017). In essence, a change in the money supply essentially represents a shift in the unit of account, leaving other variables unchanged. The foundational principle of

[a]Monetary base equals currency in circulation plus reserve balances.

[b]https://www.ecb.europa.eu/pub/pdf/other/monetarypolicy2011en.pdf.

[c]In the context of the euro area, the ECB sets three key administered interest rates: (i) the main refinancing operations (MRO), which provide the bulk of liquidity to the banking system, and it is the rate banks pay when they borrow money for one week, (ii) the deposit facility rate (DFR), which banks may use to make overnight deposits, and (iii) the marginal lending facility rate (MLFR), which offers overnight credit to banks.

(continued)

the *'long-run neutrality'* of money forms the basis of standard macroeconomic models and frameworks.[d] Therefore, in the long term, income and unemployment levels are primarily determined by real supply-side factors such as technological progress, population growth, and investment in human capital. While other factors like variations in aggregate demand or commodity price shocks may influence short-term price developments, their effects can be balanced out over time.

The monetary policy transmission mechanism is the process by which monetary policy decisions impact the macroeconomy and, specifically, the inflation. Transmitting monetary impulses to the real sector involves various mechanisms and actions by economic agents (e.g. households, firms) at different stages of the process (Angeloni et al., 2003). Consequently, the impact of monetary policy decisions on prices usually takes some time. Moreover, estimating the precise effect can be difficult because the size and intensity of the different shocks can vary depending on business cycle fluctuations. As a result, central bankers often encounter long, uncertain, and variable lags in implementing monetary policy.

Identifying the transmission mechanism of monetary policy is challenging because, in practice, any economies is continually influenced by shocks from various sources (e.g. regulatory, political fragmentation). Changes in regulated prices can directly impact inflation in the short term. Similarly, global economic developments and fiscal policies may influence aggregate demand and, consequently, price dynamics (Mishkin, 2007). Additionally, financial asset prices and exchange rates are influenced by numerous factors beyond monetary policy. Therefore, monetary policy must carefully monitor the transmission chain to prevent external shocks to the financial system from disrupting the transmission of monetary impulses. The central bank must also consider all other developments that may affect future inflation to ensure they do not influence longer-term inflation trends and expectations in a way that contradicts price stability. As a result, the appropriate course of monetary policy always depends on the nature, magnitude, and duration of the shocks affecting the economy.

The Role of Banks and the Key Channels of Monetary Transmission

The 2008 GFC and the Covid-19 shocks have revived discussions about the role of banks in the transmission of monetary policy. This debate has

[d]The idea of monetary neutrality can be traced back to David Hume in the eighteenth century, but it gained widespread attention after von Hayek (1951). Keynes et al. (1971), on the other hand, rejected the neutrality of money both in the short term and in the long term. He argued that changes in the money supply could have real effects by affecting investment and employment. As of today, the New Keynesian school emphasises models in which money is not neutral in the short run, and therefore monetary policy can affect the real economy.

(continued)

intensified both in situations of financial instability (e.g. with vulnerable banks) and when dealing with the zero-interest rate lower bound.[e]

One crucial lesson drawn from recent experiences is that financial and price stability cannot always be independently targeted (Blanchard et al., 2010). It has become clear that the efficacy of monetary policy transmission mechanisms is closely linked with the health of the banking system.

In general, the process of transmitting monetary policy to the economy involves multiple channels, each with its own potential impact on inflation. As a result, central banks must navigate a big network of economics interactions. For some important regions or countries (e.g. Eurozone), the main financial institutions through which monetary policy transmission occurs are the commercial banks. We will outline these channels below.

Interest Rate Channel

As we highlighted before, the monetary policy decisions can influence inflation through a long chain of cause and effect. The first step is for the central bank to change policy interest rates that it charges on its own lending operations. These operations typically involve the central bank providing funds to banks. In practice, banks demand money issued by the central bank, known as 'base money', to meet the public demand for currency, to clear interbank balances, and to meet the requirements for minimum reserves that must be deposited with the central bank. Since the central bank has a monopoly on the creation of base money, it can control the interest rates on its operations. By changing these administered interest rates, central bankers can affect the funding cost of liquidity and commercial banks then need to pass on these costs when lending to their customers. This is known as the *'interest rate channel'* of monetary policy.

Credit and Balance Sheet Channels

Through the *'interest rate channel'*, the central bank can exert a strong impact on money market conditions and thereby steer money market interest rates (e.g. fed funds rates in the United States or Euro short-term rate €STR

[e] In June 2014, the ECB became the first major central bank to introduce negative interest rates. This meant that banks were charged negative interest rates for putting their reserves at the ECB. The move was a radical departure from conventional monetary policy, and the decision for this shift was motivated by a number of factors, including low inflation and the threat of deflation. Negative interest rates were seen as a way to encourage banks to lend more in order to stimulate output and employment. From a theoretical perspective, the existence of an arbitrage relationship between the return on short-term nominal bonds and the return on cash has long been known in the academic literature. To quote (Hicks, 1935): *'[...] So long as rates of interest are positive, the decision to hold money rather than lend it, or use it to pay off old debts, is apparently an unprofitable one'*.

(continued)

in Europe). Changes in money market rates in turn affect other interest rates, albeit to varying degrees. For example, changes in money market rates have an impact on the interest rates set by banks on short-term loans and deposits.

Furthermore, changes in policy rates may also affect the supply of credit—this is called the *'credit channel'*. Following an increase in interest rates, the risk that some borrowers cannot safely pay back their loans may increase to a level such that the bank will not grant a loan to these borrowers (the *'bank lending channel'* of the credit channel). As a consequence, such borrowers, households, or businesses are forced to postpone their consumption or investment plans. Interest rate changes also affect firms' balance sheets. An increase in interest rates leads to a lower net worth of firms which means a lower collateral value and thus a reduced ability to borrow (the *'balance sheet channel'* of the credit channel).

Risk-Taking Channel

In addition to the traditional bank lending channel, which focuses on the quantity of loans supplied, a *'risk-taking channel'* may exist when banks' incentive to bear risk related to the provision of loans is affected. The risk-taking channel is thought to operate mainly via two mechanisms. First, low interest rates boost asset and collateral values. This, in conjunction with the belief that the increase in asset values is sustainable, leads both borrowers and banks to accept higher risks. Second, low interest rates make riskier assets more attractive, as agents search for higher yields. In the case of banks, these two effects usually translate into a softening of credit standards, which can lead to an excessive increase in loan supply, a credit boom.

Empirical Knowledge on the Transmission of Monetary Policy

Understanding the transmission mechanism is paramount for monetary policy. It is, therefore, not surprising that numerous researchers have tried to analyse the complex interactions underlying it Bindseil (2004). Over time, more information, data, empirical tools and research results have become available and there is now a better understanding of monetary transmission. One of the main findings is that monetary policy affects the economy mainly through the interest rate channel. Although the use of empirical methods for the quantification of the transmission mechanism and its channels has proved to be of great help to respond to the COVID-19 crisis, the results have shed only partial light on the complex processes involved. The learning process is still underway and major central banks continue to monitor possible behavioural and structural changes.

3 The Future of Banking and Money? The Big Tech Challenge and Payment Evolution

The world is standing at a crossroads in the evolution of banking and money. The growing interest in digital currencies from major economies, such as China, Europe, and the United States, signals a profound shift (Beniak, 2019). Since the late 1990s, the payment sector has been relatively static. However, the relentless march of technology is now modifying this once-stable environment. Central bank digital currencies (CBDCs) are one of the most significant developments in this area. CBDCs are digital versions of cash that are issued and regulated by central banks.[29] They offer a number of potential benefits, such as faster and cheaper payments, increased financial inclusion, and enhanced monetary policy transmission (Zagorsky, 2018). However, there are also a number of challenges that need to be addressed before CBDCs can be widely adopted. These challenges could include: *inter alia, (i) Securing and protecting user privacy, (ii) Managing the potential impact on financial stability*, and *(iii) Addressing the role of private banking*.[30]

Traditionally, innovations in payments focused on enhancing the user experience. Platforms like PayPal set the stage,[31] with Apple Pay and Google Pay building

---

[29] CBDC is a digital form of central bank money that could be used by households and businesses to make payments. CBDC is not a new currency, but rather a digital version of the existing fiat currency. A report by the Bank for International Settlements (BIS) states that, although the term CBDC is not well-defined, *'it is envisioned by most to be a new form of central bank money [...] that is different from balances in traditional reserve or settlement accounts' (Bech and Garratt, 2017).*

[30] According to Brunnermeier et al. (2019), the ongoing digital revolution is reshaping the way we think about money. We may see an unbundling of the traditional roles of money, with separate currencies emerging to fulfil each role. For example, a currency may be used primarily for payments, while another currency may be used primarily for storing value. Alternatively, we may see a re-bundling of money, with digital currencies associated with large platform ecosystems offering a variety of payment and financial services. This could lead to a more fragmented and complex monetary system. Digital currencies could also have a significant impact on the international monetary system. Countries that are socially or digitally integrated with their neighbours may face digital dollarization, as their citizens and businesses increasingly use the US dollar for payments and savings. Additionally, the prevalence of systemically important platforms could lead to the emergence of digital currency areas that transcend national borders. They also claim that CBDCs can help to mitigate some of these risks. By providing a safe and reliable digital form of central bank money, CBDCs can help to ensure that public money remains a relevant unit of account and that the international monetary system remains stable.

[31] Historically, PayPal was founded in 1998 as Confinity, a security software firm for handheld devices. It pivoted to a digital wallet in 1999 and merged with X.com, an online finance venture, in 2000. The combined entity was renamed PayPal in 2001 and went public in 2002. It was acquired by eBay for $1.5 billion later that year. As part of eBay, PayPal expanded its reach and security measures. It also launched new products and services, such as the PayPal Secure Card and partnerships with MasterCard and Discover Card. In 2015, PayPal separated from eBay and pursued a strategy of acquisitions, partnerships, and technological advancements. It acquired Xoom Corporation, launched the peer-to-peer platform 'PayPal.Me', and purchased Honey for over $4 billion in 2020. In 2023, PayPal launched its US dollar stablecoin, known as PayPal USD.

upon it. While these changes were incremental, the introduction of Facebook's Libra signalled a tectonic shift, proposing a complete overhaul of the global monetary and financial system.[32]

The announcement of Facebook's Libra project in 2019 was met with stiff opposition from various sides. Central banks around the world questioned the project's viability and potential implications, while regulators expressed concerns about its impact on financial stability and consumer protection. In Europe, the response was particularly vibrant and critical. French Finance Minister Bruno Le Maire declared that Libra could not replace sovereign currencies and stressed the importance of consumer protection. Bank of England Governor Mark Carney emphasised the need for stringent regulation, while German MEP Markus Ferber highlighted the risk of Facebook turning into a shadow bank.[33]

The US reaction was equally intense. Concerns ranged from how Libra would address money laundering to its impact on financial stability and consumer protection. High-ranking politicians and officials, including President Donald Trump and Federal Reserve Chairman Jerome Powell, voiced their apprehensions.[34] The US House Committee on Financial Services Democrats even urged Facebook to halt Libra's development due to its potential implications for privacy, national security, and monetary policy.

Facing widespread scrutiny and the withdrawal of major corporate partners, the Libra project underwent a rebranding. By December 2020, it was renamed *'Diem'*—a term derived from Latin meaning *"day"*. However, this rebranding did little to mitigate the concerns surrounding the project. The culmination of regulatory hurdles and global skepticism, combined with internal challenges, led to the winding down of the Diem Association by January 2022.[35] Its assets were sold to Silvergate Capital, a California-based bank, for a reported USD 200 million. By the beginning of 2023, Silvergate Capital announced a writing off their entire Diem investment, and the bank itself shut down in March 2023.[36]

The tale of Facebook's foray into the world of banking and money shows the challenges of introducing a global digital currency. It also serves as a case study of how ambitious tech innovations can be met with skepticism and resistance when they enter the domain of sensitive sectors like global finance and central banking. Nevertheless, the conversations and debates sparked by Libra/Diem about the role of

---

[32] For example, see the US Congressional report entitled 'Libra: A Facebook-led Cryptocurrency Initiative' from 2019.

[33] https://www.bloomberg.com/news/articles/2019-06-18/france-calls-for-central-bank-review-of-facebook-cryptocurrency.

[34] https://web.archive.org/web/20190710233742/https://www.nytimes.com/2019/07/10/technology/fed-chair-facebook-cryptocurrency-libra.html.

[35] During this episode, Diem Association (formerly Libra Association) also encountered legal obstacles because the name and logo of the digital currency were already in use in various jurisdictions.

[36] https://www.bloomberg.com/news/articles/2023-03-08/silvergate-plans-to-wind-down-bank-operations-and-liquidate.

private entities in the banking sector, the potential and pitfalls of cryptocurrencies, and the nature of monetary sovereignty in a digitising world will likely influence the trajectory of financial innovations for years to come.

Although Facebook's project had the potential to improve financial inclusion, especially in low-income countries, the global payment system still faces major challenges. A staggering 1.7 billion adults remain excluded from the financial mainstream, despite a significant portion having access to mobile phones and the internet. These individuals are deprived of not just payment services but also other financial utilities like credit and insurance. Meanwhile, cross-border retail payments, crucial for global commerce and remittances, remain inefficient and expensive. The average cost of sending remittances globally is 6.25% of the amount sent, as of 2023. Of course, the cost of remittances varies depending on the sending and receiving countries, the payment method used, and the exchange rate.[37]

The entry of BigTechs into the financial sector has led to a reorientation of the payment systems. While this shift is disrupting traditional banking models, it also sparks concerns about monetary sovereignty, as we have seen for the case of Facebook's Libra. Emerging technologies, like the evolution from speculative crypto-assets to more stable *'stablecoins'* promise to streamline cross-border payments.[38]

Recent global stablecoin initiatives, such as Libra, have shown the challenges and risks associated with these big projects. These concerns include anti-money laundering, unfair competition, and tax compliance. As a result, international bodies such as the G7 and the Financial Stability Board (FSB) have begun to examine the regulatory implications of stablecoins. As ECB Executive Board member Fabio Panetta put it, 'Stablecoins could have a significant impact on the payments landscape, and it is important to carefully assess their potential risks and benefits'. This assessment should be conducted on a case-by-case basis, taking into account the specific characteristics of each stablecoin. The integration of BigTechs into the financial sector marks the beginning of a new era in banking and money Bains et al. (2022) and the future of private banking is being shaped today, as banks compete with BigTechs for customers and market share.

[37] https://remittanceprices.worldbank.org/.

[38] Stablecoins are a type of cryptocurrency whose value is supposed to be pegged to a reference asset. However, in practice, stablecoin issuers have yet to be proven to maintain adequate reserves to support a stable value. This is a potential risk to financial stability, as stablecoins are increasingly being used in a variety of financial applications. For example, the Terra blockchain was temporarily suspended in May 2022 following the collapse of the TerraUSD (UST) stablecoin and its sister token Luna. The event wiped out USD 45 billion in market capitalisation in a matter of days. The collapse of UST and Luna had a ripple effect throughout the cryptocurrency market, causing prices of other tokens to fall. It also raised concerns about the stability of stablecoins, which are seen as a key building block of the crypto ecosystem.

Chapter 2
Risk Management and Banking Failures

1 Introduction

As mentioned in Chap. 1, a failure occurs when a bank is unable to meet its obligations to its depositors or other creditors because it has become insolvent or too illiquid. This can happen when the market value of the bank's assets declines to a level that is less than its of its liabilities. The bank may be taken over by the regulating government agency if its shareholders' equity is below the regulatory minimum (Table 2.1). The collapse of a bank can also have a significant impact on the economy as a whole, as it can lead to financial instability and a decline in output (Laeven, 2011). As a result, banks are subject to rigorous regulation, and bank failures are of major public policy concern in all countries across the world.[1]

2 How Does the Regulator Respond to a Bank Failure?[2]

Traditionally, once a regulatory body declares a bank as failing or likely to fail (Table 2.1 and Fig. 2.1), the so-called *Resolution Authority* assesses whether it meets the remaining conditions for resolution.[3]

(a) *First*, the Authority evaluates if any alternative private sector measures or supervisory actions could prevent the bank's failure within a reasonable timeframe.

[1] https://www.worldbank.org/en/research/brief/BRSS.

[2] For a comprehensive overview, see Chap. 5.

[3] Bank resolution is the process of restructuring a failing bank in a way that safeguards public interests, including the continuity of the bank's critical functions, financial stability, and minimal costs to taxpayers: https://www.srb.europa.eu/en/content/what-bank-resolution.

N. Abidi et al., *Why Do Banks Fail and What to Do About It*, Contributions to Finance and Accounting, https://doi.org/10.1007/978-3-031-52311-3_2

Table 2.1 Conditions for bank failure declaration

Condition	Description
Authorisation	The bank is in breach of the requirements for continuing authorisation and is likely to continue to do so in the near future. This is a serious matter that could justify the withdrawal of the bank's authorisation
Assets	The bank's assets are less than its liabilities, or will be in the near future
Debts	The bank is unable to pay its debts as they fall due, or will be in the near future
Public financial support	The bank requires extraordinary public financial support (subject to certain exceptions)
Assessment Note	In its assessment, the regulator takes into account all relevant information that is available to it in its role as a banking supervisor. This includes information on the bank's financial condition, its risk management practices, and its compliance with regulations. The regulator also considers whether there are any other actions that could remedy the bank's adverse situation. These actions could include providing the bank with financial support, requiring the bank to take corrective measures, or even withdrawing the bank's license

Fig. 2.1 Failures of all institutions in the United States (1934–2023, source FDIC)

These might encompass actions like a merger or acquisition, or an investor providing fresh capital.

(b) *Next*, the Authority considers if a resolution action aligns with public interest. If no alternative measures are available and the resolution aligns with public interest, the Authority enacts a resolution action. This can involve actions like partially selling the bank's business, establishing a *'bridge bank'* for critical functions, or even creating a *'bad bank'* to manage specific assets and liabilities. If necessary, a *bail-in* might be imposed, pushing losses onto the investors and creditors. While the Resolution Authority handles these processes, the supervisory body maintains oversight as long as the bank retains its banking license, ensuring close cooperation.[4]

From a theoretical viewpoint, regulations must not prevent bank failures. In a healthy market-based economy, some banks will fail. This is an essential feature of a competitive marketplace, as it allows for the weeding out of weak and inefficient banks.[5] However, the regulator can play a role in diminishing the risks of bank collapses and mitigating their macroeconomic impact. The regulator can do this by (i) promoting sound risk management and controls at banks, (ii) ensuring that banks have sufficient capital and liquidity to withstand adverse economic conditions, (iii) identifying and intervening in banks that are at risk of failure, and (iv) developing and implementing resolution plans for failing banks. Roughly speaking, sound regulations must ensure that bank failures do not have a systemic impact on the financial system. This means that the failure of one bank should not cause other banks to fail or lead to a wider economic crisis (Fig. 2.2).

The key element is to strike a balance between preventing bank failures and allowing market forces to play in the banking system. A zero-failure policy is neither feasible nor desirable. It is not feasible because there will always be some banks that fail, no matter how well-regulated the system is. It is also not desirable because it would discourage banks from taking risks or innovating, which are essential for economic growth (Aghion et al., 2015). Therefore, the regulator's responsibility is to make sure that bankruptcies are orderly and do not have a systemic effect. For instance, this can be done by working with bankers to develop recovery resolution planning frameworks in a way that minimises disruption and protect the interests of depositors and other creditors (Table 2.1).

In terms of regulatory policy optimality, and for illustration purposes, two phenomena are worth mentioning. For example, the too-big-to-fail problem, which has been extensively studied in the literature. The 'too-big-to-fail' (TBTF) paradigm refers to the idea that certain financial institutions are so large and interconnected that their failure could have catastrophic consequences for the broader economy, and therefore, they must be supported by the government to prevent their collapse. These institutions are considered 'systemically important' because their failure

---

[4] Let us provide few recent illustrative cases:

i. Bank A: After being declared as failing, its capital instruments were revised and another financial institution acquired the bank (e.g. Banco Popular).
ii. Banks B and C: The Resolution Authority determined that public interest was not at stake for these banks. They were then liquidated as per their insolvency law, with a portion of their operations sold to another bank (e.g. Veneto Banca and Banca Popolare di Vicenza).
iii. Bank D and its subsidiary: Both entities were declared as failing, but the public interest criterion was not satisfied. In such situations, the resolution framework suggests orderly winding down based on applicable law (e.g. ABLV Bank).

[5] In a recent article, Rajan and Zingales (2023) suggest that US government decision to cover uninsured deposits at Silicon Valley Bank (SVB) weakens free market discipline: https://www.imf.org/en/Publications/fandd/issues/2023/06/POV-riskless-capitalism-rajan-zingales.

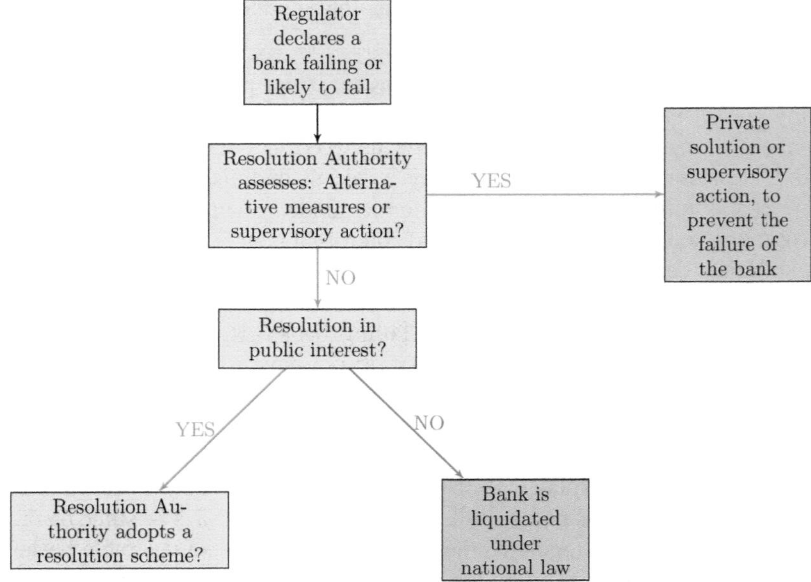

Fig. 2.2 Algorithm for declaring a bank failing or likely to fail to resolution

could trigger a domino effect, leading to a financial crisis.[6] This might lead to a moral hazard under which bankers could take excessive risk as they foresee a state bailout ex-ante, resulting into a state or tax payer implicit subsidy. Alternatively, consistent regulation of banks over time faces a challenge known as the 'too-many-to-fail' issue. When a large number of banks face failure, regulators often find it optimal in hindsight to bail them out to prevent ongoing losses. Conversely, if only a few banks fail, they can be acquired by the surviving banks instead. In this case, the crisis-prevention role of a central bank (more generally, the bank regulator) conflicts with its crisis management role due to a lack of commitment in optimal policies (Acharya & Yorulmazer, 2007).

3 Preventing Failures and Managing Banks' Risks Effectively

Historically and to prevent from collapses, banks have managed three core risks: (1) *credit risk*, (2) *interest rate risk*, and (3) *liquidity risk*. As we highlighted in Chap. 1, these risks can generally be directly linked to a specific items on banks financial statements. For example, credit risk is related to the loan portfolio, interest rate risk

[6] See for example Freixas (1999) as well as Huang and Goodhart (1999) for a theoretical analysis, and O'hara and Shaw (1990) as well as Anginer and Warburton (2011) for empirical research.

is related to the interest-sensitive assets and liabilities, and liquidity risk is related to the cash and short-term investments.

The 2008 GFC also led to increased awareness of the risks associated with Off-balance Sheet ('OBS') activities (Fender & Mitchell, 2009). OBS activities, while not directly reflected on a bank's balance sheet, can still introduce significant vulnerabilities. For example, a bank might engage in a derivative contract that exposes it to potential interest rate or currency fluctuations. Related to this, and more recently, there has been an evolution in banking risks, with emerging challenges like cyber vulnerabilities. Cyberattacks can jeopardise a bank's operational integrity and result in financial losses (Dupont, 2019), trigger a bank run[7] (Duffie & Younger, 2019), as well as undermine the trustworthiness in the financial system as a whole. Meanwhile, the impacts of climate change, such as severe weather events, can damage assets or disrupt banks' operations (Ramakrishna, 2023; Monasterolo, 2020). The following sections provide a comprehensive overview of the banking sector's risk profile, covering both traditional and contemporary challenges.

1. **Credit Risk**
   The genesis of modern banking can be anchored on the flourishing financial epicentres of Florence, Siena, Lucca, and Venice. Initially, bankers' activities were principally centred around underwriting agricultural outputs, primarily because of their tangible nature and ease of valuation, resulting in a relatively contained credit risk environment (Kindleberger, 1993). As the banking sector became more advanced, so did its risk profile. Banks began to diversify their operations, with warfare financing emerging as a pivotal function (Ferguson, 2008). In spite of this shift, they continued to adopt risk-mitigating measures, relying mainly on collaterals ranging from tangible assets like jewellery to more structured mechanisms like tax rights or city endorsements. Having said that, such safeguards offered limited protection, especially when the borrower belonged to the royal class.
   Over time, the nature of lending activities evolved. The early banking model was similar to pawnbroking, with loans predominantly being fully collateralized. This paradigm moved with the advent of investment banking, which is a distinct institution with a different approach to traditional credit facilities.[8] Investment banking ushered in an era where banks did not just act as lenders but also as investors in industries, which often meant taking on more risks, including equity investments. The ability to assess the risk associated with a loan has since become a cornerstone of modern banking practices. The 2008 GFC highlighted the

[7] A bank run occurs when customers of a financial institution simultaneously withdraw their deposits due to concerns about the institution's financial stability. With more people withdrawing their funds, the likelihood of default rises, leading to even more withdrawals. In severe situations, the institution's reserves might be insufficient to meet the withdrawal demands.

[8] In continental Europe, the practice of universal banking developed in the nineteenth century, with institutions such as the Société Générale de Belgique and the Caisse Générale du Commerce et de l'Industrie (founded by Laffitte in France).

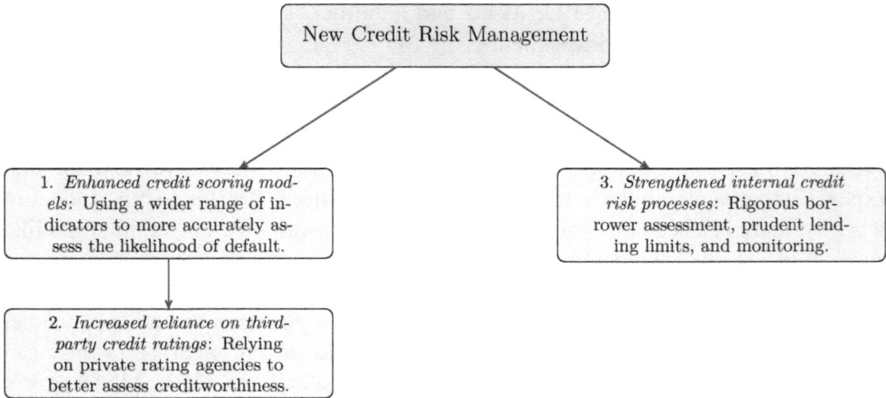

Fig. 2.3 Updated banks' credit risk management

critical importance of effective credit risk management. Indeed, banks that were heavily exposed to subprime mortgages were particularly hard hit by the housing bust (Lo, 2012). In the aftermath of the mortgage meltdown, there was a renewed emphasis on credit risk management, with banks and other financial institutions taking steps to strengthen their frameworks. The COVID-19 pandemic has also presented new challenges for credit risk management. The pandemic has caused widespread economic and financial disruptions, leading to a sharp increase in the number of borrowers who were struggling and unable to repay their debts. Figure 2.3 below presents the main credit risk management strategies that banks have adopted in response to recent shocks:

In addition to these adaptations, banks have also implemented a number of mitigation measures to reduce their exposure to credit risk, such as the five presented below (Fig. 2.4):

Credit risk continues to arise when borrowers are unable or unwilling to meet their obligations. This challenge is constantly evolving, requiring banks to constantly re-calibrate their risk management approaches in line with economic changes and shifting borrowers' behaviour. The COVID-19 pandemic highlighted the importance of effective credit risk management. As we move forward, banks must not only be adaptable, but they must also explore technological advancements such as artificial intelligence and big data analytics to improve their risk assessment capabilities and enhance their resilience.

2. **Interest Rate and Liquidity Risks**

   As explained in the first chapter, banks play a pivotal role in the economy by borrowing short term from depositors and lending long term to borrowers. This act of borrowing over short durations and lending over long periods is referred as *'maturity transformation'*. While this is essential for facilitating economic activities, it simultaneously exposes banks to two primary risks: *interest rate risk* and *liquidity risk*.

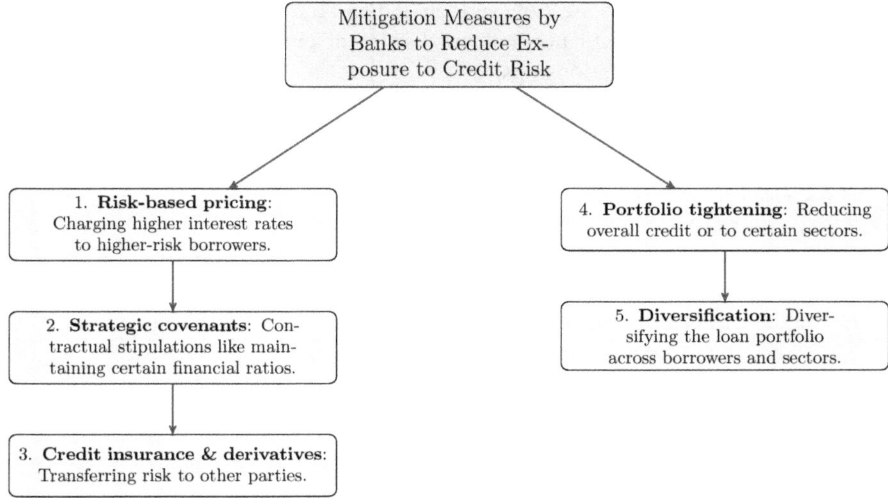

Fig. 2.4 New mitigation measures by banks

(a) *Interest Rate Risk*: Banks typically profit from the difference between long-term interest rates received on loans and short-term interest rates paid on deposits. However, when they borrow short and lend long, they face the risk that a rise in interest rates might diminish the value of their long-term fixed-rate assets. If interest rates increase, the present value of returns from these long-term assets decreases, thereby posing an *'interest rate'* or *'duration risk'* to the bank's net worth. This risk intensifies with the heightened volatility of interest rates, a trend observed since the termination of the Bretton Woods fixed exchange system.[9] Banks use various sophisticated methods, such as Asset-Liability Management (ALM), to tackle this risk by better aligning the maturities and interest rates of their assets and liabilities.

(b) *Liquidity Risk*: While banks can generally meet regular withdrawal demands, they cannot cater to all depositors simultaneously asking for their money back, which could occur during 'bank runs'.[10] This risk emerges when depositors, anxious about a bank's solvency, rush to withdraw their funds. Even if a bank's assets are above its liabilities, it may not be nimble enough

[9] The Bretton Woods system of fixed exchange rates, which was established in 1944, began to unravel in the early 1960s. The US dollar, which was the anchor currency of the system, became increasingly overvalued due to a combination of factors, including the Vietnam War and President Lyndon Johnson's Great Society programs. The overvaluation of the dollar led to a growing balance of payments deficit for the United States, as other countries were unwilling to purchase increasingly expensive dollars. In August 1971, US President Richard Nixon announced the 'temporary' suspension of the dollar's convertibility into gold. This marked the end of the Bretton Woods system, and by March 1973, the major currencies had begun to float against each other.

[10] See the Box, Diamond-Dybvig Model (1983).

to liquidate assets to meet the sudden demand for money. Such runs not only jeopardise individual banks but can disrupt the entire economy by unsettling borrower-lender relationships.

Diamond-Dybvig Model (1983)—Understanding Bank Runs and Financial Crises

The Basic Model:

The Diamond-Dybvig model (1983) offers a clear examination of bank runs. By presenting the liquidity mismatch between banks' assets and liabilities, the model captures the vulnerabilities that can lead to self-fulfilling panics. Let L represent long-term investments and D represent short-term deposits.

$$L_t = \text{Return on long-term investments at time } t$$

$$D_t = \text{Value of deposits withdrawn at time } t$$

Banks face a liquidity mismatch because $D_t < L_t$. If depositors, anticipating others will also withdraw, decide to pull their money out immediately, the bank may not have sufficient liquid assets. Such an event can lead to a bank run.

Main Assumptions:

(a) Banks hold long-term assets and offer short-term liabilities.
(b) Depositors may need to withdraw funds before assets mature.
(c) Depositors withdrawing early receive a lower return than those withdrawing later.
(d) In a bank run, all depositors try to withdraw simultaneously.

Nash Equilibrium and Bank Runs:

Under normal circumstances, only a fraction f of depositors will withdraw early:

$$f < 1$$

However, if depositors believe that others will also withdraw (due to external shocks or rumours), f approaches 1. This belief becomes self-fulfilling, leading to a bank run. In equilibrium:

$$D_t = \begin{cases} fL_t & \text{if no run} \\ L_t & \text{if run} \end{cases}$$

(continued)

Policy Implications:
To avoid bank runs:

1. **Liquidity Requirements**: Mandate banks to hold a fraction of their assets in liquid form.

$$\text{Liquid Assets} \geq \lambda D_t$$

where λ is the liquidity ratio.[a]

2. **Deposit Insurance**: Guarantee a fraction or all of the depositor's money to mitigate panic withdrawals.

$$\text{Insurance} \geq \delta D_t$$

where δ is the deposit insurance coverage ratio. However, full insurance ($\delta = 1$) might introduce moral hazard.[b]

3. **Lender of Last Resort**: Central banks can act as lenders of last resort, offering emergency liquidity assistance to banks.

---

[a]The Basel III liquidity framework introduced two required liquidity ratios:

* The Liquidity Coverage Ratio (LCR), which requires banks to hold sufficient high-quality liquid assets (HQLA) to cover their total net cash outflows over a 30-day stress period.

$$LCR = \frac{\text{HQLA}}{\text{Total net liquidity outflows over 30 days}} \geq 100\%$$

* The Net Stable Funding Ratio (NSFR), which requires banks to hold sufficient stable funding to exceed the required amount of stable funding over a one-year period of extended stress.

$$NSFR = \frac{\text{Available amount stable funding}}{\text{Required amount of stable funding}} \geq 100\%$$

The LCR and NSFR are designed to ensure that banks have sufficient liquidity and funding to withstand a period of financial stress. The LCR focuses on short-term liquidity, while the NSFR focuses on longer-term funding. The Basel III liquidity framework is an important step towards improving the resilience of the global financial system. By requiring banks to hold more liquid assets and stable funding, the framework helps to reduce the risk of bank runs and financial crises.

[b]In the US, FDIC deposit insurance is automatic for any deposit account opened at an FDIC-insured bank. The standard insurance amount is $250,000 per depositor, per FDIC-insured bank, for each account ownership category.

(continued)

Case Studies:

1. **In the United States**: The creation of FDIC in the aftermath of the Great Depression serves as a testament to the model's relevance and implications.[c]
2. **Cryptocurrency Exchanges**: These platforms, lacking traditional safeguards, show vulnerabilities similar to bank runs.[d]

The Diamond-Dybvig model remains a cornerstone in understanding banking vulnerabilities, drawing a bridge between macro-financial issues.

[c] https://www.chicagobooth.edu/review/bank-runs-arent-madness-this-model-explained-why.

[d] See for instance the run on the FTX cryptocurrency exchange in the late-2022: https://www.wsj.com/articles/crypto-has-reinvented-bank-runs-11668019310.

A notable instance was the 2023 run on Silicon Valley Bank (SVB), where concerns over the bank's solvency following a significant loss led to rapid, electronic withdrawals, culminating in the bank's takeover by regulators.

The Run on Silicon Valley Bank (1)

Case Study of a Twenty-First Century Bank Run

Silicon Valley Bank (SVB) was a large $200 billion bank that specialised in serving the tech sector. It grew rapidly during the tech boom (Fig. 2.5), following a large influx of uninsured deposits from venture capital and tech firms. These deposits were used to meet payroll and operating expenses. SVB largely invested these deposits in long-term bonds, especially Treasury bonds and US government agency mortgage-backed securities, in an effort to increase yield and bank earnings at a time when interest rates were very low. This brought SVB's investments to about half its total assets.[a] However, the values of these bonds were highly sensitive to interest rate increases.[b]

The 2021–2022 surge in inflation prompted the Federal Open Market Committee (FOMC) to raise the federal funds rate target range from 0%–0.25% on March 16, 2022 to 4.75%–5% by March 23, 2023. This increase in interest rates caused the value of SVB's long-term bonds to sharply decline, resulting in a $1.8 billion loss on the sale of $21 billion of these securities. The bank also announced a plan to raise capital, which was seen by some as a sign of distress.

[a] At the average bank, that figure is around one-quarter.

[b] For an excellent review of the events: https://www.stlouisfed.org/publications/regional-economist/2023/may/interest-rate-risk-bank-runs.

(continued)

Uninsured depositors became concerned about the bank's financial health and began withdrawing their funds (Jiang et al., 2023). This led to a run on the bank, with customers withdrawing more than $40 billion in a single day. SVB was unable to sell or borrow enough against its assets to meet the demands for deposits, and the California Department of Financial Protection and Innovation seized the bank on March 10, 2023.

The run on SVB was a major event that shook the financial world (Dewatripont et al., 2023). It highlighted the risks of banks that are heavily exposed to one sector (i.e. concentration risk) and that invest heavily in long-term bonds (i.e. interest-rate risk). The run also raised concerns about the stability of the financial system and the effectiveness of deposit insurance.

Lessons from the Run on SVB

The run on SVB provides several important lessons for banks and policymakers.

First, regulators seem to be better equipped at crisis management than prevention. As we have sent, the risks that contributed to SVB's failure, such as liquidity risk and interest rate risk, are long-standing and not specific to large banks. The run by uninsured depositors is a stark reminder of the importance of liquidity risk management (Fig. 2.6). Interest rate risk has become more relevant as higher rates have caused the value of many bank-held securities to fall. Concentration risk can amplify these other risks, as SVB's exposure to the tech industry as shown. Regulators have not publicly disclosed what steps they took to address these risks before SVB's failure, but it is clear that they need to do more to prevent similar events from happening in the future.

Second, political influence can amplify systemic risk. As Rajan and Zingales (2023) highlight, SVB's clientele included powerful and politically connected venture capitalists and firms.[c] This political clout may have shielded SVB from closer regulatory scrutiny and made it more difficult to resolve the bank's failure in a timely manner. Therefore, policymakers need to develop better metrics for measuring and limiting the political power of financial institutions.

Finally, tighter monetary conditions can expose vulnerabilities built up since the 2008 GFC. After years of low interest rates, more restrictive monetary policy is challenging banks' risk management in securities portfolios and loan exposures. With few signs of inflation abating, most central banks are expected to continue tightening. This will create a challenging environment for banks (and nonbank) financial intermediaries that are poorly managed,

[c]https://www.imf.org/en/Publications/fandd/issues/2023/06/POV-riskless-capitalism-rajan-zingales.

(continued)

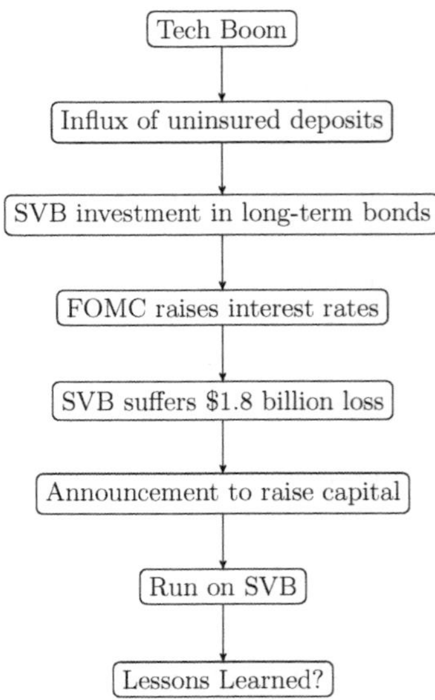

Fig. 2.5 Flow of events leading up to the run on Silicon Valley Bank

as evident in the newfound focus on unrealised interest rate-driven losses in securities portfolios. Some institutions are simply unprepared for the higher rate environment.

Did we learn the lessons from the run in order to prevent similar events from happening in the future?

It remains to be seen. Regulators have taken some steps to address the risks identified above, but more needs to be done. Regulators also need to be mindful of the potential for political influence to amplify systemic risk. And financial institutions need to ensure that their risk management practices are robust enough to withstand tighter monetary conditions.

Banks use several tools to manage these intertwined interest rate and liquidity risks:

The integration of liquidity with interest rate risk management is essential because variations in interest rates can significantly impact banks' liquidity position. For example, higher interest rates may increase borrowing costs or lower investments' value, affecting liquidity. Conversely, falling interest rates may lead to surplus in liquidity that can be invested for better adjusted risk-return assets. In other words, effective liquidity management involves a combination of strategies, tools, and risk assessment techniques tailored to a bank's idiosyncratic needs and risk tolerance.

Regular monitoring, stress testing, and scenario analysis are essential components of a robust liquidity management framework to ensure a bank remains

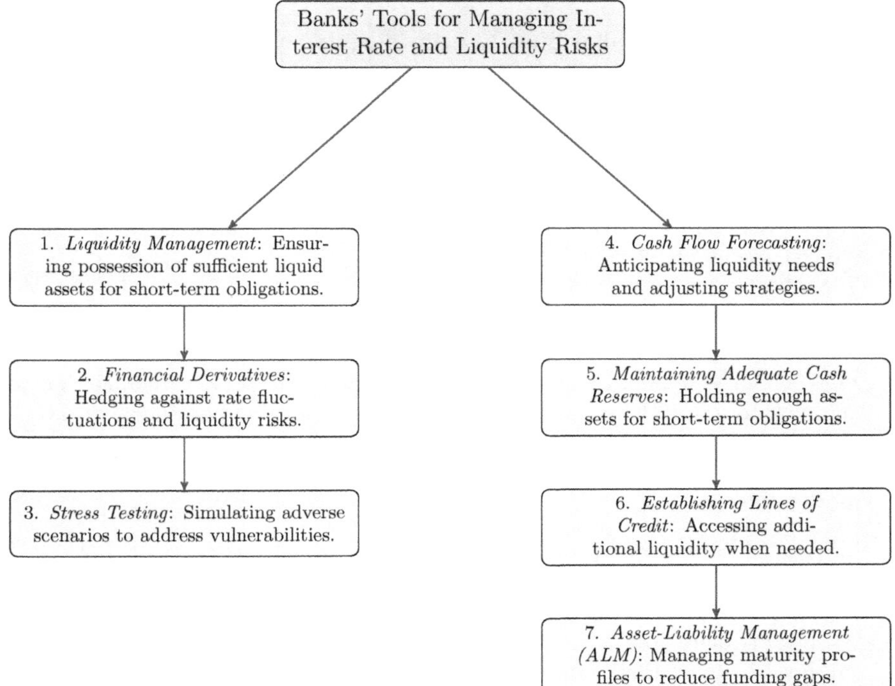

Fig. 2.6 Banks' tools for managing interest rate and liquidity risks

financially sound in the face of typical risks. The broader financial system supports banks by implementing policies that reduce the frequency, intensity, and impact of bank runs. In advanced economies, two central instrumental policies are:

(a) *Emergency Lending Facilities*: Banks can receive central bank credit (i.e. lender of last resort) not only through monetary policy operations but exceptionally also through emergency liquidity assistance.
(b) *Deposit Insurance*: Institutions like US FDIC guarantee deposits up to a specific amount, reducing the impetus for depositors to rush for withdrawals at the first hint of instability.

Despite strengthening their risk management strategies since the 2008 GFC, banks continue to face significant challenges from interest rate and liquidity risks. This was evidenced by the recent collapse of SVB in 2023, which was caused in part by liquidity issues.

The Run on Silicon Valley Bank (2): How Regulators Handled the Crisis?
In the first half of 2023, the United States experienced the abrupt insolvency of three prominent regional banks: Silicon Valley Bank (SVB), Signature Bank, and First Republic Bank. These failures marked the second, third, and fourth largest bank failures in US history. The insolvencies of these banks have raised concerns about the oversight and stability of the US banking system. This box provides a comprehensive review of the federal response to these failures, with a focus on the role of the FDIC.

The FDIC's Role in Bank Insolvency
The FDIC is a federal agency that insures deposits in US banks. It also has the authority to take over and resolve insolvent banks. When a bank fails, the FDIC typically appoints itself as receiver of the bank. The FDIC then has the authority to sell the bank's assets, pay off its depositors, and pursue any legal claims against the bank's directors or officers.

In the case of the three banks that failed in 2023, the FDIC used a variety of resolution strategies.

(a) For SVB, the FDIC entered into a purchase and assumption (P&A) agreement with First-Citizens Bank & Trust Company. Under a P&A agreement,[a] the FDIC sells the failed bank's assets and deposits to a healthy bank.
(b) For Signature Bank, the FDIC entered into a loss-share agreement with Flagstar Bank.[b] Under a loss-share agreement, the FDIC shares some of the losses that Flagstar incurs on the assets it acquires from Signature Bank.
(c) For First Republic Bank, the FDIC entered into a P&A agreement with JPMorgan Chase & Co. and a loss-share agreement with the bank's creditors.[c]

The Policy Response to the Bank Failures: The Way forward?
The failures of SVB, Signature Bank, and First Republic Bank have led to calls for reform of the US financial system. Several options are possible such as increasing the FDIC's deposit insurance limit, requiring banks to hold more capital or creating a new federal agency to oversee systemically important financial institutions. While vivid debate is still ongoing, even though there is still much debate, other policy considerations should be taken into account, such as:

[a]https://www.fdic.gov/news/press-releases/2023/pr23023.html.

[b]https://www.fdic.gov/news/press-releases/2023/pr23021.html.

[c]https://www.fdic.gov/news/press-releases/2023/pr23034.html.

(continued)

(a) *Strengthening bank safety and soundness regulations*: The failures of SVB, Signature Bank, and First Republic have raised concerns about the adequacy of existing bank safety and soundness regulations. Congress could consider strengthening these regulations, such as by requiring banks to hold more capital or by imposing stricter limits on their risk-taking activities.
(b) *Clawback authority for bank executives*: The failures have also increased awareness about the lack of accountability for bank executives who are responsible for their banks' failures. Prudential authorities could consider granting the FDIC the authority to claw back compensation from bank executives who are found to have engaged in misconduct that contributed to their institutions' failures.
(c) *Reforming the FDIC's receivership powers*: The FDIC's resolution of the 2023 regional bank failures has been criticised by some for being too costly and disruptive. Policymakers could consider reforming the FDIC's receivership powers to make them more efficient and less disruptive.

3.1 New Risks: Climate Change

Climate change affects banks through two main channels (Fig. 2.7). The first involves *physical risks* arising from the direct impact of climate change, such as more extreme weather events, sea level rise, and changes in agricultural yields. These risks can damage property, infrastructure, and land, also leading to financial losses for businesses and households. The second, *transition risk*, results from the transition to a low-carbon economy. This transition could lead to changes in assets' prices (e.g. commodity prices) and could also lead to structural shifts in consumer and investor behaviour. These risks could therefore impact firms' profitability and the assets banks hold.

Prudential authorities around the world are taking a leading role in ensuring that banks manage climate risks effectively. For instance, the ECB has already published a number of guidelines and recommendations on climate risk management, and it is conducting supervisory exercises to assess banks' progress in this area.[11]

At a high level, banks' supervisory expectations for climate risk management are based on a set of core principles:

(a) Have a clear understanding of their exposure to climate risks
(b) Have robust governance and risk management frameworks in place to manage climate risks

[11] https://www.bankingsupervision.europa.eu/press/speeches/date/2022/html/ssm.sp220922~bb043aa0bd.en.html.

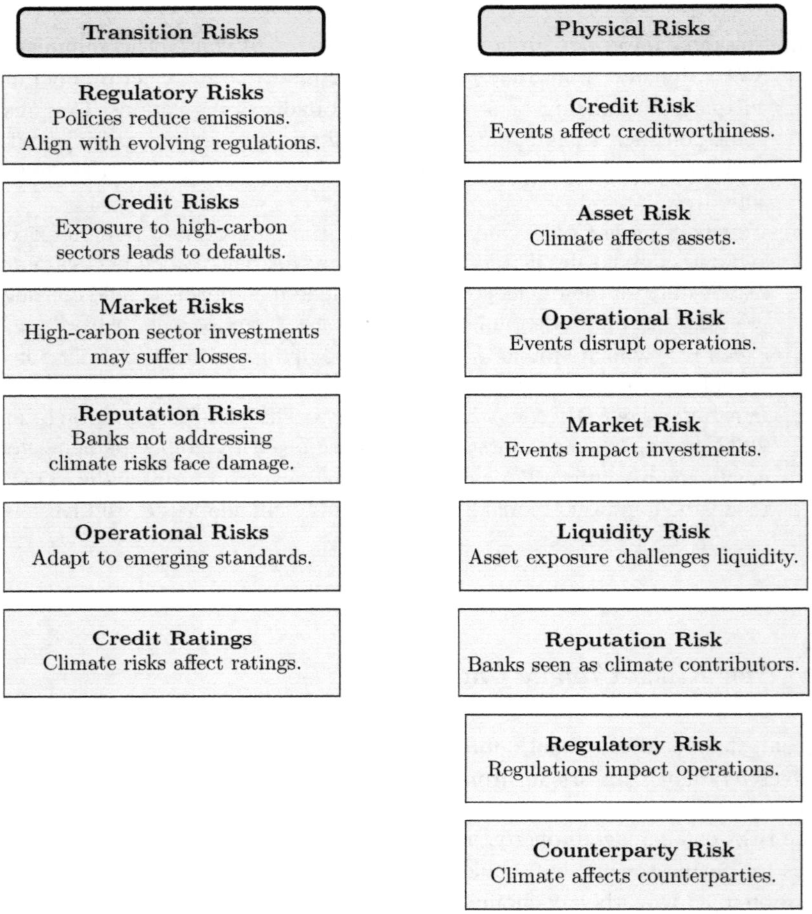

Transition Risks

Regulatory Risks
Policies reduce emissions.
Align with evolving regulations.

Credit Risks
Exposure to high-carbon sectors leads to defaults.

Market Risks
High-carbon sector investments may suffer losses.

Reputation Risks
Banks not addressing climate risks face damage.

Operational Risks
Adapt to emerging standards.

Credit Ratings
Climate risks affect ratings.

Physical Risks

Credit Risk
Events affect creditworthiness.

Asset Risk
Climate affects assets.

Operational Risk
Events disrupt operations.

Market Risk
Events impact investments.

Liquidity Risk
Asset exposure challenges liquidity.

Reputation Risk
Banks seen as climate contributors.

Regulatory Risk
Regulations impact operations.

Counterparty Risk
Climate affects counterparties.

Fig. 2.7 Overview of banking climate-related risks

(c) Disclose their climate risk exposures and management strategies
(d) Have robust governance and risk management frameworks in place to manage climate risks

Over the last few years, policymakers, governments, and supranational institutions have devoted increasing attention to environmental factors, introducing *ad-hoc* regulations and initiatives aimed at reducing CO2 emissions.[12] All of these

[12] Among the most important initiatives: At the worldwide level, the Paris Agreement signed in December 2015 by 195 nations to keep the rise in mean global temperature well below 2 °C above pre-industrial levels and ratified during the 26th Conference of the Parties (https://ukcop26.org/uk-presidency/what-is-a-cop/). At the European level, the European Central Bank (ECB)

initiatives share the overarching goal of combating climate change and protecting human well-being. The transition to a low-carbon economy is a long, uncertain, and complex process. It involves the development and deployment of new technologies, infrastructure upgrades, and changes in energy production, distribution, and consumption patterns.[13] It also entails promoting energy efficiency and implementing policies that incentivise the adoption of renewable energy solutions.

Banks play a significant role in this transition. As we have shown, they are key in allocating resources to businesses and have the power to influence the investment decisions through adjustments in loan quantities and/or prices. However, many major banks continue to support a substantial share of fossil fuel-based corporations. According to Kacperczyk and Peydró (2021), since 2015, 60 major banks have allocated USD 4.6 trillion to the fossil fuel industry, including USD 742 billion to oil, gas, and coal in 2021 alone.

Therefore, the banking system is both vulnerable to the impacts of climate change and plays a role in the transition to a low-carbon economy. Central banks and financial regulators need to take on new responsibilities to support this transition and facilitate the necessary reorientation of fund flows.[14] This balancing act is delicate. Indeed, central banks and financial regulators should use all available measures to facilitate the required redirection of capital resources, but they must be mindful of the limits of their policy tools and mandates, as well as the risks, frictions, and side-effects of their decisions (Demekas & Grippa, 2021).

At a high level, regulators have sought to incentivize banks and to incorporate environmental considerations into their lending practices, thereby promoting green lending. This approach has been motivated by the need to drive investments in infrastructure, technology, and equipment that can support a transition to a lower-carbon economy (Stiglitz et al., 2017). However, this approach presents significant trade-offs. It can help banks to tilt their portfolios toward greener lending but it can also increase uncertainty, given the measurement, risk assessment, and technical nature of green lending. This could lead to an increase in informational asymmetries and frictions in the performance of banks, as their ability to effectively reallocate funds and manage risks may be negatively affected.

---

published its 'Guide on climate-related and environmental risks' in 2020. It sets out the ECB supervisory expectations for banks' risk management and disclosure in this domain. This guide establishes a clear framework for European banks to accurately measure, mitigate, and disclose climate-related and environmental risks. (https://www.bankingsupervision.europa.eu/ecb/pub/pdf/ssm.202011finalguideonclimate-relatedandenvironmentalrisks~58213f6564.en.pdf). In addition, the ECB has adopted a climate agenda and started to carry out climate-stress tests in 2022, designed to prepare banks for both upcoming regulatory changes and climate related-risks, most notably transition and physical risks (https://www.bankingsupervision.europa.eu/ecb/pub/pdf/ssm.202212_ECBreport_on_good_practices_for_CST~539227e0c1.en.pdf).

[13] https://www.ipcc.ch/.

[14] https://www.imf.org/en/Publications/fandd/issues/2021/09/isabel-schnabel-ECB-climate-change.

The concept of a *'preferred habitat'* in lending refers to banks' tendency to concentrate their lending activities in specific sectors or markets. This concentration reflects banks' perceptions of risk-return trade-offs and comparative advantages, which are influenced by a variety of variables, including banks' expertise, information, and regulatory requirements. The concept of a preferred habitat closely aligns with the idea of specialisation, wherein a bank focuses on a specific market or lending activity where information plays a crucial role.

For instance, specialised green banks play an important role in promoting a transition to a lower-carbon economy by providing financing and expertise to green projects. These banks are dedicated to sustainable or environmental finance and have well-defined strategies and frameworks for prioritising funding for environmentally friendly projects. They conduct assessments of the environmental impact and sustainability of potential borrowers and direct their lending to green projects.

The green transition is now calling for banks that are not specialised in such lending to increasingly incorporate green lending practices into their operations.[15]This shift introduces a range of fundamental uncertainties for banks when extending credit to environmentally responsible firms. These uncertainties have far-reaching implications for financial evaluations, investment levels, and risk assessment and oversight processes. In particular, corporate carbon risk data and disclosure inadequacies pose significant challenges to the proper and effective measurement of risk (Hahn et al., 2015; Boffo & Patalano, 2020; Griffin & Jaffe, 2022). More specifically, these challenges include, *inter alia*, (i) Inconsistent Reporting Standards (e.g. absence of standardised reporting frameworks for carbon risk disclosure), (ii) Measurement and Data Challenges (e.g. Companies often encounter difficulties in obtaining accurate emissions data, especially concerning Scope 3 emissions), (iii) Forward-Looking Assessment (e.g. Current carbon risk disclosure predominantly centres on historical emissions), and (iv) Lack of Verification and Assurance (e.g. absence of independent verification or assurance mechanisms for carbon risk disclosure raises doubts regarding the reliability and accuracy of the reported information).

Data deficiencies and poor corporate carbon risk disclosure hinder effective risk management and alter the credibility of green and environmental, social, and governance (ESG) standards. Efforts are already underway to address these shortcomings, but designing comprehensive and adaptable disclosure frameworks is a long journey. Outdated industrial policies and regional disparities in disclosure coverage can lead to unbalanced competitive advantages and greenwashing. Contradictory and ambiguous information for investors could further exacerbate uncertainty and problems in decision-making.

Ultimately, banks face a formidable challenge in effectively assessing and managing climate-related risks due to the prevailing uncertainty regarding climate policies. This uncertainty also casts a shadow over their investment evaluations, with adverse consequences such as a negative impact on net present values and an

[15] https://www.nrel.gov/state-local-tribal/basics-green-banks.html.

increase in the cost of capital. This, in turn, affects negatively the ability of investors to finance low-carbon activities, as emphasised in Berg et al. (2023).

In short, climate policy uncertainty and regulatory fragmentation challenge banks' risk assessment and investment decisions for green projects563.2, impeding low-carbon financing. Clear and consistent policy frameworks that provide insights into the forthcoming regulatory environment are essential for banks to comprehensively evaluate the potential impact of climate-related risks on their portfolios.[16] Without such clarity, banks may encounter difficulties in accurately gauging and quantifying the risks associated with issues like stranded assets, carbon pricing, or shifts in market demand for carbon-intensive industries. Banks could also display reluctance to allocate capital toward long-term projects or technologies that heavily rely on supportive climate policies (Battiston et al., 2021; Monasterolo et al., 2022).

A recent study by Buchetti et al. (2023) finds that European banks perceive lending to green companies as riskier than to brown companies, a phenomenon the authors label as the *'green-transition risk'*. This study sheds light on a potential dilemma banks face. On the one hand, they are incentivised to increase green lending to align with regulatory expectations and requirements (Demekas & Grippa, 2021), as well as broader sustainability goals. On the other hand, they face a number of challenges, such as lack of specialisation or long-term predictability into the green lending business. As of today, green lending remains predominantly the domain of specialised banks that focus on sustainable and environmental finance and the transition to a green economy, catalysed by the shift toward sustainability, necessitates that non-specialised banks increasingly integrate green lending practices into their operational set-ups. Today, policymakers are playing a key role in addressing these obstacles by providing clear and consistent regulatory frameworks. This would enable banks to more effectively assess and manage climate-related risks.

Climate Risk Stress Testing

Major supervisors and central bankers have initiated a comprehensive climate risk stress test for banks' balance sheets. This is part of a broader plan to integrate climate change considerations into monetary policy and financial stability strategies. The key objectives of the stress test are to:

- Evaluate the banks' financial risk profiles in light of climate change.
- Enhance the banks' capabilities in assessing climate-related risks.
- Understand the implications of various monetary policy portfolios, such as corporate bonds, covered bonds, asset-backed securities (ABSs), and collateralized credit operations.

(continued)

[16] https://www.bankingsupervision.europa.eu/about/climate/html/index.en.html.

Methodological Framework:
Scenarios: The stress test used scenarios are usually developed in collaboration with international organisations to assess the resilience of the financial system and the central bank to climate-related risks. Specifically, the scenarios examined the impact of changes in climate policy, physical risks from extreme weather events, and transition risks from the shift to a low-carbon economy.

- The long-term scenarios consider the impact of climate change over a 30-year horizon and vary in terms of climate policy implementations and the expected materialisation of climate risks.
- The short-term scenarios focus on the impact of specific climate events, such as a flood or a disorderly transition to a low-carbon economy.

Analytical Approach:
The state-of-the-art methodology incorporate credit risk shocks specific to each type of financial exposure. The general model used for estimating credit risk shock can be represented as:

$$\Delta CR_i = \alpha + \beta_1 \times TR_i + \beta_2 \times PR_i + \varepsilon_i$$

where

- ΔCR_i is the credit risk change for asset i.
- TR_i is the transition risk for asset i.
- PR_i is the physical risk for asset i.
- ε_i is the error term.

Market shocks can also be factor in, by taking into account changes in risk-free interest rates (ΔRF) and corporate bond spreads (ΔCBS).
Key Insights:

- Both transition (TR) and physical (PR) climate risks notably influenced the bank's balance sheet risk profile.
- Under adverse scenarios, risk estimates (RE) can be modelled as:

$$RE = \gamma + \delta_1 \times TR + \delta_2 \times PR + \zeta$$

Where ζ is the error term. In general, corporate bonds linked to climate-vulnerable sectors could be a significant driver of risk in the financial system. Banks' holdings of these bonds may reflect broader market risk dynamics. For instance, covered bonds and asset-backed securities (ABSs) may be more sensitive to physical risks, such as those arising from extreme weather events, due to their exposure to the housing market. In contrast, collateralized credit operations may have lower risk due to their inherent double default nature.
Strategic Implications and Forward Outlook:

(continued)

- Periodic climate risk stress tests will become standard for assessing the bank's balance sheet.
- Future endeavours will likely witness refined methodologies and a broader spectrum of financial exposures.
- Incorporating climate risk insights will become crucial for the bank's overarching risk management strategy.

Although there is no consensus on the precise implications of climate change for financial stability, it is clear that a comprehensive understanding of all potential risks, including those stemming from climate change, is essential for ensuring a robust financial system. Ongoing rigorous academic research on the intertwining of climate change and economic outcomes is therefore essential.

4 New Risks: Digitisation, Technology, and the Financial Sector

The rapid evolution of technology within the financial industry and the associated transformation of market structures pose significant risks to the entire financial system and notably to established banks. Over the past few decades, credit, investment, and intermediation have all been transformed (Rajan, 2006) by several factors such as: (i) technological advancements (e.g. declining costs of processing and storing information), (ii) deregulation and the removal of entry barriers, and (iii) institutional changes (e.g. rise to new types of financial entities like fintech companies and shadow banks).

As mentioned in previous sections, the digital revolution presents a dilemma for policymakers, banks, and regulators alike. On the one hand, it offers the opportunity to enhance financial inclusion and create a more competitive financial system. On the other hand, it raises new challenges to financial stability[17] and consumer protection. Consequently, we must all remain collectively vigilant in identifying potential new systemic risks. Strong forces are currently reshaping the banking sector and redefining banks' business models. For instance, banks have been facing structural difficulties, such as a prolonged low interest rate environment and the costs of excess capacity.[18] In addition, banks need to deal with more recently developing challenges such as the entrance of new competitors from platform-based rivals, fintech companies, and emerging big tech players (Vives, 2019).

[17] For instance, the pressure on traditional banks' profit margins may necessitate risk-taking.

[18] More recently, however, interest rate increases by global central banks to contain the biggest inflation outbreak in four decades generated strains for banks.

Recent research has explored the drivers of digital disruption in the financial sector, as well as the impact of financial technology (fintech) on efficiency. Some studies have examined the effects of increased adoption of information technology (IT) by banks, particularly its influence on corporate lending and implications for financial stability. Other studies have investigated how fintech drives efficiency (Pierri and Timmer, 2022; Branzoli et al., 2023). Indeed, the adoption of new technologies has profound implications for the welfare of market participants, as it reduces costs in financial intermediation, lending, payment systems, and insurance (Berg et al., 2018; Buchak et al., 2018). For example, fintech enables banks to (i) better assess potential borrowers using big data, (ii) address information asymmetries, (iii) engage in more targeted price discrimination, and (iv) provide financial services to less developed regions that were previously constrained by financial resources.

5 New Risks: Cyber Risk and the Financial Sector

5.1 The Emergence of Cyber Risk for Banks

Together with the technological adoption, institutions become as well exposed to a new range of information security or cyber risks.[19] Cyber risk has been gradually and increasingly considered as one of the highest operational risk concerns.[20] The empirical literature on this topic is burgeoning with new findings. Authorities recognise cyber risk as an important channel for systemic risk. Examples are numerous. First, a strand of research aims at theorising and modelling optimal investment in information protection and cyber security (Gordon & Loeb, 2002; Varian, 2014; Anderson & Moore, 2006; Acquisti et al., 2007; Do et al., 2017; Anand et al., 2022), as well as empirically explore the implications of cyberattacks and information security risk (Gogolin et al., 2021; Jamilov et al., 2021). Second, another area of research investigates on the financial stability implications of Cybersecurity (Kashyap & Wetherilt, 2019; Duffie & Younger, 2019; Eisenbach et al., 2022; Welburn & Strong, 2022; Florackis et al., 2023). As of today, we all now understand the threat of cyber risk and its potential to disrupt critical financial services and operations and as a result impair the provision of key economic functions. Cyber risk can significantly impact banks and financial stability in several ways (Fig. 2.8):

The 2023 ransomware attack on Silicon Valley Bank (SVB) was a stark reminder of the escalating cyber threats faced by the banking sector.[21] Such attacks can manifest in various ways, with potentially devastating consequences. As shown

[19] Cyber risk is commonly referred to any risk of financial loss, disruption, or damage to the reputation of an organisation resulting from the failure of its information technology systems.

[20] See Risk.net, 'Top 10 operational risks for 2018', as well as for 2019, 2020 and 2021.

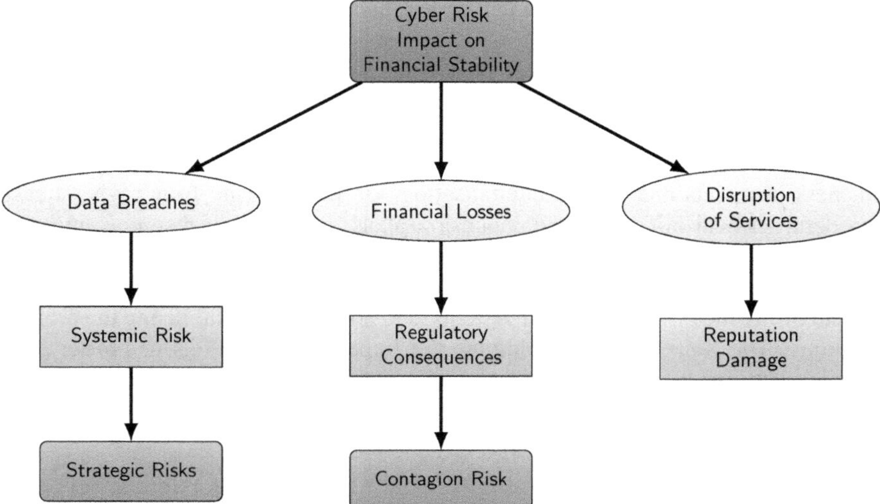

Fig. 2.8 Overview of banking cyber-related risks

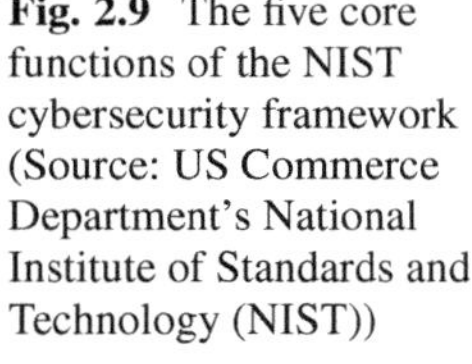
Fig. 2.9 The five core functions of the NIST cybersecurity framework (Source: US Commerce Department's National Institute of Standards and Technology (NIST))

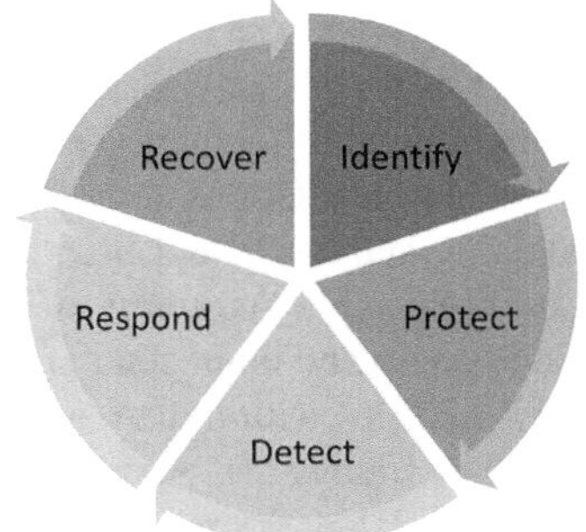

in Fig. 2.9, data breaches can expose sensitive customer information, including personal and financial details, leading to financial losses, legal liability, and also reputational damage. Direct financial losses can also result from fraudulent fund transfers, transactional manipulations, or systemic disruptions. Similarly, operational disruptions can prevent customers from accessing their accounts or digital banking services, potentially amplifying financial stress, especially if multiple banks are affected at the same time. Given the interconnectedness of the global financial system, a cyberattack on a single bank can have contagion effects across the industry. In short, a significant breach or operational disruption at a major bank

[21] https://www.bleepingcomputer.com/news/security/cybercriminals-exploit-svb-collapse-to-steal-money-and-data/.

could pose systemic risks, impacting a wide range of financial institutions, markets, and the overall economic stability.

From a regulatory perspective, banks are subject to stringent cybersecurity requirements. A cyber incident can lead to regulatory scrutiny, investigations, hefty fines, and even legal proceedings. Additionally, the reputational damage from a cyberattack can be long-lasting, eroding customer confidence and impacting business prospects and market capitalisation. On the strategic front, cyberattacks can derail critical initiatives and expansion plans, especially if resources must be diverted to address cyber threats. Finally, there is the risk of contagion, whereby cyber disruptions in the banking sector can spread to other industries, compromising critical infrastructure and payment systems, and potentially destabilising the broader economy. The SVB incident highlights the imperative for banks to bolster their cybersecurity infrastructure, implement robust security protocols, and cultivate a culture of cybersecurity awareness among their workforce.

5.2 Key Regulatory and Policy Considerations and Ways Ahead

The NIST Cybersecurity Framework

The NIST Cybersecurity Framework, developed by the US National Institute of Standards and Technology (NIST), offers guidelines for mitigating cybersecurity risks in organisations and enhancing Critical Infrastructure Cybersecurity. Based on existing standards and practices (Gordon et al., 2020), this framework presents a comprehensive taxonomy of cybersecurity outcomes and a methodology for their assessment and management. It also provides guidance on safeguarding privacy and civil liberties within the realm of cybersecurity.

This framework serves as a universal language, enabling both internal and external stakeholders to comprehend, manage, and communicate cybersecurity risks effectively. It aids in the identification and prioritisation of actions to reduce these risks, aligning policies, business strategies, and technological approaches. It can also be applied organisation-wide or focused specifically on critical service delivery.

The fundamental components of the NIST approach are based on five main functions, structuring essential cybersecurity activities at their most fundamental level. These functions, namely *Identify, Protect, Detect, Respond, and Recover*, assist organisations in articulating their cybersecurity risk management. They do so by organising information, facilitating risk-related decisions, mitigating threats, and enhancing strategies based on past experiences. These functions also harmonised with established incident management methodologies and demonstrate the effectiveness of cybersecurity investments. For instance, investments in planning and exercises bolster swift response and recovery measures, ultimately minimising the impact on service delivery.

The five framework core functions are defined below. These functions are not intended to form a serial path or lead to a static desired end state. Rather, the functions should be performed concurrently and continuously to form an operational culture that addresses the dynamic cybersecurity risk.[22]

Identify—Develop an organisational understanding to manage cybersecurity risk to systems, people, assets, data, and capabilities. The tasks within the Identify Function form the cornerstone of the Framework's effective implementation. Grasping the business context, comprehending the resources essential for critical functions, and recognising the associated cybersecurity risks empower an organisation to concentrate and rank its initiatives. This alignment with the organisation's risk management strategy and business requirements ensures a targeted and prioritised approach. Examples of outcome categories within this Function include:

- *Asset Management*: The identification and management of data, personnel, devices, systems, and facilities crucial for achieving organisational objectives. This management aligns with their importance to business goals and the organisation's risk strategy.
- *Business Environment*: Understanding and prioritising the organisation's mission, objectives, stakeholders, and activities. This information informs cyber roles, responsibilities, and risk management decisions.
- *Governance*: Comprehension of policies, procedures, and processes for managing and monitoring regulatory, legal, risk, environmental, and operational requirements. These aspects inform the management of cyber risk.
- *Risk Assessment*: Understanding cyber-related risks to organisational operations, assets, and individuals, including their impact on mission, functions, image, or reputation.
- *Risk Management Strategy*: Establishment of organisational priorities, constraints, risk tolerances, and assumptions used to support operational risk decisions.
- *Supply Chain Risk Management*: Establishment of organisational priorities, constraints, risk tolerances, and assumptions guiding decisions related to managing supply chain risk. Implementation of processes for identifying, assessing, and managing supply chain risks is in place.

Protect—Develop and implement appropriate safeguards to ensure delivery of critical services. The Protect Function aids in restricting or mitigating the impact of a potential cybersecurity incident. Examples of outcome Categories within this Function include: Identity Management and Access Control, Awareness and Training, Data Security, Information Protection Processes and Procedures, Maintenance, and Protective Technology.

- *Access Control*: Access to assets and associated facilities is restricted to authorised users, processes, or devices and is limited to authorised activities and transactions.

[22] Please see list and details on Appendix 1 in the NIST Framework Version 1.1:https://doi.org/10.6028/NIST.CSWP.04162018.

- *Awareness and Training*: The organisation's staff and partners receive education in cybersecurity awareness and are adequately trained to fulfil their information security-related duties and obligations in accordance with relevant policies, procedures, and agreements.
- *Data Security*: Information and records (data) are handled in line with the organisation's risk strategy to preserve the confidentiality, integrity, and availability of information.
- *Information Protection Processes and Procedures*: Security policies, which encompass purpose, scope, roles, responsibilities, management commitment, and coordination among organisational units, as well as processes and procedures, are upheld and utilised to oversee the protection of information systems and assets.
- Maintenance: Maintenance and repairs of industrial control and information system components are carried out in adherence to established policies and procedures.
- Protective Technology: Technical security solutions are administered to ensure the security and resilience of systems and assets, maintaining consistency with relevant policies, procedures, and agreements.

Detect—Develop and implement appropriate activities to identify the occurrence of a cyber event. The Detect Function allows for the prompt identification of cybersecurity incidents. Examples of outcome Categories within this Function include: Anomalies and Events, Security Continuous Monitoring, and Detection Processes.

- *Anomalies and Events*: Unusual activities are promptly identified, and the potential impact of events is comprehended.
- *Security Continuous Monitoring*: The information system and assets are regularly monitored to pinpoint cyber events and validate the efficacy of protective measures.
- *Detection Processes*: Processes and procedures for detection are upheld and tested to guarantee timely and comprehensive awareness of abnormal events.

Respond—Develop and implement appropriate activities to take action regarding a detected cyber issue. The Respond Function aids in managing and minimising the impact of a potential cybersecurity incident. Examples of outcome Categories within this Function include: Response Planning, Communications, Analysis, Mitigation, and Improvements.

- *Response Planning*: Processes and procedures for response are carried out and kept up-to-date, ensuring a timely reaction to identified cybersecurity incidents.
- *Communications*: Response efforts are coordinated with relevant internal and external parties, potentially involving external assistance from law enforcement agencies.
- *Analysis*: In-depth analysis is conducted to guarantee an effective response and to support recovery actions.
- *Mitigation*: Actions are taken to prevent the escalation of an event, minimise its impact, and completely eliminate the incident.

- *Improvements*: Organisational response activities are enhanced by integrating insights gained from ongoing and past detection/response efforts.

Recover—Develop and implement appropriate activities to maintain plans for resilience and to restore any capabilities or services that were impaired due to a cybersecurity incident. The Recover Function facilitates swift restoration to regular operations, minimising the impact of a cyber events. Examples of outcome Categories within this Function include: Recovery Planning, Improvements, and Communications.

- *Recovery Planning*: Processes and procedures for recovery are implemented and upheld to guarantee the timely restoration of systems or assets affected by cyber events.
- *Improvements*: Recovery planning and processes are enhanced by integrating insights gained from past experiences into future activities.
- *Communications*: Restoration activities are synchronised with internal and external entities, including coordinating centres, Internet Service Providers, operators of attacking systems, affected parties, other Computer Security Incident Response Teams (CSIRTs), and vendors.

Digital Operational Resilience Act (DORA): What Lies Ahead for the Financial Sector

The DORA[23] addresses a critical issue within the framework of financial regulation in the European Union. Prior to the implementation of DORA, banks managed operational risk categories by allocating capital but did not comprehensively address all parts of the so-called operational resilience. With DORA, banks are now obliged to adhere to specific regulations pertaining to safeguarding, identifying, containing, recovering from, and rectifying issues related to incidents involving Information and Communication Technology (ICT). DORA also explicitly recognises the significance of ICT risk and prescribes regulations governing ICT risk management, incident reporting, operational resilience testing, and the monitoring of third-party ICT risks. This regulation acknowledges the potential for ICT incidents and lapses in operational resilience to endanger the stability of the entire banking system, even when capital adequacy is ensured for conventional risk categories.

Article 1 of DORA, titled 'Subject Matter', outlines the key objectives as follows:

To establish a robust standard of digital operational resilience, this Regulation lays down consistent requirements concerning the security of network and information systems that underpin the operational processes of financial entities. These requirements include:

- Mandated provisions for financial entities concerning:
  - Management of ICT risks

[23] Officially designated as Regulation (EU) 2022/2554.

  - Reporting of significant ICT-related incidents and voluntary notification of substantial cyber threats to the relevant competent authorities
  - Reporting of major operational or security incidents related to payment systems to the competent authorities by financial entities[24]
  - Implementation of digital operational resilience testing
  - Facilitation of information and intelligence sharing concerning cyber threats and vulnerabilities
  - Implementation of measures for the effective management of ICT-related third-party risks

- Stipulations regarding contractual arrangements between ICT third-party service providers and financial entities
- Guidelines governing the establishment and operation of the Oversight Framework for critical ICT third-party service providers when they provide services to financial entities
- Regulations governing cooperation among competent authorities, as well as rules regarding supervision and enforcement by competent authorities in relation to all matters covered within the scope of this Regulation

DORA has the potential to form the *kernel* of the digital finance package—a large set of measures designed to foster and support the potential of digital finance in terms of innovation and competition while at the same time addressing the associated risks. This initiative aligns with the priorities of the European Commission to modernise Europe for the digital age and cultivate an economy that is well-prepared for the future and benefits all citizens.

Contained within the digital finance package is a novel strategy aimed at digital finance in the EU financial sector. The primary objective of this strategy is to ensure that the EU fully embraces the digital transformation and leads it with innovative European companies, thereby extending the advantages of digital finance to both consumers and businesses. In addition to the proposal under consideration, the package incorporates several other elements, including a proposal governing markets in crypto assets, a proposal outlining a pilot regime for distributed ledger technology (DLT) market infrastructure, and a directive intended to clarify or modify specific EU financial services regulations.

Within the financial sector, digitalization and operational resilience are closely linked. The adoption of ICT introduces both opportunities and risks, necessitating thorough comprehension and management, particularly during periods of high financial stress. To address these obstacles, policymakers and supervisors have progressively turned their attention to risks arising from reliance on ICT. Notably, efforts have been made to bolster firms' resilience through the establishment of standards and the coordination of regulatory and supervisory activities. These endeavours have been undertaken at both the international and European levels,

[24] Mentioned in Article 2(1), points (a) to (d).

spanning various industries and specific sectors, including new and traditional financial services.

However, ICT-related risks persistently challenge the operational resilience, performance, and stability of the EU banking system. Over the past decade, post-financial crisis reforms such as the Single Rulebook seem to have strengthened the financial health of the EU financial sector, with only indirect consideration of ICT risks in certain areas, as part of broader measures targeting operational risks.

These measures had several characteristics that limited their effectiveness. For instance, they were often designed as directives with minimum harmonisation or principles-based regulations, leaving room for divergent approaches across the Single Market. Furthermore, there was limited or incomplete focus on ICT risks within the context of operational risk coverage. Moreover, these policies varied across sector-specific financial services legislation. Consequently, the EU-level intervention did not entirely align with the requirements of European financial entities for managing operational risks effectively in the face of ICT incidents or equip financial supervisors with the most appropriate tools to prevent financial instability arising from ICT risks.

The lack of comprehensive and detailed EU-level rules on digital operational resilience (DOR) has led to a proliferation of national regulatory initiatives, such as DOR testing and supervisory approaches to address dependencies on ICT third parties. However, national actions are limited in their effectiveness due to the cross-border nature of ICT risks. Moreover, these uncoordinated national initiatives have resulted in redundancies, inconsistencies, duplicate requirements, high administrative and compliance costs–especially for cross-border financial entities–or undetected and unaddressed ICT risks.

This fragmentation could negatively affect the Single Market, the stability and integrity of the EU banking sector, and places consumers and investors at risk. Hence, it is critical to establish a comprehensive and detailed EU DOR framework for banks. This framework will deepen the digital risk management dimension of the Single Rulebook. Specifically, it will improve and streamline banks' management of ICT risks, institute rigorous testing of ICT systems, heighten supervisors' awareness of cyber risks and ICT-related incidents, and empower supervisors to oversee risks arising from banks' reliance on ICT third-party service providers. The proposal will also establish a uniform incident reporting mechanism to reduce administrative burdens for banks and strengthen supervisory effectiveness.

US Cyber Security Strategy Takes a New Regulation for the Cloud

One of the challenging aspects of the current environment is the lack of clarity regarding the security measures implemented by cloud providers, which leaves both government entities and businesses in the dark. The US Treasury Department has pointed out the *'insufficient transparency'* provided by cloud firms, making it difficult for due diligence and risk monitoring. This ambiguity has raised concerns within the White House, as the cloud is increasingly viewed as a significant security vulnerability.

In response to these concerns, the United States is taking unprecedented steps to formulate a comprehensive plan aimed at regulating the security practices of major cloud providers such as Amazon, Microsoft, Google, and Oracle. These companies play an important role by offering data storage and computational resources to a diverse clientele, ranging from small and medium-sized enterprises to government agencies as critical as the Pentagon and CIA. Recently, the Biden administration emphasised its intention to further intensify cloud regulations, shedding light on its commitment to maintaining the integrity of cloud services. Rather than shunning the cloud, the administration's objective is to ensure that the rapid expansion of cloud technology does not introduce new security vulnerabilities.

As we said, cloud security has become a top priority for policymakers, given the cloud's essential role in the global economy. Senior officials, such as Acting National Cyber Director Kemba Walden, have highlighted the potential for catastrophic economic and government disruption if cloud services were disrupted. This has led to concerns about the 'too-big-to-fail' status of cloud providers. Another concern is the interconnected nature of cloud services. A failure at a single cloud provider could have a cascading effect, disrupting the entire Internet infrastructure. This is especially concerning given the reliance of many businesses and governments on cloud services. One challenge complicating the cloud security landscape is the practice of cloud providers charging customers extra fees for enhanced security protections. This practice not only capitalises on the necessity for heightened security but also creates vulnerabilities when organisations opt not to invest in these additional safeguards. This was evident in the SolarWinds attack, where agencies affected by the Russian hacking campaign had not opted for the added security features offered by Microsoft. Also, policymakers have raised concerns about the focus of major cloud providers on promoting the security of individual products rather than addressing the collective risk associated with the integration of multiple products and services. This is why we are facing an urgent need for a more comprehensive and coordinated approach to cloud security in the evolving digital architecture.[25,26]

[25] https://www.politico.com/news/2023/03/10/white-house-cloud-overhaul-00086595.

[26] https://home.treasury.gov/news/press-releases/jy1252.

Chapter 3
The Role of the Accounting Information in Banking Failures

1 Introduction

History has witnessed the catastrophic impacts of financial misinformation, from the Great Depression (1929–1939) to the more recent Great Financial Crisis (2008). The aftermath of these events was not merely economic. They led to a crisis of trust, questioning the very foundations upon which modern financial institutions are built and their transparency in disclosing financial information.

As stakeholders, how can we scrutinize bank behaviour? How do we navigate the maze of numbers to discern the true financial health of a bank? It is vital to recognise the tools and tactics that might obscure this truth. In every business, there is a balance between presenting oneself optimally and crossing the line into deceit or manipulation. Banking, with its intricate web of transactions, and complex financial instruments offer a fertile ground for 'accounting manipulation'. But why might banks employ such tactics? At the core, it often stems from the incessant pressure to meet targets and satisfy investors. These pressures are heightened by the high-stakes nature of banking, where a shift in depositor sentiment can provoke bank runs.

In the financial world, meticulous accounting is essential. It offers shareholders, depositors, and all stakeholders a comprehensive view of a bank's health. However, when this data is compromised (e.g., by overstating assets or underreporting liabilities), the consequences can be severe. This chapter examines the repercussions of inaccuracies or intentional distortions in a bank's financial statements and how they can trigger or exacerbate banking failures.

We will commence by distinguishing between the financial statements of commercial banks and investment banks. By capitalising on these differences, we aim to explore how banks might inflate asset values, thereby misleading stakeholders and incurring potential long-term risks. Indeed, precise valuation is indispensable given the varied financial instruments that banks manage. The procrastination in recognising bad loans, combined with the misevaluation of complex assets as witnessed in the MPS and Lehman Brothers cases, underscores the inherent risks.

N. Abidi et al., *Why Do Banks Fail and What to Do About It*, Contributions to Finance and Accounting, https://doi.org/10.1007/978-3-031-52311-3_3

Lastly, we delve into the specifics of these tactics. We begin with the notorious 'Lehman 105 Repo Scandal', a financial stratagem that contributed to one of the most significant bankruptcy filings in US history. We will also explore the subtle mechanisms of special purpose entities (also known as special purpose vehicles) that enable banks to move items off their balance sheets. Additionally, we will address the strategies that banks employ at quarter-ends, delve into the nuances of accrual accounting, and discuss the phenomenon known as income smoothing. Each of these aspects provides insights into the motivations, techniques, and consequences of financial misrepresentation.

2 The Financial Statement of Commercial and Investment Banks

Before delving into the methodology for estimating assets and liabilities in banks, and understanding the inherent risks in this process, let us review a simplified version of a bank's financial statement (hereafter referred to as FS).[1] Figure 3.1 displays the FS for both a commercial bank (hereafter referred to as CB) (Panel A) and an investment bank (hereafter referred to as IB) (Panel B).

- Commercial banks (CBs) principally focus on retail banking. CBs accept deposits (Column 2—Liabilities) from individuals and businesses and extend loans (Column 1—Assets). While these banks do invest in securities (Column 1—Assets), such assets typically are not the dominant item on their balance sheet (hereafter referred to as BS). Their primary revenue streams come from the interest spread between their lending and deposit rates. When a CB's interest income from loans (Column 3—Revenues) exceeds the interest it pays on deposits (Column 4—Costs), the CB earns a profit. Figure 3.2 Panel A graphically displays the main items of a CB's BS. As we can observe, lending and deposits are the two largest items on the BS.
- Investment banks (IBs) primarily aid corporations in raising capital, offer advisory services on mergers and acquisitions (M&A), manage the underwriting of securities, and execute trades on behalf of their clients. Unlike CBs, IBs do not accept deposits from the general public. Instead, they source funds mainly through short-term debt instruments (Column 6—Liabilities) from sophisticated investors and deploy these funds into various securities (Column 5—Assets). Their revenue streams come from a combination of service fees, trading activities, and advisory services. Figure 3.2 Panel B graphically depicts the primary components of an IB's BS. Naturally, the exact structure of the FS of banks will vary depending on the specific activities each bank engages in. For instance, a CB

[1] To simplify our analysis, we exclude several items typically found in Commercial banks and Investment banks, for example, intangible assets (e.g., goodwill, core deposit intangibles), premises and fixed assets, and retained earnings.

Commercial bank (Panel A)

Balance Sheet

Assets (Column 1)	Liabilities (Column 2)
a) Loans (Main Item) • residential mortgages • commercial loans → Risk of accounting manipulation in terms of delaying the recognition of bad loans • consumer loans b) Investment securities • Level 1 → Low risk of accounting manipulation • Level 2 → Medium risk of accounting manipulation • Level 3 → High risk of accounting manipulation c) Cash	d) Equity • share capital • share premium e) Deposits (Main Item) • checking • savings f) Short-term Debt • interbank loans • certificate of deposits g) Long-term Debt • bonds • subordinated debt

Income Statement

Revenues (Column 3)	Costs (Column 4)
h) Interest Income (mainly interest income from loans)	I) Interest Expenses (mainly Interest paid on deposits)

Investment bank (Panel B)

Balance Sheet

Assets (Column 5)	Liabilities (Column 6)
a) Investment securities (Main Item) • Level 1 → Low risk of accounting manipulation • Level 2 → Medium risk of accounting manipulation • Level 3 → High risk of accounting manipulation b) Cash	c) Equity • share capital • share premium d) Short-term Debt (Main Item) • broker-dealer borrowing • repurchase agreements (REPOS) • interbank loans e) Long-term Debt • bonds • debentures

Income Statement

Revenues (Column 7)	Costs (Column 8)
f) Income (derived from trading revenues, investment banking fees (like M&A advisory fees), asset management fees, and commissions)	g) Expenses

Fig. 3.1 FS Banks

that engages in some IB activities (as many large CBs do) might have an FS that combines features of both. Similarly, an IB that has a CB branch will incorporate elements of both in its FSs.

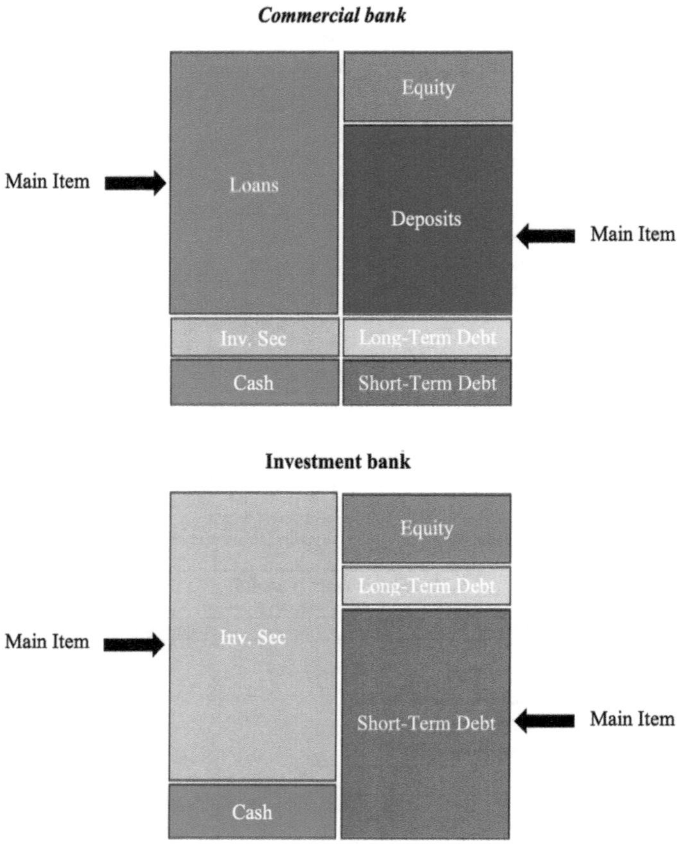

Fig. 3.2 Balance sheet composition commercial vs investment banks

3 Mechanics of Accounting Misrepresentation

3.1 Overstatement of Assets

The accurate representation of asset values is pivotal in ascertaining a bank's true financial health. In recent years, top bank executives, for various reasons (some of them elaborated upon in the subsequent chapter), have strategically inflated their banks' asset values (see Fig. 3.1, Column 1 and Column 5). This strategic increase can mislead stakeholders ranging from regulators and supervisors to shareholders, depositors, and customers. While these inflated values might offer a short-lived perception of financial stability and robustness for a bank or group of banks, long-term repercussions can be severe. To comprehend the magnitude of this problem, we first need to understand the mechanics behind banks' BS compositions.

Why is the measurement of asset values in banks so significant?

The nature of banking operations provides the answer. Banks manage vast portfolios of both basic (e.g., loans, government bonds, liquid securities, foreign exchange, and gold reserves) and advanced (e.g., exotic derivatives and Asset-Backed Securities) financial instruments. The precise valuation of these instruments is crucial. A misrepresentation or miscalculation can distort the perception of a bank's financial health. Overestimating assets or underestimating liabilities can paint a falsely prosperous picture of its financial well-being. As mentioned in Chap. 1, 'Loans and securities are the primary assets on a bank's BS'.

Accounting manipulation of assets poses one of the primary risks banks face. This can manifest in two main ways:

(a) Delayed recognition of bad loans.
(b) Incorrect valuation of sophisticated financial instruments.

Both of which can artificially inflate a bank's BS asset value. Regarding the first aspect, which is the delay in recognising NPLs, this predominantly impacts CBs with substantial deposits and a limited number of Level 2 and 3 assets on their BSs. After major financial crises, regulatory bodies introduced stricter and more proactive provisioning rules, such as IFRS 9 (by the International Accounting Standards Board (IASB)) and the US's Current Expected Credit Losses (CECL) standard (by the Financial Accounting Standards Board (FASB)). These regulations mandate banks to rapidly identify and set aside funds for anticipated losses. Adopting a forward-looking perspective, banks must estimate the expected credit losses over the lifespan of a financial instrument from the moment of its origination or purchase. This approach contrasts with the older incurred loss models, which recognised losses only when they seemed imminent.

A salient example of the risks tied to delayed bad loan recognition is the Monte dei Paschi di Siena (MPS) case (2010–2015). MPS, Italy's oldest bank, faced profound financial difficulties post the 2008 financial crisis. At the heart of MPS's challenges was its exposure to late-recognised NPLs and highly sophisticated financial derivatives. MPS engaged in a series of complex transactions to obscure some of these issues, effectively concealing the true scale of its losses. These tactics enabled MPS to portray a more favourable financial health than was actually the case. When these actions were exposed, it greatly harmed the bank's reputation and financial position, leading to substantial capital injections and bailouts. The lack of transparency and procrastination in addressing the deteriorating loan portfolio highlighted the perils of delayed recognition of NPLs in the banking sector.

In a document from the 'Inquiry Commission of the Italian Senate of the Republic', details about the MPS Bank are provided.[2] The report suggests severe financial turbulence for MPS, especially from credit risks:

"From the second half of 2008, the effects of the crisis began to manifest. Between 2008 and 2011, the Bank of Italy conducted ten inspections at MPS, three of which were focused on credit risks and two on financial risks. One of these inspections (conducted between March and July 2008; doc. 26), focused on residential mortgages and consumer credit, notes that 'in the residential building loan sector, there is a prevalent incidence of operations carried out in derogation of the automatic granting criteria and, in particular, of the 40% limit set for the instalment-income ratio'. Another (conducted between December 2008 and May 2009; doc. 63 and 69), dedicated to the analysis of corporate credit, extends to loans granted by Antonveneta. With reference to these, there emerged "delays in identifying customers characterized by critical issues and in taking initiatives to facilitate their return," "despite the more prudent guidelines of the Parent Company." The inspection also indicates that from the last months of 2008 there has been a degradation even of the "historical loans of the MPS group," given, among other things, "the significant increase in restructuring requests made by major clients." Both inspections conclude with an intermediate judgment (page 7).

"The financial risks seriously troubled MPS; however, in the long run, it was the credit risk that most profoundly undermined its financial stability" (page 3)

Another potential source of accounting manipulation arises from the incorrect valuation of highly sophisticated financial instruments. The International Financial Reporting Standards (IFRS) offers a detailed framework for measuring and reporting the fair value of assets and liabilities. As delineated by IFRS 13, assets appraised at fair value are classified into three distinct levels (see Fig. 3.1, Column 1 and Column 5):

- **Level 1:** 'Assets for which the valuation is derived directly from prices observed in active markets (liquid markets)'. These values are transparent and readily available, leaving little to no room for ambiguity or opacity. Examples of these assets include government bonds, liquid securities, foreign exchange holdings, and gold reserves. These instruments benefit from well-established, active, and notably liquid markets, ensuring a continuous flow of buy and sell orders. Consequently, their prices are immediately available and mirror current market sentiments. This promptness in pricing ensures that banks' stakeholders have a clear and timely understanding of an asset's value at Level 1.
- **Level 2:** 'Assets whose valuation primarily hinges on observable market inputs other than Level 1 prices'. Although these assets maintain a certain level of

[2] Italian Senate of the Republic—Chamber of Deputies Parliamentary Inquiry Commission on the Banking and Financial System Law of July 12, 2017, no. 107 Monte dei Paschi di Siena Bank Carmelo Barbagallo Head of the Banking and Financial Supervision Department of the Bank of Italy. https://www.bancaditalia.it/pubblicazioni/interventi-vari/int-var-2017/Barbagallo-22112017.pdf.

transparency, they might be subject to slightly more interpretative variation because of the nature of the inputs used. Assets and liabilities in this category do not have consistent market valuations. However, they can be fairly valued using prices from less active markets or models with observable parameters, such as interest rates or default frequencies. Interest rate swaps are typical examples of Level 2 assets.

- **Level 3:** Perhaps the most complex category to understand and explain, 'these assets are valued based on non-observable market data'. The valuation of Level 3 assets lacks the direct visibility of the previous categories. This absence of 'direct observable inputs' can introduce potential for manipulation, sometimes resulting in overestimations or undisclosed financial shortfalls. Level 3 assets comprise complex instruments such as mortgage-backed securities (hereafter MBS), private equity stakes, exotic derivatives, and distressed obligations. Their valuation is predominantly anchored in the mark-to-model methodology (i.e. sophisticated financial models which are based on assumptions and projections).

It is important to remember that from an accounting perspective the key differentiation between these levels is the source and transparency of the valuation inputs. Level 1 assets are directly observable (low risk of accounting manipulation), level 2 assets have indirect observability (medium risk of accounting manipulation), and level 3 assets lack observable inputs (high risk of accounting manipulation).

Of these three levels, 'level 3' assets pose the most significant risk in the context of banking failures. Because they rely on non-observable data, these assets can easily be manipulated, an action also referred to as 'Fair Value Accounting Manipulation'. This provides a distorted view of a bank's actual financial position. When stakeholders base their investment decisions on such inflated or manipulated values, it paves the way for a banking crisis. If a significant portion of a bank's portfolio consists of misvalued Level 3 assets, it can set off a domino effect, eroding trust and liquidity, eventually leading or exacerbating a banking failure.

In relation to this second aspect, the imprecise valuation of complex financial instruments primarily impacts IBs with significant Level 2 and 3 assets on their BSs. A prime example of the risks associated with manipulated valuations of these complex financial tools is the 2008 collapse of Lehman Brothers, once the fourth-largest investment bank in the United States.

A significant factor in this crisis was Lehman's inflated valuation of its Level 3 assets. As previously mentioned, these assets are notoriously difficult to value due to their lack of transparent market pricing. Lehman held a substantial portfolio of these complex assets, with MBS being predominant. To determine their value, Lehman utilised a combination of internal models (i.e. models devised in-house by the bank's employees) and third-party evaluations. As the real estate market in the United States began its decline, the verifiable worth of these assets became challenging. By the end of Q2 2007, level 3 assets constituted 104% of the bank's equity. This proportion surged to 170% by Q1 2008, with MBS accounting for 60% of that total. Such valuation intricacies understandably led to growing investor apprehension. The uncertainty surrounding the value of Lehman's assets eroded investor and market confidence, accelerating the bank's default.

4 Creative Accounting, Underreporting of Liabilities and Off-BS Position

Drawing from the preceding discussion, the accurate representation of asset values is fundamental in determining a bank's genuine financial health. However, from an accounting perspective, it is also crucial to note that obscuring or under-representing obligations can paint an overly rosy picture of a bank's financial health. Below are some 'accounting tricks' that banks employ to conceal their real financial situation.

I. Accounting Trick, the 'Lehman 105 Repo Scandal' a pivotal, yet often under-highlighted factor in the debacle of Lehman was their deceitful application of 'Repo 105'. Typically, in Repos transactions, an entity temporarily sells securities with a commitment to repurchase them at a predetermined price. In essence, this transaction mirrors a short-term collateralized loan. However, Lehman's approach with Repo 105 diverged from this standard. Instead of recording it as a loan, they treated these transactions as true sales, effectively removing around $50 billion off their BS. By strategically employing 'Repo 105' just ahead of the quarterly financial disclosure deadlines, Lehman portrayed healthier liquidity and improved leverage metrics. Once the reporting period ended, the securities were promptly bought back, restoring their original position on the BS.

Cases and Examples

- Imagine a bank, let us call it 'Bank LB'. As the quarter-end approaches (e.g., Q2), Bank LB has total assets of $200 billion and liabilities of $190 billion, making its total equity $10 billion (i.e. $200 billion – $190 billion). We can say that Bank LB is carrying a significant debt on its BS. The Bank LB wishes to present a healthier leverage ratio to the investors for Q2.

Original Position Bank LB (Before 'Repo 105')
Total Assets Bank LB: $200 billion
Total Liabilities Bank LB: $190 billion
Total Equity Bank LB: $10 billion (Assets – Liabilities)
Leverage Ratio (Before Q2) = 190/10 = 19
This means that for every dollar of equity, Bank LB has $19 in liabilities.

- To artificially bolster its BS, Bank LB decides to use the 'Repo 105' tactic, similar to what Lehman Brothers did.

(continued)

- Bank LB engages in a 'Repo 105' transaction, where it 'sells' to 'Bank AP' \$50 billion worth of securities with a commitment to repurchase them shortly after the Q2-end. So, on paper, its assets decrease to \$150 billion from (because Bank LB 'sold' \$50 billion of securities). Since it received cash for the sale, its liabilities would also decrease by a similar amount, let us say down to \$140 billion (from \$190 billion).
- With these revised numbers, Bank LB now presents a BS at the Q2 showing assets of \$150 billion and liabilities of \$140 billion, leading to total equity of \$10 billion. This presents a far healthier leverage ratio than before.

After the Repo 105 Transaction:
Total Assets: \$150 billion
Total Liabilities: \$140 billion
Total Equity: \$10 billion (Again, Assets – Liabilities because equity has not changed) Leverage Ratio (End Q2) = 140/10 = 14
After the Repo 105 transaction, for every dollar of equity, Bank LB has \$14 in liabilities.

- However, shortly after the reporting period ends, Bank LB repurchases the securities for approximately the same price, restoring its balance sheet to the original position with \$200 billion in assets and \$190 billion in liabilities. This manipulation offers only a temporary relief, as the numbers will revert back after the repurchase, but for the period of reporting, the bank appears in a healthier financial state than it truly is.

II. Special Purpose Entities (SPEs) or Special Purpose Vehicles (SPVs) Banks can create these off-BS entities to manage assets or debt without these items appearing directly on the bank's own BS. When not transparently disclosed, this can give a misleading view of the bank's real financial health. Like many other important financial institutions, during the years 2000–2008, Bank of America (BoA) utilised SPVs to manage their MBS. In other words, rather than having these MBS on the BoA's main BS, they were placed in these separate entities known as SPVs. For BoA, the downturn in the US housing market meant that many of the underlying mortgages in the MBS held by the SPVs were becoming non-performing. This decline in value reverberated back to BoA, putting stress on its liquidity and capital positions, despite these assets being off its main BS. Following the global financial crisis of 2007–2008, there were notable shifts in accounting regulations, particularly within the IFRS and the US GAAP. These updated guidelines imposed stricter criteria, making it challenging for banks and other financial entities to maintain specific assets and liabilities off their primary BSs without any disclosure to the stakeholders.

Cases and Examples

- Initial Situation: Bank B Main BS: Contains $1 trillion in assets. Desire to Optimise BS: Banks often want to make their financial health look better to stakeholders.
- Creation of Separate Entities (SPVs): Purpose: By creating SPVs, banks can move certain assets off their main BS, making it look leaner and potentially more attractive.

Action: Bank B transfers $100 billion in MBS to these SPVs. These MBS are now off Bank B's main BS.

- The Consequence of a Housing Market Crash:

Decline in Value: Due to the downturn in the US housing market, let us say $20 billion of the MBS in the SPVs become non-performing.
Reverberation to BoA: Although these problematic MBS are in SPVs and not on Bank B's main BS, the bank still faces indirect risks. If the SPVs cannot manage the losses, Bank B might need to cover them, straining its liquidity.
Post-Crisis Accounting Changes:
New Rules Introduced: After the 2007–2008 financial crisis, stricter accounting regulations were set in place.
Result for BoA: With the new regulations, Bank B has to report some of the assets and liabilities from its SPVs on its main BS. For illustration, let us say it is now showing $1.05 trillion on its main balance sheet, including some previously off-BS assets.

III. Banks' Borrowing Tactics (Also Referred to in Jargon as 'Window Dressing of the Balance Sheet') This typically occurs when banks reduce their short-term borrowing just before the end of a quarter (or reporting period) to appear less leveraged. Once the new quarter begins, banks increase borrowing again. During the peak of the Eurozone crisis, certain European banks were observed engaging in this behaviour. This tactic, while reminiscent of the 'Repo 105' strategy, involves genuine transactions.

IV. Accrual Accounting and the Risk of Inappropriate Discretion Building upon conventional accounting methodologies within the banking industry, financial institutions frequently choose to amortize significant expenses across several accounting periods. By doing so, instead of absorbing the full impact immediately (i.e. decreasing profits), thus tempering the effect on profitability for each respective period. However, the potential for manipulation arises if executed without 'due diligence' (i.e. the bank does not follow the standards rigorously or try to use discretion inappropriately), this strategy can give a transient and possibly misleading boost to the perceived financial robustness of a bank.

Cases and Examples

Accrual Accounting and the Risk of Manipulation: A Case Study

- Bank Overview:
  - Let us call our bank 'Bank EZ'.
  - Bank EZ has a major expense this year, say a loss of $10 million from a bad loan.
- Standard Approach Without Accrual Accounting:
  - If Bank EZ recorded this loss all at once, its profits for the year would decline by $10 million immediately.
  - Investors and stakeholders might be concerned about this sudden drop.
- With Accrual Accounting:
  - Instead of taking the full hit in one go, Bank EZ decides to spread this loss over 5 years.
  - This means each year, only $2 million of the loss will be recorded.
  - As a result, the annual financial statements look more stable, and the bank seems to be more profitable than it would if it had absorbed the whole loss at once.
- Potential for Manipulation:
  - Suppose the standard accounting principle suggests that such a loss should only be spread over 3 years, but Bank EZ stretches it to 5 years to make its books look even better.
  - By doing this, Bank EZ is not following standard protocols rigorously and is using its discretion inappropriately.
- Consequences:
  - Short term: The bank appears financially robust, which might attract more investors.
  - Long term: The bank will have to account for the loss eventually. If stakeholders find out about the manipulation, it can erode trust and damage the bank's reputation.

This method provides a temporary boost to Bank EZ's perceived financial health but may lead to long-term issues if the bank is not transparent about its accounting practices.

V. Income Smoothing This happens when banks (also done from NFCs) adjust revenues and costs to show steady and consistent earnings, rather than reflecting the inherent volatility of profits (i.e. masking the real ups and downs). For instance, if a bank faces a particularly profitable quarter, it might increase its provisions for loan losses. By doing this, the bank tempers its high earnings, making it appear more consistent with previous quarters, even if the actual profit was higher. This happens because investors prefer banks (and NFCs) with steady and consistent financial performance.

Cases and Examples
Income Smoothing: Simplified Case

- Scenario:

'Bank S' makes a high profit of $20 million one quarter, typically earning only $12 million.

- Without Smoothing:

Reporting $20 million would show a big earnings spike.

- With Smoothing:

Bank sets aside $8 million for future loan losses.
Reports $12 million profit, aligning with typical earnings.

- Why?:

Makes earnings seem steady.
Investors trust consistent earnings.

- Outcome:

Short-term trust from investors.
Possible long-term scrutiny if overused.

Chapter 4
Corporate Governance and Banking Failures

1 Introduction

In this chapter, we explore the interplay between corporate governance (hereafter CG) deficiencies and banking failures. Specifically, we focus on the central roles that inadequate risk oversight by the board and unchecked directorial greed can play in precipitating banking crises. Drawing upon the theoretical framework proposed by Buchetti and Santoni (2022a), we delve deep into the complex realm of CG within the banking sector, elucidating its significance and the profound ramifications of its shortcomings. The intricate web of relationships between stakeholders—from shareholders to depositors—gives rise to unique agency costs that can lead to significant banking failures if not properly managed.

Two primary agency costs emerge in the banking industry: one where the interests of shareholders and depositors diverge from those of bank directors, and the other highlighting the tension between depositors on the one side and shareholders and directors on the other. At the heart of these issues are poor risk management by the board and unchecked ambition of directors, both of which can potentially trigger banking crises.

The Wells Fargo and Washington Mutual (WaMu) CG failure cases, among others, exemplify how agency problems can lead to large-scale disasters. Through this lens, we underscore the essential need for robust, transparent, and effective CG systems within the banking industry.

Leveraging insights and comprehensive measures outlined by Buchetti and Santoni (2022a), we provide a roadmap for enhancing CG, aiming to prevent past missteps and lay the foundation for a more resilient and ethical banking landscape

N. Abidi et al., *Why Do Banks Fail and What to Do About It*, Contributions to Finance and Accounting, https://doi.org/10.1007/978-3-031-52311-3_4

2 What Is Corporate Governance in the Banking Sector?

Robust CG is pivotal for the optimal functioning of the banking industry and the broader economy. While no universal approach exists for exemplary CG, multiple national and supra-national institutions[1] have provided guidelines and regulations in recent years that emphasise the significance of a clear and well-structured CG framework for banks. A key international entity setting standards for the oversight of banks is the Basel Committee on Banking Supervision (BCBS).[2]

Over the past years, the BCBS has issued a series of guidelines for banks and their supervisors, aimed at correctly evaluating a bank's CG framework. Notably, in 1999, the BCBS introduced the 'Enhancing Corporate Governance for Banking Organizations' as the first international CG guideline for banks. This guidance was later updated in 2006 and 2010. In 2015, the BCBS rolled out the 'Corporate Governance Principles for Banks'. The 13 principles[3] outlined in the guideline provide a framework for banks and their supervisors to ensure strong and transparent risk management and decision-making. Moreover, this guideline highlights the principal role of CG in banks, stating: 'The primary objective of corporate governance should be safeguarding stakeholders' interest in conformity with public interest on a sustainable basis. Among stakeholders, particularly with respect to retail banks, shareholders' interest would be secondary to depositors' interest'.

We can observe a clear distinction between banks and non-financial corporations (hereafter NFCs) regarding the role of CG in safeguarding key stakeholders. In particular, banks recognise depositors as a distinct stakeholder category. The BCBS underscores this difference, emphasising that in the banking context, the interests of

---

[1] Examples of Supra-national institutions are the Basel Committee on Banking Supervision (BCBS) and the Organisation for Economic Co-operation and Development (OECD). In Europe we find the European Banking Authority (EBA) and the Single Supervisory Mechanism (SSM). In the United States we mainly find The Federal Reserve System one recent guideline issued from this institution was the 'Supervisory Expectations for Boards of Directors' in 2017, clarifying the roles and responsibilities of boards of bank holding companies, savings and loan holding companies, and state member banks.

[2] Established in 1974 by the Group of Ten's central bank chiefs, the Basel Committee on Banking Supervision (BCBS) acts as a collaborative body for banking oversight authorities. It expanded its membership notably in 2009 and again in 2014. As of 2019, the BCBS brought together 45 regulatory representatives across 28 jurisdictions, combining central banks and dedicated banking regulators. The BCBS serves as the leading international body for setting standards for the prudential oversight of banks and offers a platform for consistent collaboration on matters related to banking supervision.

[3] Principle 1: Board's overall responsibilities; Principle 2: Board qualifications and composition; Principle 3: Board's own structure and practices; Principle 4: Senior management; Principle 5: Governance of group structures; Principle 6: Risk management function; Principle 7: Risk identification, monitoring and controlling; Principle 8: Risk communication; Principle 9: Compliance; Principle 10: Internal audit; Principle 11: Compensation; Principle 12: Disclosure and transparency 36; Principle 13: The role of supervisors 38.

shareholders are secondary to those of depositors. This unique role of banks arises mainly from their duty to manage citizens' funds, a topic explored in the initial two chapters. Mismanaging these funds can pose grave risks to the broader economy, underscoring the distinction between banks and NFCs. In fact, in NFCs, directors—appointed at the Annual Shareholders' Meeting (hereafter ASM)—operate with the primary objective of maximising shareholder value, as posited by the shareholder theory (Friedman, 2007). Failure to achieve this can lead to their replacement in subsequent ASMs. In contrast, directors in banks have a more nuanced duty: they must balance shareholder value maximisation with the protection of depositor interests. To fully understand the role of CG in curbing directors' opportunistic tendencies, especially in the banking domain, it is invaluable to examine the agency theory, a cornerstone often referenced in CG research.

3 Corporate Governance: Insights from Agency Theory

Agency theory holds a central role in CG, providing an analytical perspective into the dynamics of directors' and top managers' actions and their implications for a firm's success. This theory is rooted in the seminal work of Fama and Jensen (1983), which explored the challenges stemming from the separation of 'ownership' (represented by shareholders) and 'managerial control' (embodied by directors and top managers). Within this paradigm, the principal (shareholders) entrusts specific tasks to an agent (directors and top managers).

The agent's primary responsibility is to achieve the objectives set by the shareholders (principal), usually framed in terms of value creation and wealth maximisation (Jensen and Meckling, 1979). However, this separation of ownership and control can give rise to conflicts of interest. As agents rise to leadership positions in the company, they might become enticed by personal benefits, leading to a 'moral hazard'. This situation highlights agents' inclination towards rational self-interest, often favouring personal financial gains rather than shareholders' wealth maximisation.

For proponents of agency theory, the board of directors' pivotal role is to supervise and reduce any tendencies of managerial self-interest, ensuring that their actions align with shareholders' goals (Fama and Jensen, 1983). This divergence in objectives can be better defined by comparing the primary ambitions of shareholders (principal), centred on financial returns, against those of managers (agent), which may be influenced by short-term incentives, career objectives, and other considerations not directly tied to enhancing a firm's financial returns.

In settings where ownership is dispersed,[4] such as in publicly traded firms with fragmented shareholding, overseeing managerial actions becomes particularly challenging, leading to agency costs. These costs manifest when management's actions prioritise personal gains over enhancing the firm's value (the primary goal of shareholders). In fact, in companies with a fragmented ownership structure, the power of individual shareholders to monitor and influence directors' behaviour is often limited. For instance, a singular shareholder in such companies might lack the power to oust a director—during the ASM—that is favouring personal financial gains rather than shareholders' wealth maximisation.

Consider a scenario where a company has 100 shareholders, each possessing only 1% of the total shares. This represents a clear case of fragmented ownership. Under such a configuration, a single dissenting shareholder lacks the power to effectively oversee or oust the directors. It is important to note that pivotal decisions at the ASM, like director nominations, commonly mandate a majority vote, often exceeding 50.01%. Given this, there is an inherent risk in such companies: directors once appointed may act primarily in their own interests, understanding that individual shareholders, due to their minimal stakes, are unlikely to challenge their decisions. Figure 4.1 illustrates the prevalent disconnect between ownership and managerial control in firms with such dispersed ownership.

4 Agency Costs: How to Reduce Them

When faced with misalignment, the literature suggests that dispersed shareholders might opt for multiple strategies to protect their investment in the company.

Firstly, shareholders have the option to sell their holdings, often referred to as the 'exit strategy' (or the 'Wall Street walk'). When shareholders offload their shares, it can drive down the stock price. An informed investor, recognising the company's undervaluation resulting from managerial misbehaviour, may grasp the opportunity to acquire a significant stake or even all shares, getting the majority in the ASM and subsequently initiating changes to the Board of Directors (BOD) (i.e. appointing new members). This dynamic creates a deterrent against opportunistic actions by the directors. It is worth noting, however, that this mechanism applies only to publicly traded companies.

Secondly, it is often suggested (and sometimes mandated) that companies include a specific quota of independent directors on their BOD. Corporate governance codes lay out varied requirements that directors must meet to be labelled (and appointed)

[4] 'Ownership dispersion' refers to a scenario where shares are distributed among a large number of shareholders, with no single entity or individual possessing a controlling stake. In essence, it is an ownership structure without significant shareholders (often termed 'blockholders') who can exert influence over the Annual Shareholders' Meeting, and consequently, the approval or removal of directors. This kind of structure is typical for large public companies particularly in the Anglo-Saxon context.

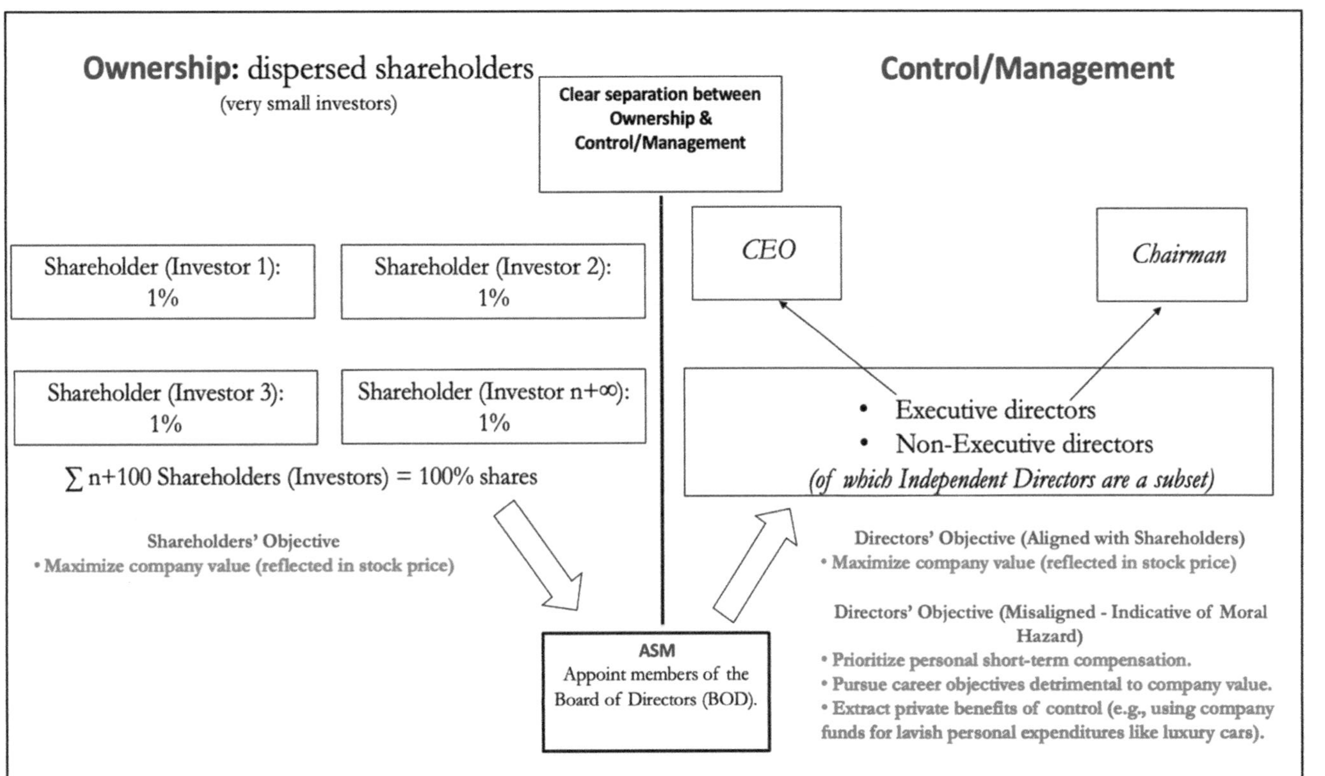

Fig. 4.1 Source: Authors' own representation

as independent directors. For instance, the New York Stock Exchange (NYSE) provides a precise definition for this role. According to the NYSE, an independent director is 'a member of the board who has no material relationship with the firm, either directly or indirectly'. This implies that such an individual should not be associated with the firm as a shareholder, partner, or officer. Moreover, they should not have affiliations with corporations that maintain significant ties to the company under consideration.

Many corporate governance codes require that companies—with equity securities listed—have a board of directors composed of a majority of independent directors (minimum of one-third of board members in Europe). For example, the New York Stock Exchange (NYSE) requires that companies with equity securities listed on the NYSE have a board of directors composed of a majority of independent directors.

Such a recommendation aims to bolster oversight. The underlying rationale is that these independent directors, in their pursuit to maintain their professional standing in the independent directorship market, will likely make decisions free from bias. This objectivity empowers them to efficiently monitor and mitigate any potential self-serving behaviours by fellow (executives) board members. In other words, the primary role of independent directors is to oversee management and curtail any opportunistic actions by executive directors, thus safeguarding shareholders' interests and protect their reputation as independent directors. In fact, if they do not act appropriately, there is a risk that they will not be re-elected to the BOD or that their reputation might be compromised (they will not be elected to other BOD of other companies as independent directors). Consequently, independent directors are often selected from individuals with solid experience and a strong commitment to integrity and transparency, such as high-profile international consultants, renowned academics, military officers, and other experts in their field of expertise. To fulfil this responsibility effectively, it is imperative that they maintain their independence.

Third, bolstering the presence of blockholders (also called 'large shareholders'), greatly impacts the dynamics and decisions within ASM. When a shareholder holds a significant stake, they wield substantial influence, enabling them to propose resolutions, exercise dominant voting rights, and even control the appointment or removal of directors. This control stems from their ability to dictate outcomes during these meetings and their capacity for direct dialogue with management. To illustrate, imagine a situation where a shareholder elevates their ownership from a negligible 10% to a commanding 51%. Such a shift not only demonstrates the profound leverage that comes with larger shareholdings but also highlights the extent of influence it provides in steering company decisions and oversight. However, situations characterised by highly concentrated ownership, such as when a family holds the majority of shares (this happens many times in European companies), can present distinct agency costs. In this case, the agency costs may arise between dominant shareholders (the family) and minority shareholders. In such configurations, the controlling shareholder (i.e. the family members) may act in ways that serve their interests at the expense of the minority shareholders.

For instance, instead of channelling resources into projects yielding positive net present value, they might divert undue bonuses to their board affiliates, practices also called ‘extracting private benefits of control’. Such imbalances arise from the limited power of minority shareholders. To address these challenges, experts in the field have proposed measures, including guaranteeing representation for minority shareholders on the BOD or bolstering the number of independent directors unaffiliated with the dominant shareholders.

Fourth, compensating directors and senior executives with long-term stock options help align the objectives of shareholders and directors, especially with respect to enhancing stock value. This approach links directors’ compensation directly to the company’s performance, ensuring shared interests in its success. Consequently, directors are less motivated to engage in actions (reflecting moral hazard) that might negatively impact the firm’s stock value.

As we have observed, there are various strategies to address the agency costs stemming from the divergence of ownership and management, particularly in the context of a fragmented ownership structure. Now, we will explore how these agency costs manifest and transform within the banking sector.

5 Corporate Governance and Banking: The Role of Agency Costs

Interestingly, agency theory is the predominant theoretical framework in studies examining the role of CG in banking outcomes (Buchetti & Santoni, 2022b). In the banking context, while the agency theory retains its core principles, its costs and implications significantly evolve. As underscored by the BCBS guidelines, directors of banks face the intricate challenge of optimising shareholder value while concurrently ensuring the protection of depositor interests. It is worth noting that in this setting, depositors appear as a new class of principals.

Given their inherent characteristics, banks are often seen as opaquer and more complex than NFCs. This leads to intensified agency issues, as outlined by Morgan (2002). Multiple elements feed into this complexity, making it arduous for stakeholders to effectively oversee operations. For instance, stakeholders grapple with the task of evaluating a bank’s loan portfolio quality or unravelling the intricacies of advanced financial instruments, such as Asset-Back-Securities (ABS) or specific types of derivatives. Such complexities diminish monitoring and exacerbate the challenges of governance. Furthermore, scholarly works suggest that safeguards such as deposit insurance (Merton 1977) and implicit state guarantees (Gandhi and Lustig 2015) inadvertently encourage bank stakeholders and directors to indulge in riskier ventures (Thakor 2014; Merton 1977), further intensifying agency problems.

The prevalence of significant agency costs in banking underscores why much of the academic inquiry into CG within the banking sector relies heavily on agency theory. Buchetti and Santoni (2022c) illuminated the intricacies of agency costs in banks by introducing a unique classification of pertinent subjects within the banking CG framework—a classification we also adopt in this book. Specifically, they detail the objectives and attributes of three subjects:

- Depositors: Individuals or entities who place their money in banks. Primarily concerned about the safety of their deposited amounts and the bank's operational efficiency and growth, as this ensures continued interest earnings on their deposits.
- Bank Shareholders: Owners of a portion of a bank's equity. Their primary goals are twofold: to protect bank deposits, thereby preventing potential bank runs (a concept expanded upon in Chap. 1 and 2), and to enhance the overall value of the bank, ensuring an increase in their returns on investment.
- Bank Directors: Key managerial personnel appointed to oversee a bank's operations and strategies. Their primary responsibilities and goals include safeguarding depositors' funds to prevent potential bank runs, enhancing the bank's valuation in line with shareholder expectations, and advancing their own professional stature and influence within the industry.

6 Agency Dilemma I: Shareholders and Depositors vs Directors

Figure 4.2 presents a comparative view of the objectives of depositors, shareholders, and directors.

Issues arise when the objectives of these different subjects misalign, leading to agency costs. According to Buchetti and Santoni (2022a), the first agency problem stems from the divergence between the interests of depositors and shareholders (as principals) on the one side and the bank's directors (as agents) on the other. Moral hazard surfaces when directors prioritise their own financial goals (action 'C.2' in Fig. 4.2) by leveraging their authoritative power, potentially jeopardising both the bank's value and the safety of deposits. The temptation of momentarily increasing bank risks (and, by extension, profits)—which could boost their short-term compensation—often entices bank directors.

A significant impediment (for principals) to oversight stems from the intrinsic complexity of banks. This opaqueness hampers the efforts of shareholders and depositors in scrutinising the bank's lending practices and deciphering intricate financial products like derivatives. The existing frameworks of depositor insurance and inferred state guarantees further disincentivise vigilant monitoring by reducing the imminent threat of bank runs and potentially fostering self-interested pursuits by directors (agents).

An example of such behaviour in the banking sector was the Wells Fargo 'Fake Accounts Scandal' starting around 2002 and intensifying until 2016. During this period Wells Fargo employees opened millions of unauthorised checking and savings accounts, credit cards, and lines of credit without customers' knowledge or

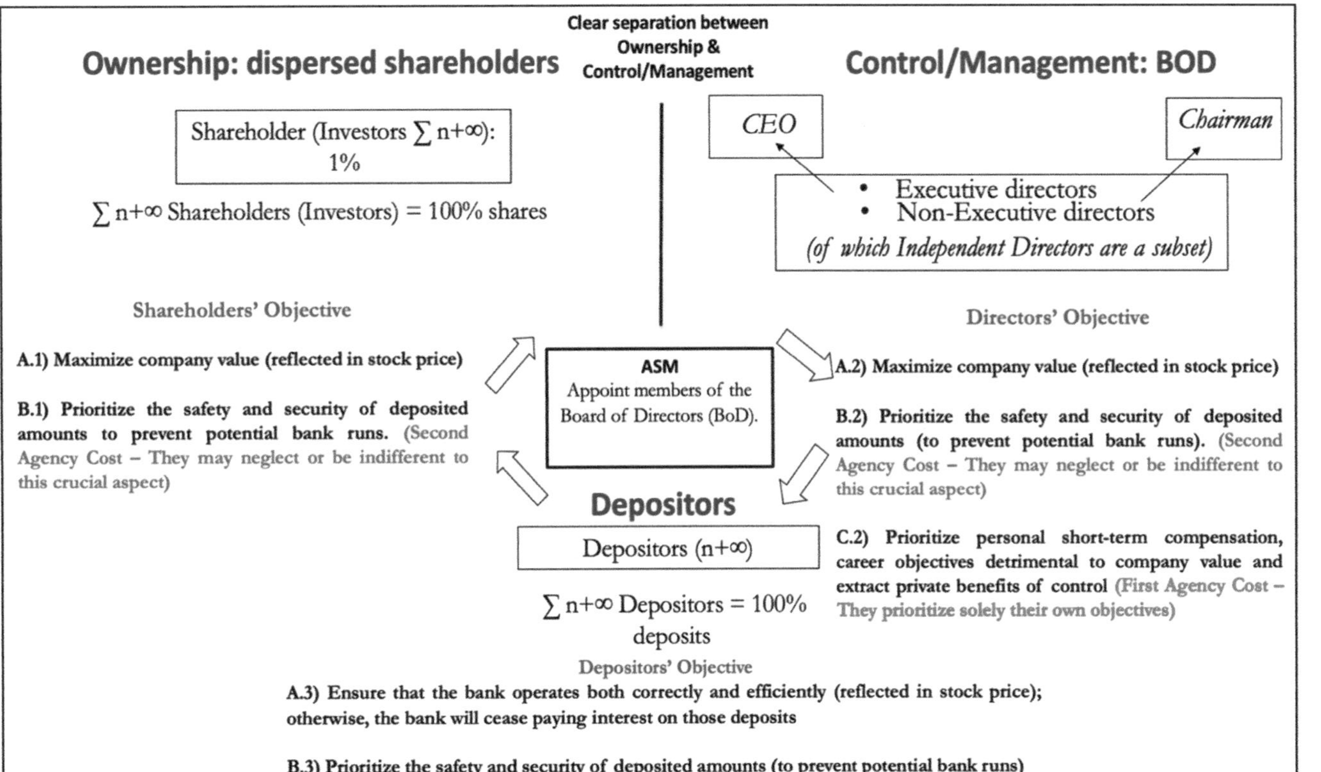

Fig. 4.2 Source: Authors' own representation

permission. This practice was primarily driven to meet the bank's aggressive sales targets and earn incentives. While initially framed as misconduct by lower-level employees, subsequent investigations revealed that the pressures and incentives leading to this behaviour were shaped by decisions made by upper management. This includes high-ranking executives keen on achieving bonuses tied to sales targets (action 'C.2' in Fig. 4.2). Furthermore, shareholders were totally unaware of the vast scale of the unethical practices occurring within the bank, believing instead that its high account growth was a sign of robust business operations. The bank was hit with a massive fine of $100 million.

For shareholders and depositors, the Wells Fargo scandal is a clear reminder of the potential agency problems in large banks, where executive decision-making can sometimes prioritise short-term gains over long-term ethical and sustainable growth.

Buchetti and Santoni (2022d) outlined a comprehensive set of measures or actions aimed at curbing this type of moral hazard in the banking sector. These seven strategies or actions provide a roadmap for enhancing CG in banks.

(a) First, 'Enhanced Transparency Regarding Bank Risk-Taking': Regulators should mandate comprehensive risk-related disclosures to diminish the veil of opacity surrounding banks and their risk-appetite. With heightened clarity, both depositors and shareholders can engage in more effective oversight. Examples of such risk-related disclosures can be observed in both Europe and the United States. In Europe, the European Banking Authority (EBA) and the European Union (EU) have adopted the Basel III framework. This mandates banks to routinely disclose information about their risk exposures and risk management processes under its Pillar 3 requirements, such as capital adequacy, leverage ratios, liquidity ratios, among others. In the United States, the Dodd–Frank Act, introduced in 2008, mandates banks to offer thorough risk disclosures, undergo stress testing, and provide regular reporting, particularly aimed at averting crises in the derivatives market. Additionally, the Securities and Exchange Commission (SEC) enforces various regulations that require publicly traded companies, including banks, to disclose risk factors. An example is the Form 10-K, an annual report mandated by the SEC, which compels companies to delve into their risk factors, giving investors a more lucid insight into the potential risks tied to the company.

(b) Second, 'Balanced Safety Mechanisms': Regulators should fine-tune the framework for deposit insurance and state-backed guarantees. Excessive guarantees can reduce the incentive for active oversight and inadvertently encourage directors to pursue self-serving actions.

(c) Third, 'Strengthened Board Independence': Regulators should advocate for a robust representation of independent directors within the board. Such individuals, as observed in the paragraph 4.4, uninfluenced by internal dynamics, can act as a protection for shareholders and depositors against potential self-serving tendencies of executive directors.

(d) Fourth, 'Empowering Shareholders': Regulators can bolster shareholder oversight by advocating a concentration of shareholding. In fact, a concentrated ownership often translates to more stringent directorial oversight (stricter directorial scrutiny). However, similar to the NFC scenario, an excessive concentration of shares among a few dominant blockholders might introduce other agency problems. In these setups, the majority shareholder could potentially prioritise their own interests over those of minority shareholders. For example, rather than allocating resources to projects with a positive net present value, they might unduly reward their board affiliates with bonuses. Such discrepancies emerge due to the diminished influence of minority shareholders.

(e) Fifth, 'alignment of Director Compensation': Banks should be pushed to structure director remuneration, particularly stock options, in a way that mirrors both shareholder and depositor interests. For instance, options could be contingent on achieving profitability without elevating the bank's risk exposure.
(f) Sixth, 'Depositor's Exit Strategy': Depositors, when they perceive a divergence from their interests, can resort to a withdrawal of their funds—a potent 'exit strategy'. This latent threat of a bank run can serve as a deterrent against the board's potential opportunistic actions.
(g) Seventh, 'Shareholder's Exit Strategy': Fragmented shareholders, discerning the misalignment of directors, might opt to divest their holdings. Such a divestiture can precipitate a decline in stock value. Informed investors, identifying this undervaluation as a consequence of BOD shortcomings, could be incentivised to acquire substantial holdings and push for board restructuring. This mechanism acts as a potent counterbalance, discouraging directors from embarking on self-serving actions.

7 Agency Dilemma II: Shareholders and Depositors vs Directors

The second agency cost emerges from the dichotomy between the interests of depositors and on one side, positioned as principals, and the combined interests of the bank's directors and shareholders, who act as agents. In this case, the moral hazard problem arises when directors and shareholders prioritise their own financial objectives leveraging on their authoritative power, potentially compromising the security of deposits.

The agents may elevate the bank's risk-taking, driven by the allure of short-term dividends (for shareholders) and enhanced short-term compensation (for directors).

In other words, while shareholders and directors are more focused on maximising short-term bank's value, depositors are primarily concerned about the security of their accounts. Given the safety nets of state interventions or the costs primarily borne by depositors during a bank failure, a dual moral hazard arises to reach short-term bank's value:

Shareholders, in their pursuit of short-term greater returns, might heighten the bank's risk tolerance, targeting immediate increase in earnings and fees. This can be realised for example by intensifying the risk parameters set out in the bank's regulatory mandates (overlooking the objective 'B.1' as described in Fig. 4.2).

In a parallel vein, directors, motivated by this same quest for yield, could expand the bank's risk tolerance with an aim to boost short-term revenues and associated fees, thereby increasing the short-term bank's value. For example, the authors suggest that this objective can be accomplished by modifying the risk thresholds embedded in the bank's strategic objectives and capital planning (overlooking the objective 'B.2' as described in Fig. 4.2).

One of the most prominent examples of such behaviour in the banking sector was the Washington Mutual (WaMu) collapse in 2008. Founded in 1889 in the United States, Washington Mutual (also known as WaMu) had become one of the nation's largest lenders of subprime mortgages by the early 2000s. Executives and loan officers at WaMu were heavily incentivised based on the volume of loans they originated, not on their quality. This led to a surge in riskier lending practices (e.g. subprime lending and adjustable-rate mortgages). The short-term profits from these loans led to generous bonuses, creating a perverse incentive structure that disregarded long-term risks (overlooking the objective 'B.2').

Furthermore, shareholders of WaMu were initially content with the profitability stemming from the surge in subprime lending and other high-risk assets. Instead of intensifying their oversight of directors' actions, they actually incentivised this system by approving bonuses for top managers based on the bank's short-term profits (overlooking the objective 'B.1').

Unfortunately, as the housing market began to collapse, many of WaMu's loans started defaulting. The riskiness of its loan portfolio began to be apparent, and confidence in the bank started to wane. In a span of about ten days in September 2008, WaMu experienced a bank run, with depositors withdrawing approximately $16.7 billion in deposits. The rapid outflow of deposits and the bank's deteriorating financial condition alarmed regulators. On September 25, 2008, the Office of Thrift Supervision (OTS) seized WaMu. This was the largest bank failure in US history ($307 billion). The bulk of WaMu's assets were sold to JPMorgan Chase for $1.9 billion.

Also in this case the authors suggest a comprehensive set of measures aimed at curbing this type of moral hazard in the banking sector. First, enhancing transparency regarding the bank's risk threshold (similar to the measures taken for the initial agency cost). Second, by optimising the balance between state-backed insurance on individual deposits and other governmental assurances (mirroring actions from the primary agency cost). Third, by mandating that equity incentives align with the interests of depositors (in line with the approach for the initial agency cost). Fourth, by ensuring depositors have a voice, either on the board or in pertinent committees—this could involve establishing a committee specifically for representing depositor interests. Fifth, depositors have the option to retract their deposits (akin to the solution for the primary agency cost). The looming threat of a mass withdrawal or 'bank run' acts as a deterrent against self-serving decisions by bank directors and shareholders.

Notably, the strategies to address both agency problems bear resemblances. This suggests that with proper implementation, regulators have significant leeway to curtail agency challenges effectively.

Chapter 5
Banking Resolution and Its Key Concepts and Tools

1 What Is so Special About Banks and Why We Need Resolution Regimes

No matter how strict banking supervision is and how much banks are prepared to undergo a swift recovery in case of distress, it will never be possible to entirely rule out the possibility that a bank might result to be failing or likely to fail. Failures, although less likely to happen in the presence of an effective supervision regime (Ben Bouheni, 2014; Kandrac & Schlusche, 2021), are events that might affect banks, as well as any other firms in the market (Petitjean, 2013).

Recent times brought this lesson back to our mind. After almost 15 years from the financial crisis of 2007–2008, bank failures have not disappeared. Despite the constant trend to tighten banking supervision and impose higher capital requirements, there are always unpredictable circumstances that may trigger a failure. After the lift of the restrictions imposed during the Covid-19 pandemic, banks worldwide have been generally very profitable. In this general trend of good profits, while probably many bank executives were corking champagne bottles to celebrate their bonuses, some notable failures still materialised. In March 2022, as a consequence of the start of the conflicts in Ukraine, the European Union subsidiary of the Russian Sberbank did not manage to continue its operations. Exactly 1 year later, in the first quarter of 2023, other notable failures worried financial markets. In the United States, Silicon Valley Bank filed for bankruptcy after suffering from the rise in interest rates. As the bank was overly exposed to US Treasury bonds issued in previous years at lower interest rates, when it was forced to sell them to repay deposits it had to book huge losses on its balance sheet. In the same quarter, Credit Suisse, once one of the largest and most profitable banks in the world, following a constant decline in its share value driven by poor performance and reputational issues, underwent a write down of its balance sheet and was acquired by the Swiss competitor UBS.

The impossibility to completely offset the risk of bank failures is just one side of the coin. The other pertains to the specific risks posed by the failure of a

N. Abidi et al., *Why Do Banks Fail and What to Do About It*, Contributions to Finance and Accounting, https://doi.org/10.1007/978-3-031-52311-3_5

large bank to the entire financial system, risks that would not be correlated with the failure of another company, although very large and deeply interconnected with other parties. The failure of a large company may certainly entail very negative consequences for the employees, creditors, business partners, or any other interconnected counterparty. In addition to that, the failure of a bank directly hits financial stability, with negative spill-over effects on a wider range of households and companies through the channel of the financial system.

To say it differently, a failure is a bad thing, a banking failure is even worse. In fact, if banks share with other firms the characteristic of being economic agents aiming to maximise their profits, they also display important distinctive features that make them crucial for the market and society at large (Bossone, 1999), with a positive correlation between a robust banking system and well-established creditors' rights on side and potential for long-term growth on the other (Levine, 1998, 1999; Rousseau & Sylla, 2003; Liang & Reichert, 2012), which has been also confirmed through historical back testing in different jurisdictions (Sandberg, 1978; Levine & Zervos, 1998; Triner, 2000; Arestis et al., 2001; Lucchetti et al., 2001; Miwa & Ramseyer, 2002; Fulford, 2015).

First, banks are transmission channels for the monetary policy, which is something no other firm can do (Werner, 2005, 2014), if not in the case of other financial intermediaries and up to a limited extent (Milic, 2021). To regulate the monetary supply in the economy, central banks pass through banks, with a system of deposit taking and lending of liquidity at different interest rates. Second, banks perform critical functions towards the entire society, thus being the infrastructure of the market in which they operate. If we think about our everyday life, there is little chance we can carry our regular activities – at least with twenty-first century standards – without passing through banks. Our revenues are held in bank accounts, to be later at least partially invested in (hopefully) lucrative financial assets via bank intermediation. We often buy our first estate property with the help of a mortgage. To do our Christmas shopping, we need a credit card to withdraw cash at the ATM, pay electronically, or purchase online (unless of course in prey of a vintage fashion we want to withdraw cash at the desk, but this does not change the fact that we are once again passing through a bank). Moreover, if instead of the latest Black Friday offer we desire to buy a new car, we will need to request a transfer from our account to the one of the car dealers. These are just few examples on the side of households, but if we look at enterprises, the role of credit institutions is even more pervasive. In addition to deposits, payments and transactions, mortgages, and loans, many firms need open credit lines to perform their activities. We are therefore at a point in which hardly any economic activity can be performed without some form of bank intermediation.[1] The regulation of the banking sector is hence designed

[1] The reader should be aware that over the last few decades alternative forms of intermediation have risen alongside traditional banking. It has been already observed that these intermediaries may also pose systemic risk (Bengtsson, 2016; Aramonte et al., 2022). This could potentially require additional regulatory attention, even in fields that traditionally were an exclusive domain of banks, such as the transmission of monetary policy (Dabrowski, 2017; Cappiello et al., 2021).

in a way to balance risk reduction, compliance costs, and the continuation of the important functions banks provide to society (see for example Barth et al., 2008; Schoenmaker, 2016; Hirtle et al., 2020).

Among the experts in this field, these very important tasks go under the name of critical functions (see also Sect. 2.1 on the origins and sources of this definition). A function is considered critical as long as its disruption would have a significantly negative impact on the economy, and its substitutability is low, where substitutability refers to the possibility of another market operator to take the function over in a reasonable timeframe. It is evident that the impact and substitutability are generally correlated with the size of a bank and its market share for a given function. The relation between the size and the impact in case of disruption is positive: The greater the activities carried out by a bank in a certain field, the greater the impact in case these were suddenly discontinued. However, the substitutability itself is correlated, although inversely, with the size and market share of a credit institution. The functions carried by a large bank in a highly concentrated market are more difficult to be taken over by another player.

Now, several banks are sufficiently large and diversified in their business model that in the same country they would provide not just one, but several critical functions, ranging from collecting deposits to providing loans and mortgages, passing through cash and payment services or wholesale activities. In case of failure, these institutions are likely to trigger a chain reaction of adverse effects, potentially affecting all sides of the economy.[2] This is the reason why until the establishment of resolution regimes, the problem of what to do with the failure of a large credit institution had been a true dilemma for scholars and policy makers. How to reconcile the rescuing of an important failing bank with the principles of fair competition on a level playing field? Advocates of bailouts (i.e. the intervention by which a failing bank is saved at the expenses of the taxpayers) would usually put the question in utilitarian terms.

From the pure perspective of resolution, some non-bank intermediaries, such as financial market infrastructure, are already subject to resolution regimes similar to those for banks. In the present chapter we focus on bank resolution only.

[2] The literature on the effects of bank liquidation is abundant and spans over decades. The specific point we want to make here is that – in addition to the risks of financial contagion – a bank liquidation is likely to affect the real economy as a whole. For example, the performance of firms depending on banks' lending is affected by capital shocks in banks (as found in Chava & Purnanandam, 2011). Another well-known consequence of an unsterilised bank failure – especially under a systemic crisis – is a steep reduction in the lending activity, which also affects households and small and medium enterprises. This phenomenon, which usually goes under the name of 'credit crunch', was well documented after the 2007–2008 financial crisis (Mizen, 2008; Brunnermeier, 2009; Hull, 2009, on secondary effects on investments and wedges Buera & Moll, 2012; Cingano et al., 2016, with an EU perspective Iyer et al., 2014, for Japan Watanabe, 2007). These negative consequences on real economy are normally experienced on top of much more intuitive immediate effects, such as the unavailability (or even not full repayment) of deposits and the suspension of certain services provided by the bank, such as for cash or payments.

From a cost-benefit perspective, it was said that the contagion effects a failing bank would pass onto real economy would significantly overcome the costs to rescue it. For example, Emilios Avgouleas and Charles Goodhart considered that rumours about a potential bail could exacerbate phenomena of panic selling and bank runs (Avgouleas & Goodhart, 2015). Mathias Dewatripont (Dewatripont, 2014), writing after the last financial crisis, even went as far as to say that rescuing troubled banks can be considered as a 'good investment' from a public perspective. In its reasoning, a public bail-out in addition to sterilising the effects of a crisis on financial stability at an early stage would also prevent that other sectors of the real economy get hit by a banking failure. The passage from a financial crisis to an economic crisis is a crucial point for public finances. The chain effects triggered by the failure of a bank can easily make several enterprises suddenly unable to continue their activities in lack of the functions provided by the bank. This puts the public welfare under pressure, especially to mitigate the consequences of a crisis on the financially weakest segments of the population. Hence, scholars like Dewatripont advocated a rapid public intervention as a second best option or – even more precisely – the lesser evil one.

We have to admit that this utilitarian argument has a certain appeal, at least on paper. However, if we looked at it more closely, we would soon realise that public bail-outs, while apparently solving the issues relating to contagion effects and financial stability, are a therapy that is worse than the disease they aim to treat.

First of all, let us assume for the sake of reasoning – although in reality it is something on which it is difficult to get thorough evidence – that the costs of saving a failing bank are effectively less than what would be disbursed to remediate its consequences.[3] Still, a public bail-out remains a controversial solution. Whatever is the total, we need to ask ourselves who pays the bill. When a sovereign rescues a failing bank, the costs are entirely on taxpayers. Are we sure that the argument of 'pay now to pay less' can be reconciled with the functioning of liberal democracies? It might be eventually possible that the automatic activation of the 'welfare option' at a later stage could turn out to be more costly than a bailout – although, as we will soon explain, also this assumption has to be handled carefully – but at least the welfare system is something on which citizens have control through political representation. The content and the extent of the welfare are subject to a political decision. A bail-out is instead an ad hoc intervention, on which there is no form of prior control at a political level. As to their effects, bail-outs are nothing different from a sort of hidden taxation.

One may still be tempted to put aside this ethical concern and state that, despite the lack of a prior public agreement on public bail-outs, a taxpayer would probably still agree ex post to the rescuing of a bank with public money, if this would cost

[3] We want to note for the sake of transparency that models in the literature also point towards the opposite conclusion. According to a model developed in 2015 (Klimek et al., 2015), considering three possible solutions for a banking failure (bailout, bail-in, and sale of business, which is also a resolution tool) as well as different levels of economic growth and employment, in no scenario a bailout is able to outperform resolution tools in terms of efficiency.

him less. After all, we delegate our representatives to take several decisions in our name and in our interest. The problem is that it is not possible to precisely compare the costs of a bailout with the marginal increase in welfare expenses caused by the liquidation of a bank. In case of crisis, a bank is either rescued or winded down. Whatever option is taken, we can only roughly estimate what would have been the outcome if we had selected the alternative.

It should also be duly considered that while there are established valuation and accounting methodologies to determine the amount of losses in liquidation passed to external creditors (direct contagion), roughly equivalent to the portion of liabilities that cannot be repaid with performing assets, we cannot go as far as to estimate with sufficient precision what would be the impact on the economy in case a failing bank is left to die (see also Sect. 4). We can certainly provide an indication, based on the number of critical functions, their scale and the readiness of a given market to re-absorb these functions through other competitors (substitutability); however, these estimations are not sufficient to run a complete cost-benefit analysis. Consequently, it is not possible to state with certainty whether a bailout will be costlier or cheaper for the taxpayers.

Furthermore, it is not only the liquidation of a bank to have side-effects; bailouts also come with problems too, whose impact has reached a sound level of consensus in the literature. Which economic agent would behave prudently when knowing that regardless of his decisions, in case of distress it will be rescued with public funds? In very simple terms, the implicit guarantee of a bailout[4] is correlated with higher risk-taking by banks (Mariathasan et al., 2014; Toader, 2015). This correlation was rather strong in the past in the banking sector, especially in times when prudential requirements were less stringent than today (measures before and after the adoption of the Dodd Frank Act are included in (Acharya et al., 2016) and even more notably in the absence of resolution regimes (Toader, 2015). It is indicative of the proportions of the debate on moral hazard in banking the fact that we refer to it with a sector-specific definition. For banks, when this type of moral hazard comes into play, it is defined as the 'too-big-to-fail' problem.[5]

[4] Literature often refers to bank bailouts as forms of implicit guarantee of banks' debt. Within this chapter, we refer to two contributions providing also estimations on the extent of this implicit guarantee. Toader measured this effect as the difference between credit rating scores with and without the expectation of public supports (note that the expectation of public support is indeed a factor considered in the credit rating). Interestingly, writing in 2015 after the adoption of the Bank Recovery and Resolution Directive (BRRD), the author noted a consistent reduction of this spread across the sample of 56 large European banks from 17 countries of the European Union, suggesting that the adoption of the European resolution regimes has had an impact on the expectations of market participants.

[5] The expression was first popularised by the US congressman Stewart Brett McKinney in 1984, in the context of a hearing concerning the intervention of the Federal Deposit Insurance Corporation to rescue Continental Illinois. Since then, the expression has entered both the public and the academic debate on the situations of moral hazard of the largest credit institutions. A review of the literature concerning the too-big-to-fail issue would probably deserve a separate chapter. However, we urge to provide the reader with some 'classical' references in case he were interested

In brief, a bank is too-big-to-fail when it is so sizeable and its functions so crucial for the entire economy, that the management can rely on the assumption that in troubled times public powers would generously tend a rescuing hand. This assumption relies on the expectation that the liquidation of a large bank is likely to spread contagion to other banks and ultimately to the real economy, which is something decision makers want to avoid at all cost.

If bailouts are an option on the table, any bank of sufficient size and relevance is subject to the sweet temptation of earning higher margins by taking up additional risks well beyond a level that would be considered prudent. Any rational economic agent would do so: If things go in the direct direction, there will be more profits to distribute, and if not, losses will be passed onto public funds.

Let us move this reasoning to its extreme consequences. Is it still possible to define something 'a risk', when effectively there is nothing to risk? The 'bailout insurance policy' practically offsets the notion itself of risk, which is one of the crucial drivers of any entrepreneurial activity on a competitive market. Without the possibility of bearing the consequences of losses, nobody will be incentivised to think twice before over-exposing himself to risky counterparties. Under this perspective, bailouts are the worst enemy of any sound risk management policy.

Even if we put aside the impact of a bailout policy on risk taking management of banks and consider it from a perspective of political economy, we would be urged to conclude that the way of bailouts is paved with great dangers for public finances. It goes without surprise that rescuing a large bank always comes at a very high cost, ranging in the order of magnitude of billions of Euro or US Dollars. However, from the point of view of market participants and rating agencies, rescuing a large failing bank would be translated into something on the line of 'taking a large exposure towards an uncreditworthy counterparty'. In other terms, through a bailout the state becomes the creditor of a bank that has been close to be insolvent and whose future cash flows (i.e. the perspective of a return to profitability) are highly uncertain. Depending on the size or the numbers of the bailouts, this may result in a rating

to gain additional knowledge on this topic. One of the earlier contributions is the one by O'hara and Shaw (1990). Appeared few years after the speech of McKinney, this article found that the declarations by the Comptroller of the Currency concerning deposit insurance for largest banks boosted their equity value, when compared to the smaller banks. While today deposit insurance is commonly considered as a key element of the safety net protecting financial stability, neutral in terms of moral hazard provided that it is clearly limited to covered deposits and excludes any other creditors (Gropp & Vesala, 2004; Schich, 2009; Demirgüç-Kunt et al., 2015), the article well outlines the relation between banks' size and moral hazard. A now classical reference in the literature concerning the too-big-to-fail issue is the book by Stern and Feldman (2004), with a foreword by Paul A. Volcker. This book is an ample monographic study on the too-big-to-fail issue, which provides the common definitions and concepts that are now used in the literature. With a historical and comparative approach, a useful reference can be found in the 2011 article by Morris Goldstein and Véron (2011), which also outlines the key differences between the too big-to-fail-issue in the United States and in Europe. For a reconstruction of the debate on the too big-to-fail-issue after the 2007–2008 financial crisis, the reader may also refer to the 2014 article by Kaufman (2014), which also reflects on the previous literature to improve the definitions of the issue.

deterioration of sovereign debt. The fact that the state is exposed to risky institutions will increase the cost of its debt, as the creditors will be willing to invest in public debt only at a higher return.

However, the increase in the interest rates of public debt would depreciate the outstanding bonds issued at lower interest rates. This depreciation would in turn impact banks themselves, for the part of their assets that they invested in government bonds, and as we observed recently with the Silicon Valley Bank case, a depreciation of outstanding issues of government bonds[6] may have serious consequences for the solvency of a credit institution. At this point, the state would find itself again at the starting line, with banks on the hedge of failure and the need for additional taxpayers' money.

This negative feedback loop has been widely examined by the literature (see for example Merler et al., 2012; Angelini et al., 2014; Mitchener & Trebesch, 2021) and formalised in economic models (see De Bruyckere et al., 2013; Acharya et al., 2014; Farhi & Tirole, 2018; Alogoskoufis & Langfield, 2019), which often refer to the doom loop between banks and sovereigns, an expression made famous by the book of the Canadian economist William Leiss (Leiss (2011), see also Alessandri and Haldane (2009) for an earlier use of this expression with the same meaning).

This is what is really puzzling with large banks in troubles: We cannot let them fail; yet we do not want them to take advantage of their particular position in the market and assume that somebody will always pay for bailing them out.

However, would not it be possible to conceive a method to preserve the critical functions of large banks, while avoiding making use of taxpayers' money? This question became extremely urgent after the terror spread by the 2007–2008 financial crisis and did not take long to gain a wide echo in the academic and political debate. It was with this question in mind that in a day of January 2010 two prominent bankers, Paul Calello and Wilson Ervin, published a magazine article (Calello & Ervin, 2010), where taking inspiration from the Lehman Brothers case they asked themselves what would have happened if instead of going to bankruptcy the bank had been recapitalised converting around the 15% of the claims of bondholders into new capital. In its essential terms, the bail-in tool was born.

Calello would pass away not long after, in November of the same year, without having the opportunity to fully appreciate the legacy of his co-authored article. However, favoured by the increased public attention, this idea of a third way to deal with a failing or likely to fail bank kept circulating among the policy community, becoming increasingly popular.

A few months later, in July 2010, the newly adopted Dodd–Frank Act would have already contained provisions on the prohibition to bailout swap dealers and on

[6] In the recent case of Silicon Valley Bank, the depreciation of government bonds was caused by an increase of monetary interest rates in the market and not by a deterioration of the rating of the US Treasury bonds. However, we refer to this case to show in concrete what are the consequences of a bond depreciation on banks' balance sheet. It has to be noted that most of the literature on the doom loop was published in a period of low interest rates. Raising interest rates coming on top of a doom loop depreciation would most likely act as an amplificatory effect.

the need to prepare resolution plans. It was however in 2011 that the cornerstone of all resolution regimes we know today was set by the Financial Stability Board, with the publication of the Key Attributes of Effective Resolution Regimes for Financial Institutions (hereafter referred to as 'KA'). Although they would be subject to amendments in 2014, the KA in 2011 already included the essence of what we now understand as resolution, along with its key concepts, tools, goals, and terminology.

In this chapter we will go through the main elements that together shape the world of banking resolution. To do so, we base this chapter on the wording of the FSB KA (FSB, 2011), although we also make – where relevant – some references to legislation reflecting the KA.

2 The Resolution Objectives

The lessons learnt from the financial crisis have been reflected in the objectives that resolution procedures need ensure when a bank is failing or likely to fail ('FOLTF'). In relation to banks,[7] the KAs state[8] that resolution regimes should:

1. Ensure the continuity of critical functions.
2. Recognise the same protections applicable in insolvency proceedings (e.g. by not affecting covered deposits) and protect the assets owned by clients.
3. Eliminate the recourse to or the expectations of public interventions.
4. Make shareholders and creditors bear the losses, in line with the applicable insolvency hierarchy.
5. Avoid unnecessary destruction of value, minimising the resolution costs.
6. Entail credible and feasible resolution strategy, whose fast and transparent implementation should be enhanced by ex ante planning and testing.
7. Entail forms of cooperation between home and host authorities.

[7] The KAs have a scope (KA1) that goes beyond banks, including also other types of financial institutions. In the present chapter, wherever we refer to the KA, we only select those parts pertaining to the resolution of banks, which are those reflected in the various bank resolution regimes. Hence, the reader should not be surprised to find a longer list of objectives within the KA.

[8] The KAs also make a distinction between the objectives of resolution regimes, included in the Preamble, and objectives of resolution authorities in KA2, with the second list being a subset of the first. As a matter of fact, the legal texts do not make this difference and refer to the 'resolution objectives'. See for example Art. 31 of Directive EU 2014/59 of the European Parliament and of the Council of 15 May 2014 establishing a framework for the recovery and resolution of credit institutions and investment firms, the so-called Bank Recovery and Resolution Directive (BRRD). The terminology used in this list should be seen as a simplification of the wording used in the KA for illustrative purposes.

8. Keep the possibility for non-viable banks to be orderly liquidated.
9. Prevent contagion[9] and maintain market discipline.

The way these objectives are formulated in different jurisdictions might vary to a certain extent, depending on the wording of the relevant legal texts. However, these objectives are the core framework of any resolution regime. Differently said, it might be true that in any resolution regime they might be formulated differently, but at least all these key concepts will be present.

Furthermore, the resolution objectives are not a mere declaration of intent. Typically, they would also have legal relevance, as it is against these objectives that resolution authorities formally assess the credibility of a resolution procedure, both in the actual implementation and in the resolution planning phase.

2.1 Preservation of Critical Functions

Resolution actions should make sure that the critical functions a bank performs towards society are preserved, even though the entity is FOLTF. Keeping these functions alive means that the troubles of a bank shall not negatively affect the real economy or the rest or the financial system.

That being said, there are some key concepts that need to be clarified around the preservation of critical functions. First of all, when is a function considered critical? Resolution authorities, based on the legislation in their respective jurisdictions, have traced their identikit of what a critical function is and operationalised their approach to the criticality assessment. Without entering into jurisdiction-specific aspects, there are two common features that are once again rooted in the FSB soft law and more precisely into the Guidance on Identification of Critical Functions and Critical Shared Services (FSB, 2013). A function towards third parties is considered critical when (a) its disruption would severely affect the economy or the financial system and (b) the same function cannot be taken over by another provider in a reasonable timeframe. In order to determine whether functions are critical, resolution authorities go through these two conditions, in steps that, respectively, go under the name of impact assessment and supply-side analysis.

The impact assessment is aimed to reach a conclusion on the importance of a certain function in the market in which a bank operates. The indicators used to perform this assessment typically refer to the ‘size’ of the function exercised by a bank. Depending on the type of function, the indicators could include the market share, the volume of transactions, the outstanding amounts associated with the

[9] To be precise, in the wording of the KA the contagion prevention is not listed as an objective of resolution regimes or resolution authorities, but it is itself an overarching objective included at the beginning of the Preamble and constituting a motivation for the adoption itself of the KA. We choose to include it along the others, because this is the approach normally taken by the legal texts reflecting the KA.

function, the number of clients, or any other factors that are relevant to estimate how large would be the impact in case of discontinuation.

However, the 'size' of a function is not everything that matters in terms of criticality. If a certain service is offered on highly standardised terms and there are many other competitors offering comparable solutions, even though the impact of the function discontinuation could potentially be high, it is not unreasonable to think that the negative effects on a market level can be overall mitigated by the fact that clients could move to another bank. This is what resolution authorities assess in the second step of the supply-side analysis. The relevant indicators in this case are typically the operational or legal barriers to switch to a different provider, the market concentration, or the time expected for substitution. The propensity of the function provided by a certain bank – or its substitutability – is inversely proportional to its criticality. On the contrary, it is also possible that even in the presence of a more downscaled function size, the barriers to substitutability are so high or the market so concentrated that the assessment goes in favour of the criticality of the function. In summary, the criticality of a function exercised by a given bank is determined by the combination of its relevance for the reference market and the possibility to replace it in a reasonable timeframe.

Note that among the factors for determining the criticality there is no mention of the content or the 'nature' of a certain function. This is because it is not the type of function to determine its criticality, but the market structure where it is performed and the relative position of the bank performing it in that specific market. The criticality assessment is hence a bank-specific assessment. It is well possible that within the same jurisdiction a function is considered critical for certain banks but not for others.

Following the reasoning up to this point, the reader will have certain realised that the combination of impact in case of disruption and substitutability might leave a certain margin of appreciation. What if for example the impact analysis returns a medium–low result, but substitutability is also assessed to be medium–low? It is fair to say that on the outcomes of the criticality assessment there is a role for expert judgment. To conclude on the criticality of a borderline case, it will be necessary to get additional evidence on the client base and the modalities in which the function is provided, as well as to run benchmarking analyses.

Such a process would be too lengthy in an actual crisis case when resolution authorities are mandated to prepare a resolution scheme as rapidly as possible. This is the reason why the criticality assessment is performed upfront, being an integral part of the annual resolution planning cycles. In the regular preparatory work carried by resolution authorities with credit institutions, there is all the necessary time to exchange material, run dedicated meetings, and exchange views on the criticality of a certain function.

In many jurisdictions, banks are asked to report their functions during the resolution planning cycle and perform a first level assessment of their criticality. As to the taxonomy of this reporting requirement, the operational guidance by the FSB indicates the following high-level categories of critical functions:

(a) Deposit-taking
(b) Lending
(c) Payments, clearing, custody, and settlement
(d) Wholesale funding markets
(e) Capital markets and investment activities

The same FSB guidance document also clarifies that the criticality assessment will depend on what effectively feeds into these five blocks. For example, in relation to deposit-taking, the FSB guidance specifies that 'different types of depositors may exhibit different kinds of behaviour'. By 'different type of depositors', we can for example think of institutional and retail depositors. However, even within retail the behaviour of SMEs might differ from the behaviour of individuals. It is not only the counterparty that matters but also the type of service. Lending can mean loans as well as mortgages, which are different types of function.

Regulators and resolution authorities have therefore broken down these five categories in multiple functions. For instance, the European Banking Authority (EBA) has elaborated a template for the reporting of critical functions,[10] with a minimum taxonomy of 23 functions to analyse and the possibility for banks to report additional functions if not perfectly covered by the 23 standard functions (leasing and factoring are key examples of functions often reported as additional functions).

Prevention of Contagion Effects

The Lehman Brothers case demonstrated that in lack of a resolution regime the failure of a bank might have serious consequences also for other credit and financial institutions (see for example Chakrabarty & Zhang, 2012; Dumontaux & Pop, 2013; Wiggins & Metrick, 2014). Intuitively this might happen due to the interconnections between different financial operators. If a bank is exposed towards an insolvent counterparty, this means that a portion of its assets will turn to be defaulting. Depending on the amount of defaulting exposures due to the failure of this counterparty, a bank originally viable might face financial troubles as well. In substance, when a bank is failing or likely to fail, it is not only its viability to come into question but also financial stability at large.

This is why the KAs (2.3) state that resolution authorities 'should pursue financial stability'. However, we need to properly understand what pursuing financial stability means for resolution authorities. Central banks and other regulators are also mandated to ensure financial stability. In the context of resolution, the wording used by the European legislation on banking resolution can provide some clarifications.

[10] European Commission Implementing Regulation (EU) 2018/1624 of 23 October 2018, laying down implementing technical standards with regard to procedures and standard forms and templates for the provision of information for the purposes of resolution plans for credit institutions and investment firms pursuant to Directive 2014/59/EU of the European Parliament and of the Council and repealing Commission Implementing Regulation (EU) 2016/1066.

According to Article 31 of the Banking Recovery and Resolution Directive (BRRD), when applying the resolution tools and exercising the resolution powers, resolution authorities shall 'avoid a significant adverse effect on the financial system, in particular by preventing contagion [...] and by maintaining market discipline'. In the context of financial crisis, contagion is defined as 'a situation whereby instability in a specific market or institution is transmitted to one or several other markets or institutions' (Constâncio, 2012). From the standpoint of resolution authorities, pursuing financial stability means preventing the negative spill-over effects arising from an insolvent bank might endanger other financial market operators.

Now, we can argue that when a failing bank undergoes a resolution procedure, the objective of preventing contagion has higher chances to be met, in comparison to what would happen if the bank were liquidated. This is because typically in resolution external creditors would bear lower losses. We will come back extensively on these conclusions (in particular in Sect. 4); however, we can already detail some key implications of opting for a resolution procedure instead of liquidation.

When a bank is liquidated, this means that not only the capital will be depleted but also many creditors will see their claims completed eroded. What is left on the asset side will be distributed to creditors according to the hierarchy of their claims, from the most senior to the junior. In this situation, some of the creditors (normally the junior ones) will never see any of their money back.

In resolution the capital is also likely to be written down, at least partially. But then, what happens to debt instruments? In the case the bank is sold to another company via the sale of business tool, the external acquirer will take over the debt of the insolvent bank. In this case, creditors will assist to a change in the counterparty, but the book value of their claims would remain largely unaffected. In the case of the bail-in tool, debt will be converted into new capital, but its book value also in this case will be largely unaffected.

We say largely because the exact resolution outcome will evidently depend on the amount of losses, there including also the hypothetical case of losses exceeding the total capital of a bank, with part of the debt instruments being written down to absorb losses. In fact, we do not want to say that losses passed to external creditors will always be lower in resolution than in liquidation. More precisely, we affirm that it is reasonable to expect that on average resolution is less likely than liquidation to pass losses onto external creditors.

However, this is an element of non-secondary implications. Banks are in fact exposed to each other through debt rather than through capital. In this respect, it is worth nothing that holdings in the capital of a bank above a certain threshold (i.e. a qualifying holding) need to undergo the approval of the prudential supervision authority, which will assess the viability and reputation of the acquirer. As a matter of fact, a bank more willingly enters this assessment in cases where it aims to gain control of another bank. Otherwise, a bank will more likely retain on its asset side debt rather than capital instruments issued by another bank. As resolution appears less prone to affect the book value of debt instruments held by creditors, it will also be better tailored to cope with direct contagion effects.

This different interplay of liquidation and resolution with contagion can also be read in the other direction. If resolution authorities need to prevent contagion, in the choice between a resolution and a liquidation procedure, they will need to consider what are the risks of contagion. Is the failure of a bank likely to affect materially the soundness of other credit institutions? If so, this will be one of the arguments in favour of resolving a bank rather than liquidating it.

The link between a resolution procedure and the need to limit contagion effects is explicit in the European resolution framework. The contagion risk is one of the key components to determine whether there is a public interest to resolve the bank. We will come back on how the public interest assessment (or PIA) is performed. However, even without entering the details of the methodology, we want to highlight that the PIA is not carried out for the first time during a crisis case. Considering the complexities that this assessment entails, it would be unreasonable to think that over the time of a weekend – the time usually associated with resolution actions – resolution authorities could reach a conclusion on the existence of a public interest to resolve a bank, without having prepared in advance. The PIA is part of the annual cycles of resolution planning, in which resolution authorities design the presumptive path of what they would do in a crisis case. It will of course be repeated in a crisis case, but with the benefit of having prepared in advance in respect of bank-specific characteristics.

Under this spirit, the Single Resolution Board (SRB), i.e. the resolution authority of the significant credit institutions of the European Banking Union, has published a policy document explaining the approach to the PIA (SRB, 2019b), which applies to both the ongoing resolution planning and the crisis management after a failure. The PIA is an aspect on which the BRRD remains to a high level, without entering the details of what should be assessed within the PIA. Hence, the SRB has disclosed its own methodology for operationalising the PIA, which envisages two types of contagion risk, direct and indirect.

Among these two types, direct contagion is the one we explained at the beginning of this subsection. It materialises through the exposures of a bank towards another bank that is failing or likely to fail. When looking at indirect contagion, the SRB considers the risks passed to the solvency of other institution through the financial markets. For example, the SRB distinguishes between the first round effects on banks directly exposed to a failing or likely to fail bank (direct contagion), from the second or third round effects on other market operators, which might be exposed to an institution hit in the first round. Still, the extent of indirect contagion considered by the SRB goes well beyond that, including a number of quantitative and qualitative dimensions.

Among quantitative factors, the PIA covers for example the correlation in the bond spreads with other banks, the effect of widespread fire sales, or the amount of ex post contributions other banks would be called to pay in case of activation of the deposit guarantee scheme. The qualitative analysis looks for example at the reputation effects that a failing or likely to fail bank might ingenerate also for institutions of similar size and business model.

Conclusively, for how dramatic a crisis case might be, one of the primary tasks of resolution authorities is to make sure that the effects of it are sterilised sufficiently in time and before the transmission to the rest of the financial system. The potential impact of a failure on the overall financial stability is in fact one of the elements which make a failing or likely to fail bank something more than a headache for its creditors, i.e. a question of general public interest.

2.2 *Protection of Taxpayers*

The fact that a resolution action might be in the public interest does not mean however that its financing should happen at public expenses. We have already outlined above what are the threats posed by public bailouts. By contrast, resolution regimes should be built in a way that internalises the costs of resolving a failing bank to the failing institution and its creditors.

The KAs give ample importance to this objective, which along with the continuation of critical functions and the prevention of contagion is mentioned at the very beginning of the foreword. However, the objective of protecting taxpayers in the KA is particularly ambitious. In fact, according to the KA (Preamble and 2.3), resolution regimes should 'not rely on public solvency support and not create an expectation that such support will be available'. The second part of this sentence is a key point. Resolution regimes in respect of the taxpayers' protection should be actually established in a way that orients the expectations of market operators against the perspective of a bailout.

However, how does this deterrent function operate in reality? We can detect at least two levels at which this mechanism of incentives works. On a first level, it is the post-financial crisis legislation itself that states black on white that public money is no longer an option when it comes about banking crises. In the United States the Dodd Frank Act includes two provisions about taxpayers' protection. When outlining the functioning of the Orderly Liquidation Authority (OLA, i.e. the set of tools, powers, and procedures to resolve a failing bank), the legal text (see 12 U.S.C. §5394, Dodd–Frank Act §214) clarifies that 'taxpayers shall bear no losses'. An analogous provision (15 U.S.C. §8305, Dodd–Frank Act §716) prohibits the bail-out of swap banks at the expenses of the Federal Government. Including these provisions in the legislation is the first way to orient the expectations of market operators about what would happen in case of a crisis. It has been empirically highlighted (see for example Berg et al., 2018) that even before an actual crisis case, the shift in the US legal framework and the inclusion of an explicit bailout prohibition have contributed to improve the capital ratios and risk-taking of banks.

In addition to this first level of incentives, resolution authorities themselves have operationalised and implemented the legal framework in a way that protects taxpayers. We can argue that if the prohibition of bailouts is a negative measure, the work performed by resolution authorities on an ongoing basis is the active side of taxpayers' protection. In concrete terms, during the annual resolution planning phase, banks and resolution authorities design a presumptive course of action to take in case of failure. This presumptive course of action is called preferred resolution strategy (PRS). When preparing the PRS, banks and resolution authorities shall work under the assumption that no public intervention would take place. In the European Union, where resolution plans are prepared by resolution authorities themselves, the legislation (Art. 10, 15, and 16 BRRD) requires to identify in advance the financing means for resolution, excluding any kind of public support. The SRB has further commented on these provisions by stating in its public guidance on resolution planning (SRB, 2016) that 'resolution authorities have to prepare resolution plans detailing how a bank will be resolved, in a way that achieves the resolution objectives, while ensuring taxpayers avoid carrying the burden'.

The requirement to plan for a PRS excluding public support has two orders of consequences. On the one hand, such as the bailout prohibition, it orients the expectations of market operators as to what would happen in case of resolution. However, the inclusion of taxpayers' protection in resolution planning goes even beyond that. As we will examine in Sect. 7, preparing (and regularly updating) resolution plans is a recurring task aimed to ensure the readiness of the resolution tools in case of crisis. This is a demanding process, engaging both banks and resolution authorities on a continuous basis to detail operational step and financing arrangements in case of resolution, without any recourse to public money. Resolution planning orients the behaviour of banks in going concern, making them aware that 'if things go bad' nobody will 'come and rescue them for free'. As already noted, this influences the propensity to take risk.

In addition, resolution planning has the goal to prepare banks and resolution authorities to a resolution action. Under this perspective, banks are requested to perform preparatory exercises and simulations of a resolution action. In performing these tasks, banks are confronted with the operational and financial aspects of the implementation of a resolution scheme, where there is no space for any form of public support. Hence, resolution authorities and banks work side by side to make sure that a resolution action will function properly, without the need of any external support. Under this perspective resolution planning is an active form of taxpayers' protection: It does not only predict what would not happen (i.e. a bailout) but should also demonstrate how the resolution of a failing bank would be possible without costs to be borne by public finances.

2.3 *Protection of Covered Counterparties, Insolvency Hierarchy and Segregation of Client Assets*

Although it is clear that to avoid the burden of a crisis being passed to taxpayers the costs of resolution need to be internalised to the institution, equally not all the liabilities of a bank may concur to the financing of the procedure. We will explain for example that the write down and conversion or bail-in of capital instruments and eligible liabilities includes certain mandatory exclusions from their scope. However, within the resolution objective themselves, we find a specific reference to covered depositors and investors, which need to be protected while performing a resolution action.

In many jurisdictions the deposits of households – and often also those of small and medium enterprises – are covered up to a maximum level. The maximum level is either defined in relation to each deposit held at a certain bank or – more frequently – as an aggregate level per depositor for all his deposits held at a certain bank (e.g. EUR 100.000 per depositor in the European Union and USD 250.000 per depositor for each category of deposit for the clients of US banks covered by the Federal Deposit Insurance Corporation). If a bank had to be liquidated and the insolvency estate were not sufficient to repay completely covered deposits, these would be repaid in any case. The full reimbursement is ensured by specific mechanisms organised for this specific purpose and financed by banks, with ex ante contributions and the constitution of a fund or ex post contributions after a default event. These mechanisms are referred to as deposit guarantee or deposit insurance.

The reasons for establishing deposit guarantee and the debate on its effect on financial stability will be discussed more extensively in Sect. 5 on the resolution tools. The consideration we need to make in relation to the resolution objectives is that – even proceeding by common sense – if certain liabilities are worthy of protection in liquidation, it would be unreasonable to accord them a worse treatment in the context of resolution. A different treatment in resolution would be equivalent to conclude that these creditors would be better off in liquidation. As we will see when outlining the safeguards to resolution, the no-creditor-worse-off principle imposes that resolution procedures are performed according to the limit that no creditor should receive less than what he would get if the bank were liquidated (this is not only for covered depositors but also for all creditors of the bank). If this was not the case, a resolution procedure would entail a redistribution of the costs of the failure across creditor classes, which is something that cannot be left at discretion of a resolution authority. Furthermore, from the position of any creditors, it would be against any principles of fairness to force them to bear additional costs due to a decision by a government body to start a resolution procedure instead of an insolvency one. As we will often repeat in the rest of this chapter, resolution is framed as an exception to the general presumption that a failing bank should undergo a liquidation procedure. The decision in favour of resolution must be motivated by the existence of a public interest that would be endangered in liquidation. However, in jurisdictions characterised by the rule of law, a public administration cannot receive an unlimited delegation to establish on a case by case basis when a public interest should prevail on individual rights. The no-creditor-worse-off principle acts as a safeguard, ensuring that while mandated to protect the public interest, resolution authority cannot violate the individual rights that creditors have against a failing entity.

This is the reason why the Preamble of the KA among the resolution objectives also includes the respect of the insolvency hierarchy in all actions involving a write down of capital instruments and eligible liabilities. When a shareholder or a creditor is written down, it means that he will bear a loss. The sequence by which these losses are borne will therefore mirror the insolvency hierarchy in reverse order (e.g. as in liquidation shareholders are the last in the hierarchy of rights on the insolvency estate, in resolution they will be the first to bear losses).

Similarly to covered deposits, there may be certain investors that receive a form of protection against the insolvency of a bank, which need to be protected also in resolution. An example can be one of the investor compensation schemes in the European Union,[11] conferring a protection of EUR 20.000 per investor. In the United States,[12] securities and cash under brokerage are protected up to a value of USD 500.000 for securities and USD 250.000 for cash. The protection is not to cover investors from credit or market risk, i.e. from the default of the debtor[13] or the loss in value of its shares or securities. These are the inherent risks of investments, which each investor needs to be prepared to endure. This compensation instead is foreseen in very specific situations, such as for example fraud cases or criminal conducts leading to the disappearance of the shares or security of the investor or an insufficient segregation of the client assets under management from the balance sheet of the bank, which in case of liquidation could make it very difficult to recover these assets.

It has to be said that as a matter of fact covered investors may have a lesser relevance from the strict point of view of the comparison between resolution and liquidation for at least two reasons. First, although the activation of these mechanisms is not infrequent, they only seldom relate to cases of bank insolvency, with the most notable exception being the activation of the investor protection in the United States after the collapse of Lehman Brothers (when however resolution procedures were not yet in place and the regulatory framework was less tight than today). For the few instances in which it was activated for banks in recent times, the cases involved smaller banks, for which a resolution procedure is in any case unlikely.

A more substantial argument concerns the difference between covered deposits and covered investments. Covered deposits are liabilities of the bank; covered investments are assets of the clients. Resolution powers and tools for their financial aspects are applied to the assets and liabilities of the failing bank. The assets of the clients are completely out of the equation. This distinction is also reflected in a separate resolution objective, which prescribes the protection of client assets and client money. This objective is largely self-explanatory: How can we imagine to ask a creditor to use its own money to repay other creditors of the same debtor? We can think about three young brothers and name them John, Susy, and Andrew. Let us

---

[11] Directive 97/9/EC of the European Parliament and of the Council of 3 March 1997 on investor compensation schemes.

[12] Securities Investor Protection Act of 1970, 15 U.S.C. §78aaa et seq. The initial level of coverage was USD 100.000, then increased for securities, and expanded to cash in 1980.

[13] We are not referring to shares or bonds issued by the failing entity but shares and bonds owned by clients of that entity and kept in custody at that entity.

imagine that John borrowed 15 dollars from Susy and Andrew to open a lemonade business with the promise to give 16 dollars back to his siblings. To complete the picture, let us assume that it is January, snow falls heavily, and the entrepreneurial initiative of our adventurous John does not encounter any demand at all for cold lemonade. Would the mother ask Andrew to sell his Pokemon cards or any of his toys to share the proceedings between him and Susy? What about John? Will he come out clean after having lost the money saved by Susy and Andrew, who decided not to spend their entire five-dollar-a-week grant on chocolate and candies? At the most, it will be John to be requested to resell his lemonade equipment to recover at least part of the capital lent by Susy and Andrew.

In liquidation and resolution, a bank is not different from this lemonade business: the claims of Susy, Andrew, and thousands of other creditors will be repaid based on the recovery of the assets of the bank. The difference instead is that a grown-up Andrew does not own Pokemon tradable cards, but tradable securities. These tradable securities are not held under his bed but custodied at an intermediary, often the same bank where he deposited his money and of which he may also have bought a handful of shares. Now, in this situation Andrew can suffer from a write down of the shares of the bank he owns, and he may see a conversion of his deposits exceeding the coverage limit into new capital; but for what concerns the other securities in its portfolio, he shall bear no consequence.

2.4 Efficiency of Resolution

While it is clear that in resolution costs are internalised to the banking sector and that taxpayers should never bear losses, resolution authorities should also keep an eye on the cost efficiency of resolution actions, in order to 'avoid unnecessary destruction of value' (Preamble and KA 2.3). In a resolution case, this means to limit the application of resolution tools imposing losses to shareholders and creditors down to the minimum amount necessary to absorb the external losses and recapitalise the failing bank up to a level at which it can confidently continue to operate.

Naturally, under the tight constraints and little time available in an actual resolution case, there would be very few alternatives on the table for resolution authorities to pick up the most efficient one. For this reason, this objective becomes of even greater importance in the planning phase, during which resolution authorities and banks are mandated to design the course of action that they would likely take in resolution.

Efficiency in resolution has both a procedural and a financial meaning. On the procedural side, in order to facilitate the implementation of the overall resolution strategy, the powers of resolution authorities should be exercised only as far as it is strictly necessary to resolve the banks. In practical terms, this means that in the resolution planning phase, among different alternative courses of actions, resolution authorities should privilege those implying the fewest operational steps. A resolution scheme always includes a set of authoritative measures. Although being adopted on the basis of the mandate and powers conferred to resolution authorities, these measures would come as an external alteration of the natural course of events, if the bank were left alone. Therefore, all of them entail a certain execution risk because it is not possible to be certain a priori that they will produce the predicted outcomes. In the implementation of a resolution scheme, it might be the case that an unforeseeable or an inculpably ignored factor could alter the final result. Therefore, it is reasonable to assume that the feasibility of a resolution action is inversely correlated with the number of operational steps necessary to perform it. Even intuitively, it can be said that for resolution the easier the better. To make things even clearer, we can say with good approximation that if the same (or a reasonably comparable) outcome can be reached either with a combination of resolution tools or with a single resolution tool, the second option should be generally preferred, since it is conditioned by a lower execution risk.

Next to the operational side, efficiency should also be ensured on a financial level. In this case – even more intuitively – resolution authorities are mandated to select the least costly option for shareholders and creditors of the bank. Similarly as to what has been said for the operational efficiency, if a similar outcome can be reached through different alternatives, the less costly one is to be preferred.

That being said, if operational and financial efficiency are easy to grasp on paper, we need to flag that in reality they are not as much effortless to be ensured. In particular, it should be noted that the interplay between these two aspects might in some cases be puzzling. In fact, a procedurally simple strategy is not necessarily the least costly. To give a concrete example, we might think of the operationalisation of the bail-in (for the functioning of this tool please refer to Sect. 5.1). In case of losses that do not completely deplete the capital of a bank, wiping out the entire remaining capital before converting debt would be procedurally easier than diluting existing shareholders, because it would simplify the recapitalisation of this entity, without the need to estimate too precisely the exact extent of the dilution. This argument could appear very promising especially in a case where the existing shares have a peculiar legal nature. We may think for example about the shares of a cooperative bank: Issuing new capital alongside the existing one would require additional steps, such as the conversion of the existing shares into ordinary shares. However, writing down the capital exceeding losses will always be more costly for shareholders than diluting them with converted debt. Furthermore, we started from the assumption that losses do not completely deplete capital. Writing down capital beyond the loss absorption needs (i.e. the remaining capital) would put a resolution authority in a dangerous territory, with the risk of breaching the no-creditor-worse-off principle, according to which no creditor should bear in resolution losses that are greater than in liquidation.

The trade-off between procedural and cost efficiency works also the other way round. Using the sale of business tool with a share deal (i.e. the case when an acquirer buys the entire bank or banking group in resolution, see Sect. 5.2) would be very efficient from the standpoint of costs. In this situation, debt holders are likely to remain unaffected. However, preparing a bank for a sale under resolution entails a number of preparing measures, aimed at making the resolving institution more marketable in terms of expected profitability. This transformation process can be sometimes very far from being operationally simple.

Given these complexities in conjugating procedural and cost side, it is emblematic the way efficiency is framed in the BRRD (Art. 31 BRRD). Rather than constituting an objective per se, the efficiency of resolution actions is rather included as a residual clause that remains subordinated to the achievement of the other resolution objectives. That is consistent with the KA (2.3), where in relation to the statutory objectives of resolution authorities, it is said that cost minimisation and unnecessary destruction of value need to be pursued 'where that is consistent with the other statutory objectives'.

2.5 Other Objectives Included in the Key Attributes

The KAs further include other objective that we choose to examine all together here, under the disclaimer that within the legal texts they may not always be presented as resolution objectives as such, but as standalone provisions concerning the functioning of resolution.

One of these objectives pertains to the credibility (Preamble) and feasibility (Preamble and KA 2.3) of a resolution procedure. Both these qualities are deeply interrelated with the concept of resolvability, which we will examine in the next section, and they refer to the possibility of resolving a failing bank by continuing its critical functions and limiting the impact on financial stability and real economy.

Drawing a line between credibility and feasibility of resolution may not be so obvious. If we wanted to make a distinction, we would say that the credibility pertains to the overall results of a resolution procedure, while the feasibility relates to the possibility of implementing it.

The credibility of a resolution procedure has to be assessed against the hypothetical counterfactual of an insolvency proceeding. It is therefore not an absolute quality, but a conclusion relative to the baseline outcome that would be produced if no action is taken and hence the bank liquidated. Once again applying a common sense approach, a therapy must be at least better than the disease to cure. If collateral effects are extremely severe and unbearable, putting the life of the patient even more at risk, it would be preferable to endure the symptoms of the disease rather than starting the cure.

The same reasoning applies to the comparison between resolution and liquidation. Resolution should address the situation in a way that it is at least not worse of what would be achieved in liquidation. We examined a similar idea with the principle of the no creditor worse off. The credibility of resolution may be seen as a generalisation of this principle, involving not only the creditors of the bank but also real economy and financial stability at large.

Now, when moving from theory to practice, it may not be so immediate to conclude about the credibility of a resolution procedure in relation to financial stability and real economy. This is the reason why resolution plans themselves include a provisional assessment of the credibility of a resolution procedure compared to insolvency proceedings. In the EU, where it is the resolution authority to draft the resolution plans, this is done through a comparison of the way resolution and liquidation can achieve the resolution objectives, with a particular attention to financial contagion. Effectively, this is part of the public interest assessment we already introduced above.

That being said, one thing is to conclude that it would be beneficial and hence credible to put a bank in resolution, and another one is to be sure that there is an effective possibility of performing the procedure. This is a crucial aspect in the comparison between liquidation and resolution. Insolvency proceedings can be very long,[14] but they are overall simpler than resolution. In fact, they entail valuation processes (such as resolution) to determine the net asset value of the failing entity and a liquidation of the remaining assets of the bank with the aim of maximising the insolvency estate. The reader should not misunderstand what we mean here: the tasks of liquidation are certainly burdensome, conditioned by the need of technical expertise and following complex legal procedures. However, if there is one thing certain about liquidation, it is that it will be always possible. In the worst (rather theoretical) case, none of the assets will be recovered and none of the shareholders or creditors will see their claims repaid, but the procedure will be closed.

For resolution things get more challenging, because the procedure is effectively about continuing the functions of a bank, either by rescuing the company or by transferring its business to a different institution. By the way it is conceived, resolution cannot end with a 'we can do nothing' statement and the drop of the pen. To trigger a resolution procedure, there is the need to be reasonably sure that its objectives will be achieved.

We will discuss about these problems when presenting the resolution tools and also explain what are the 'plan B' options resolution authorities have in store should the situation be extremely complex to address. However, the key idea to retain here is that performing a resolution procedure presupposes the possibility of implementing resolution tools. Therefore, resolution plans and testing exercises will deal with the organisational, legal, procedural, and financial aspects of resolution, in order to ensure readiness for the implementation of a resolution procedure. Banks in turn are expected to develop certain capabilities, pertaining for example to the possibility of timely providing timely and accurate information to the resolution authorities and external valuers, have in place the arrangements to perform a write down and conversion or to raise liquidity, make sure that the services underlying the performance of critical functions will continue to operate, and so on.

A particularly challenging situation is the one concerning the resolution of large cross-border groups, G-SIBs specifically (Carmassi et al., 2015; Hüpkes et al., 2016; Quaglia & Spendzharova, 2019). The resolution of these banks requires the cooperation of different resolution authorities established in various jurisdictions.

[14] For instance, the liquidation of Lehman Brothers was initiated in September 2008 and closed 14 years later in September 2022.

In this perspective, the KAs include also a resolution objective on the cooperation between the home and the host resolution authorities, where the home one is the resolution authority of the country where the group is headquartered. Without entering in excessive details about what these forms of cooperation entail, on a very high level we can say that the strategy for resolving these banks needs to be coordinated. This implies that there should be at least a minimum transferability of funds across the groups. In fact, if resolution authorities decided to proceed with a ring-fencing approach (i.e. forcing the resources of the entity in their jurisdiction to remain there and not be used for other entities in the group), this could very easily increase the resolution costs, at the expenses of creditors. The resolution of such a bank therefore requires the resolution authorities to meet in a college (for G-SIBs also referred to as a crisis management group). The college does not start to operate during a crisis case. In reality, it is already active in the ongoing planning and testing phase, being convened periodically (normally at least annually) to adopt the updated group resolution plan and decision on the loss absorption requirements.

Concerning the feasibility of a resolution procedure, it also has to be clarified that resolution does not necessarily imply the survival of the original company and its activities. As we clarified above in relation to the continuation of critical functions, the mandate of resolution authorities concerns the protection of the public interest and the financial and economic value of the failing bank. In some cases, these goals will be achieved with the resolved bank continuing to operate after the procedure. In other cases however, the failing bank has little of no chances to survive in a medium to long-term horizon. When this is the situation, resolution authorities will achieve their mandate by transferring the activities of a bank to an acquirer or a bridge institution, with the liquidation of the remaining parts of the institution that entered resolution.

This is in line with the KA objective according to which non-viable firms can exit the market in an orderly way. This objective has two orders of implications. First, if a firm is not liquidated, there should be reasons to believe that it still retains profitability drivers, which after resolution would restore its long-term viability. In other words, a bank that is left open by resolution needs to be able to sustain itself in the long run. This is why after an open-bank resolution, the institution will undergo a deep phase of re-organisation, to refocus its activities on the still profitable part of their business.

Second, this objective – for the part on the orderly exit – applies to both residual entities liquidated as an effect of resolution and entities liquidated under normal insolvency proceedings. The meaning is that a liquidation should not be a chaotic process with little or no recovery (such as in the theoretical worse case we suggested above). By contrast, also in liquidation financial stability should not be endangered and neither the performance of other economic activities. It is therefore understandable the stance taken by the EU legislation, under which also institutions earmarked for liquidation are still subject, although with a simplified approach, to resolution planning and to loss absorption requirements.

To summarise the considerations on this last objective, we can say that all failing banks are non-viable by definition. For them the default option is to be liquidated under insolvency proceedings unless there is a public interest to protect. If there is a possibility to make the bank return to be profitable after resolution, this may continue to operate. In all other cases, resolution will leave behind entities to be liquidated. Regardless of the liquidation being the main option or the by-product of a resolution procedure, the KAs require the exit from the market to be an orderly one.

3 The Concept of Resolvability (Or the Corollary to the Resolution Objectives)

3.1 The Definition

Deeply interlinked with the resolution objectives is the concept of 'resolvability'. The KAs (Appendix I, Annex 3) define a bank[15] resolvable as long as:

'It is feasible and credible for the resolution authorities to resolve it in a way that protects systemically important [i.e. critical] functions without severe systemic disruption and without exposing taxpayers to loss'.

There are two elements to highlight in this definition. First of all, the link with the resolution objectives is made evident by the direct mention of three of them, with an emphasis on the continuation of critical functions. In addition to these three objectives, the definition is also based on the feasibility and credibility of resolution. As previously outlined, feasibility and credibility are in turn concepts that embrace all resolution objectives, at the same time looking at the practical details of implementing a resolution scheme. For simplicity, we can therefore summarise the above definition by saying that a bank is resolvable as long as it can be resolved in a way that it is coherent with the resolution objectives.

Second, being resolvable is an attribute of a bank. As such, it refers to its propensity to successfully undergo a resolution action. This propensity is a bank-specific quality, whose assessment – as we will see – needs to match the general goal of successfully implementing a resolution scheme with the different and sometimes unique characteristics of any given credit institution.

[15] More precisely the KA refers to significant financial institutions, thus including large insurance companies but excluding smaller banks. This choice reflects the compromise in the KA for which the resolvability assessment is to be carried at least for the largest groups. We choose to refer to banks instead, in line with the approach taken in the European Union and other jurisdictions, where the resolvability assessment is carried for all credit institutions.

3.2 The Content

However, having noted that the concept of resolvability relates to the possibility of resolving a bank achieving the resolution objectives and that this possibility is of bank-specific nature, it remains to be clarified what is the actual content of it. When is a bank resolvable? What are the characteristics that it needs to demonstrate to be considered so? The KAs provide some insights as to the content of resolvability. The Annex 3 of Appendix I includes – as an example of what resolution authorities should assess – a list of questions divided by topics. These questions have to do on one side with the organisation and business model of a bank, but on the other also on a set of capabilities that a bank should develop in preparation of resolution. More precisely, the questions are classified into five blocks, pertaining to (1) structure and business of a bank, (2) the internal interconnectedness, (3) the access to financial market infrastructures (FMI), (4) the management information systems (MIS), and (5) the cross-border dimension.

To give some examples, these questions space from the critical functions exercised by a bank to the transferability of contracts with central clearing counterparties (CCP), passing through the outsourcing of services, the separability of various activities or entities in the group, or the ability to report precise information under stress. These questions are meant as a guidance as to what resolution authorities should assess in relation to the resolvability of credit institutions. However, we should not expect to find in them a definitive answer as to the content of resolvability, for a number of reasons.

First, the recalled Annex of the KA is addressed to resolution authorities in performing their assessment. In this sense, it provides a clue about typical questions a resolution authority should reflect upon when performing the assessment. This is the reason why the last part of the questions focusses on the relations between home and host authorities or the coordination across different legal regimes. However, the definition of resolvability in the KA, as we noted above, is based on banks rather than authorities.

Second, this list of questions is not exhaustive. The Annex itself presents them as (Appendix I, Annex 3, p. 38) 'some of the questions that, at a minimum, would need to be explored': some of them, indeed, but not all of them. This is understandable considering that the KAs are a document published by an international body with a global outreach. The actual content of resolvability needs to be defined at a more local level, taking also into account the characteristics of the economies and legal frameworks in which banks concretely operate.

Third and more importantly, this list of question is built around a series of areas that need to be under the lens of resolution authorities; however, it does not specify the features or capabilities that banks should demonstrate to be considered resolvable. To said it differently, these questions tell resolution authorities where to look, but not what to look for.

A single example is probably worth more than a thousand explanations. In relation to service level agreements, the Annex includes the following question (p. 38):

'What is the extent to which key operational functions [. . .] are outsourced to other group entities or third party service providers?'

From such a question, we get the idea that services provided to the resolving entity by other entities in the group or by an external provider might pose risks to operational continuity in resolution and that resolution authorities should look at the extent by which services are provided on the basis of these delivery models. However, this question alone would not be sufficient to tell us how a resolvable bank would look like in terms of intra-group or outsourced services. In concrete, what is the extent of externalisation that can be considered acceptable? What are the risks connected with the outsourced services (e.g. the risk of sudden interruption due to the impossibility of remunerating them)? Or conclusively, what is the relation between externalised services and resolvability?

If we limited ourselves to the KA, we would not get a definitive answer as to what a resolvable bank would look like. Other guidance documents by the FSB provide more precise indications regarding what banks need to have in place to be considered resolvable on selected areas. To name few of these documents, we can refer to the principles on external (FSB, 2015) or internal (FSB, 2017a) total loss-absorbing capacity, on bail-in execution (FSB, 2018b), on funding in resolution (FSB, 2018a), or the guidance on the arrangements to support operational continuity in resolution (FSB, 2016). These documents complement KA and give substance to the concept of resolvability, indicating with more precision what banks need to develop to be considered resolvable.

3.3 *The Policy Operationalisation of Resolvability*

Obviously, as for the list of questions in the KA, the FSB principles and guidance documents cannot account for the specificities of different jurisdictions and economic environment. The precise content of resolvability needs in fact to be further refined at a more granular level before banks can take action. In other terms, it is necessary to pass from high-level principles to implementable regulatory expectations.

Neither the resolution legislation, although mirroring the soft law of the KA, operationalises the concept of resolvability at a level sufficiently granular to be implementable. At most, it is sufficiently detailed to be directly implementable for some standardised (and quantitative) features, such as the calibration of the loss absorption requirements of the KA. For the other aspects, the policy operationalisation[16] of what banks should develop to be considered resolvable is demanded to resolution authorities themselves.

However, what does it mean concretely operationalising the concept of resolvability? In short, it means translating this ideal condition into a specific set of actions to perform and capabilities to develop, in order to make it possible – should it be the case – to perform an effective resolution procedure in a short timeframe. This type of translation of high-level principles into actionable requests takes place at the level of the policy guidance documents published by resolution authorities. To make the reader better grasp what we are referring to, some examples may be very helpful.

In the European Banking Union the SRB has operationalised the concept of resolvability in seven Resolvability Dimensions, covering (a) the governance arrangements for resolution planning and execution, (b) loss-absorbing and resolution capacity, (c) liquidity and funding in resolution, (d) operational continuity and continued access to financial market infrastructures, (e) information system

[16] We feel that in order to make the present section properly understood, we need to provide some clarifications about what we mean with policy operationalisation. References to policy operationalisation can be found across very different fields, from access to dental care (Harris 2013) to natural hazards prevention (Kumar 2020), passing through public transport (Milne et al. 2020), marine areas (Galparsoro et al. 2021b), health (Huber et al. 2016; Stucki et al. 2020), water (Lawson et al. 2020), homeland security (Murphy 2014), or sustainable aquaculture (Osmundsen et al. 2020).

Some of these authors (Harris 2013; Huber et al. 2016; Stucki et al. 2020) use the world 'operationalisation' to refer to the operationalisation of a variable at a given moment in the policy cycle, which is not the process we aim to study in this research. Even among those who use the word 'operationalisation' to describe a step in the policy cycle, there is no consensus around what it represents. For Kumar (Kumar 2020) this process covers all the aspects relating to the policy implementation and evaluation of its effects. Lawson et al. (2020) and Murphy (2014) intend operationalisation as a synonym of 'phase-in' or 'implementation' of the regulators' expectations. As in Galparsoro et al. (2021a), the policy operationalisation is a sub-step of the formulation phase. A definition of policy operationalisation that is comparable to what we intend was provided by Dinica (2004), who describes it as the process by which (p.2) 'the policy goals, means and schemes are specified in a way that implementing actors are able to work with them'. Other authors (Verschuere & Vancoppenolle, 2012) agree with the link to the implementation phase but emphasise the role of implementing actors. In brief, 'operationalisation forms a blind spot in the current literature'. Taking note of this void, Mastenbroek, Treib, and Versluis interpret policy operationalisation as the passage between the legislation and the practical implementation, and they describe it as the process 'making instruments applicable'. In this chapter we adhere to this approach and define policy operationalisation as the process by which legislation is transformed into implementable provisions. This process involves inter alia guidance documents, public statements, consultations, and informal interactions with the addresses, accompanied by the adoption of internal instructions and procedures.

and data requirements, (f) communication in resolution, and (g) separability[17] and reorganisation.

These seven dimensions are collectively illustrated in a policy document called *SRB Expectations for Bank* (SRB, 2020). The Expectations for Banks represent an organic and multi-source system of guidance, organised along the aforementioned seven dimensions, further articulated into Principles and Capabilities. This guidance system explains the tasks and preparatory work that banks had to develop according to a multi-year work programme for a transition period between 2020 and the end of 2023 in order to become fully resolvable. These expectations continue to apply also after the transition period and are subject to regular re-assessment (e.g. the annual resolvability assessment), on-site inspections, and testing exercises (i.e. simulations of a resolution procedure or of some specific aspects of it).

The Expectations for Banks system is only one example of the policy operationalisation by resolution authorities. A similar approach is used by the Bank of England, with the publication in 2019 of the policy statement named *Approach to Assessing Resolvability* (BoE, 2019). More complex is probably the case of the United States, where the word resolution was already in use before the KA with a different meaning and where the progress on the resolution regimes has seen 'different seasons' with steps made forward and backward depending on the agenda of the administration in charge. However the Federal Insurance has also published resolution handbooks and guidance for resolution planning.

The list of authorities having published guidance on the FSB concept of resolvability can grow very long and the reader can easily check these documents on the websites of the resolution authority in its jurisdiction. However, we need to add a clarification. Guidance documents are a key element – even possibly the most relevant one – of the policy operationalisation of resolvability. However, taken alone, they would not be sufficient to make sure that resolution regimes are ready to operate.

First, no matter how precise and clear a guidance statement may be, there will always be specific and complex cases requiring an interpretation of the policy. If resolution authorities limited themselves to publish a document to then remain inactive until the day a resolution procedure needs to be implemented, these documents would not be anything else than a mere declaration of intent. They could be considered as a commentary or a development of the original text (in this case the KA and the resolution legislation), but they would still be just a collection of words printed on paper or displayed on a webpage.

The guidance documents are – if you want – the foundation of policy operationalisation. However, the implementation readiness can only be achieved through

[17] Yet another '-ility' word in the resolution lexicon. Separability refers the possibility of separating different group entities without causing a disruption of their critical functions. To visualise this concept, the reader can think about different types of cookies. Some can be fractioned in parts and shared with friends. Others, if we attempt, will just break apart in many pieces. We can say that the first type is 'separable', whereas the second one is not.

the subsequent actions of the public authorities and the addressees of the guidance. In the case of resolution regimes, resolution authorities and banks continuously exchange on the interpretation of this guidance. Furthermore, the authorities request banks to provide information concerning how the various aspects of resolvability are taken into account and developed within the bank.

To go even further, the resolution plans are precisely a way to prepare the banks and the authorities to what would happen in resolution. Drafting and updating these plans require a substantial amount of information and preliminary steps to be made on both sides. In more recent times, with years of preparatory work by banks on becoming more resolvable,[18] resolution authorities have increased the efforts on testing and inspections (see for example the *SRB 2023 Work Programme*) and it is likely to continue to be the case in upcoming years.

4 The Preconditions to Resolution and the Public Interest Assessment

As noted in the introductory remarks, resolution procedures have been developed to balance the continuation of the critical functions with the need to protect public finances and limit moral hazard. However, this does not mean that any bank failure should entail a resolution procedure. Alongside failing banks that are resolved, others will end their activities through liquidation.

There are in fact three preconditions to trigger a resolution procedure, two of which are openly mentioned by the Key Attributes (KA 3.1) when saying that:

'Resolution should be initiated when [Precondition 1] a firm is no longer viable or likely to be no longer viable, and [Precondition 2] has no reasonable prospect of becoming so'.

According to first precondition, a resolution procedure can only be initiated if a bank is FOLTF. There is no possibility of triggering a 'preventive' resolution procedure in remedy of a temporary distress. Resolution and liquidation procedures are only for banks that after reaching the point of non-viability are legally declared to be failing or likely to fail and they would not be able to continue to operate. To be declared failing or likely to fail, a bank must have undergone a severe deterioration

[18] Note that we referred to years of planning, checks, and testing exercises. Ideally, all of that needs to take place before the resolution policy is effectively implemented in a crisis case. We want to stress this aspect, because when thinking about resolution regimes, the immediate association would be with crisis cases. These cases luckily appear only seldom, whereas resolution regimes entail an intense operationalisation process in a business as usual environment. We want to conclude this part on the concept of resolvability by emphasising this too often neglected aspect. We may in fact be prone to ask ourselves what are the consequences of having a resolution regime when a crisis materialises. Less evident, but certainly not less important, are however the changes in the market expectations and in the level of resilience to stress that years of crisis preparation have already produced in banks.

of its solvency or liquidity position, from which it is not possible to recover. Should there be any perspectives of restoring the viability of the bank, other procedures would be implemented, such as the activation of the recovery plan or the early intervention measures.

By contrast, resolution and liquidation procedures can only be activated in the absence of any reasonable remedies for the bank to restore its viability, as prescribed by the second precondition. As to the exact content of what resolution authorities should consider to ascertain the second precondition, this should be found in the resolution legislation based on the KA. It is worth considering for example Article 32 of the EU BRRD, which in respect of this second precondition clarifies that:

> there is no reasonable prospect that any alternative private sector measures, including measures by an IPS [institutional protection scheme], or supervisory action, including early intervention measures or the write down or conversion of relevant capital instruments and eligible liabilities [...] taken in respect of the institution, would prevent the failure of the institution within a reasonable timeframe.

The BRRD develops the second precondition of the KA in two groups of 'last-resort remedies' to try before opting for resolution (or liquidation). These two groups consist in (a) private sector measures and (b) supervisory actions, some examples of which are directly included in the Directive.

First, a failing bank can be rescued by the private sector. The BRRD mentions the institutional protection schemes, which are a specific form of cross-guarantee mechanisms established by cooperative and public banks typical of German speaking countries (on the topic see Haselmann et al., 2022). In a nutshell, the credit institutions participating to an IPS are collectively bound to provide support to any members facing solvency or liquidity problems (for more details on the IPS functioning and specificities, see Stern, 2014; Huizinga, 2022). In the presence of an IPS, resolution authorities before taking any actions will need to make sure – among other things – that the resources centralised through the cross-guarantee mechanism are already fully depleted. IPSs are just an example of mutual support between banks, but alongside them there are a number of market mechanisms, often constituted as private consortia or associations of credit institutions. As to their organisation and functioning, these mechanisms are highly heterogeneous. In some cases members are imposed ex ante contributions to a centralised fund, and in others they will be requested to contribute after a specific loss event on an affiliated member; some of these mechanisms are sectoral and their membership is limited to banks with a similar organisation and business model, and others instead are open to any bank interested to join.

Market alternatives can also be developed on an ad hoc basis, especially in case of macroeconomic developments affecting the whole banking sector. In the aftermath of the European sovereign debt crisis, some countries were particularly affected by the high volumes of non-performing loans (NPLs). While for most banks the increase in NPL levels only implied a reduction of their profitability, for a few banks in Europe it even went as far as to 'add a negative sign' before the final results. This is why in the mid-1910s many private equity funds were constituted by consociated banks on a transitory basis to achieve the specific goal of reducing the weight of NPLs and other non-performing exposures on their respective balance sheets. This was a market measure implemented by banks and other operators in response to a specific situation, whose results have proven to be satisfactory (see for example Mesnard et al., 2016; Raimondo & Tubi, 2016; Locatelli et al., 2018; with empirical evidence on 15 EU countries, see Brei et al., 2020). It would have been an unpardonable mistake to put under liquidation or resolution banks that thanks to these funds would ultimately be able to recover from the burden of high NPL stocks.

Alongside market solutions the BRRD mentions supervisory actions and it refers directly to early intervention measures or write down and conversion of capital instruments (outside the resolution action). As to the early intervention measures, these are subject to dedicated provisions within the BRRD (Articles 27–29 BRRD; for a more complete overview of early intervention measures and their use, please refer to EBA, 2020, 2021). An early intervention measure can be adopted faced to a rapidly deteriorating situation concerning the liquidity, leverage, or exposures of a certain bank, which is likely to lead to a breach of prudential requirements in the near future. In such a situation, supervision authority (resolution authorities are not yet called into question) may adopt one of the following measures (Art. 27 BRRD):

- Request an update of the recovery plan.
- Instruct the institution to implement one or more of the recovery options in the recovery plan.
- Call for a meeting of the management body or of the shareholders (should the management body fail to convene), setting the agenda and the decisions to be approved.
- Require the removal or the replacement of one or more of the members of the management body or senior management.
- Trigger a debt restructuring.
- Impose changes to the business model or legal and operational structure of the bank.
- Perform on-site[19] inspections.

In addition to the measures under Article 27, the BRRD foresees additional ones in Articles 28 and 29, respectively, on the removal of the senior management or management body and the temporary administration. While these measures might look at first similar to some of those under Article 27, there are some key differences which is necessary to outline. First, to activate one of these two additional measures,

[19] Differently from the on-site inspections carried in a business as usual situation, the BRRD clarifies that in the context of early intervention measures on-site inspections are to inform the resolution action and the valuation of assets and liabilities. In this particular case, such early intervention measure is likely to be performed in a case in which the situation is gradually heading towards resolution.

the situation of distress needs to be more severe.[20] In fact, instead of an infringement or a likely infringement of the law due to a 'rapidly deteriorating situation' as under Article 27, the removal of management or senior management of Article 28 can only be adopted face to a 'significant deterioration' or 'serious infringement', which are supposed to have already materialised. In turn, Article 29 clarifies that the temporary administration can only be adopted where the measure under Article 28 would prove insufficient, thus factoring an even more sever starting point.

Furthermore, the removal of management and temporary administration differ from similar Article 27 measures also as to their content. The removal of one or more members of the management body or senior management under Article 27 BRRD needs to be motivated by either the lack of an effective direction (Article 13 of Directive 2013/36/EU, 'CRD') or the unfitness for the job (Article 9 of Directive 2014/65/EU, 'MiFID'). By contrast, the management removal of Article 28 does not require any other precondition apart from the above recalled significant deterioration. Therefore, a decision on the basis of Article 28 will be grounded on the seriousness of the distress rather than on the effectiveness or quality of management. Furthermore, Article 28 also provides for the removal of the management body or senior management 'in its entirety', while Article 27 appears to be limited to the removal of 'one or more' management members.

Regarding the temporary administration, competent authorities may appoint any temporary administrator either to replace the management body of the institution or to work alongside them. There are a few measures under Article 27 BRRD that can be considered close to it as to their effects, such as the call for a meeting of the management body or of the shareholders, or also the changes imposed to the business model or structure of the bank. However, under Article 27, net of any changes due to the removal of one or more management members, the management is still the 'ordinary' management of the bank (although it is reasonable to assume that their decision can be largely influenced by the competent authority).

We can therefore conclude that there is a graduation in the early intervention measures, depending on the seriousness of the shock to address. In any case, before moving to resolution (or liquidation), it should be made sure that none of them, even the most intrusive ones, would be sufficient to restore the viability of the bank.

Next to the early intervention measures, the actions that need to be exhausted before moving on to resolution (or liquidation) also include the write down and conversion of capital instruments and internally issued debt (Art. 59 BRRD). We will come back to this action, as it is often associated with the bail-in tool in a resolution perspective. To the aims of the present section, it is sufficient to note that this action targets losses arising at an entity that is not designated as resolution entity, i.e. a subsidiary. If such an entity needs to be recapitalised, its capital (owned by another entity in the group) can be written down to absorb the losses, which will

[20] On this point see in particular the conclusions arising from Judgment of the General Court (Fourth Chamber, Extended Composition) of 12 October 2022, Francesca Corneli v European Central Bank, ECLI:EU:T:2022:627.

be passed to its direct parent. After that, subordinated debt instruments issued to either the direct parent or the ultimate parent will be converted into new capital. This second step financially corresponds to a downstream of capital from the parent to the subsidiary. The write down and conversion is limited to internally issued debt and does not affect external creditors, such as the bail-in tool. Differently from the other supervisory actions, the write down and conversion powers are conferred to the resolution authority, which may exercise it in combination with a resolution action or independently from it, indeed as an early intervention measure. It can be argued – but it is of course just a theoretical expectation – that it seems rather unlikely that a write down and conversion on a standalone basis would suffice to restore the viability of a bank. In fact, this would be the case only for losses arising from a single entity or a limited number of entities of a group, where the parent is sufficiently capitalised and liquid to absorb the losses and recapitalise the one or more subsidiaries in trouble. However, if the parent had the possibility to support any of its subsidiaries facing troubles, it would probably do it before any authorities would step in. Instead, if the situation is distressed at a point that early intervention measures (or more) are under the radar of competent and resolution authorities, it is highly unlikely that the troubles are limited to a subset of subsidiaries, while probably it is the main operating company itself to face the worst.

To summarise quickly what we have discussed so far, the first two conditions entail the failing or likely to fail status of a bank and the absence of market alternatives or supervisory actions that might credibly restore its viability. However, if we limited ourselves to these two preconditions, we would not be in a situation that differs from the ground for liquidation. A bank to be liquidated is also failing or likely to fail and it stands in the impossibility of being recovered with market alternatives or supervisory measures. What is then the decisive element to put a bank under resolution?

Once again, financial contagion and critical functions are a guiding criterion in the decision to trigger a resolution action. The KAs only indirectly refer to them, when clarifying that resolution regimes are for any bank that 'could be systemically significant or critical if it fails' (KA 1.1). In this formula, the KAs contain a reference to systemically significant institutions.

Regulators themselves publish annual lists of institutions they consider systemically significant (see FSB, 2017b or EBA, 2022). In the determination of significance, the size and the functions are some of the indicators to assess the financial risks posed by a credit institution. Nonetheless, one should not be too quick to match the significance status in a business as usual environment with a positive decision on resolution in case the bank is failing or likely to fail. Size is not the only thing that matters when deciding in favour of resolution. The KAs in fact indicate that the systemic significance has to be assessed in case of bank failure ('if it fails'), opening up also to the residual possibility of a bank failure being critical, although not systemically significant.

To show the difference, we need to consider that as we explained above the assessment of criticality of the functions carried by a credit institution is performed with reference to a specific economy. It is well possible that a credit institution that would be considered of medium to low size in terms of total assets when compared with major financial players is established in a small country where it has a predominant market share for certain functions, such as deposit taking or landing. In this case, the sudden discontinuation of these functions without the possibility to replace them quickly, although limitedly visible in terms of financial stability on a cross-border level, would severely affect the real economy of that country. Therefore, these functions have to be considered critical and be continued also after the failing of the bank, through a resolution procedure. Conversely, a significant bank could operate in a country with a high number of competitors, where the discontinuation of its functions could be more easily re-absorbed by the market. In this case,[21] the continuity of critical functions would not be put at risk by the failure of that bank, although it should be still considered whether its failure might put at risk financial stability through the contagion of other credit institutions.

After making the link between resolution and the expected impact of the failure on the real economy and financial system, the KA demands to the legislation setting up resolution regimes to define the additional precondition to distinguish between liquidation and resolution cases. In fact, in KA 3.1 we read that 'there should be clear standards or suitable indicators of non-viability to help guide decisions on whether firms meet the conditions for entry into resolution'.

To continue our example based on the European BRRD, Article 32 has introduced as third precondition to resolution the notion of public interest. More precisely, while both resolution and liquidation are based on the failing or likely to fail status of a bank and the absence of market alternatives or supervisory measures to restore its viability, a resolution action shall only be triggered if it is in the public interest (Article 32(1)5 BRRD). The BRRD makes explicit the link between resolution and critical functions, financial stability, and preservation of the real economy by saying that (Art. 32(5) BRRD) 'a resolution action shall be treated as in the public interest if it is necessary for the achievement of and is proportionate to one or more of the resolution objectives'. This is the crucial element that draws the line between liquidation and resolution. In that respect, it needs to be noted that within the EU legislation the resolution procedure is framed as an exception (although this does not necessary mean less frequent) in respect to the default option, which remains the recourse to insolvency proceedings (Mortágua & Solipa, 2022).

Apart from the explanation of when a resolution shall be considered in the public interest, the EU legislation does not include additional elements as to what precisely resolution authorities need to consider when assessing it. On this point, resolution authorities themselves have operationalised the public interest assessment (or PIA). To give an example, we can consider the methodology developed by the Single

[21] We need however to acknowledge that this is rather a hypothetical case. In reality, by definition systemically important banks (e.g. the O-SIIs recognised by the EBA) are institutions that pose financial risks to the system. It is therefore to be expected that for most of these banks resolution authorities anticipate to start a resolution action in case of failure. If willing, the reader can test this statement by checking what systemically significant banks disclose in their annual report in terms of the resolution strategy envisaged by resolution authorities.

Resolution Board, whose overarching elements have been disclosed in a document called Public Interest Assessment: SRB Approach (SRB, 2019b).

Considering the link made by the resolution objectives in the EU legislation, the SRB PIA methodology considers a hypothetical liquidation as the 'counterfactual' to resolution. In other words, the SRB will assess if any resolution objectives would be at risk in case the failing bank had to be liquidated. Intuitively, this means to assess whether the bank performs any critical functions and whether they would be put at risk by liquidation or if in case of wind down there could be consequences on financial stability, due to spill-over effects.

In evaluating if liquidation could be detrimental to resolution objectives, these have been subject to different degrees of operationalisation. In fact, as the reader will remember, there are objectives that are structured on multiple dimensions, while others appear to be more straightforward. The BRRD formalised five resolution objectives in Article 31, according to which resolution needs:

(a) To ensure the continuity of critical functions
(b) To avoid a significant adverse effect on the financial system, in particular by preventing contagion, including to market infrastructures, and by maintaining market discipline
(c) To protect public funds by minimising reliance on extraordinary public financial support
(d) To protect depositors covered by Directive 2014/49/EU and investors covered by Directive 97/9/EC
(e) To protect client funds and client assets

Concerning the first objective, provided that critical functions have already been identified in the ongoing resolution planning, it appears overall immediate to conclude that a liquidation would not leave room from their continuation. Note in fact, as we explained in 3.b.1. above, that the criticality assessment of banks' function is based on the scenario of a sudden discontinuation, such as it would happen in liquidation. In the degree of substitutability it is then considered to which extent the market could spontaneously reabsorb those functions in lack of resolution. As long as critical functions have been identified, it is very hard to argue that liquidation would not put them at risk.

Public support is lesser decisive in relation to the PIA, or at least it appears to be rather neutral. In fact, under liquidation by definition no public support is to be envisaged since the bank ceases to exist.[22] In resolution this objective would be achieved ex se, as long resolution authorities are mandated to adhere strictly to the resolution objectives. It is also to be noted that under this objective the SRB is not expected to protect the public sector entities from losses arising from their exposures

[22] It should be noted however that in the past it has not been infrequent that creditors of a liquidated bank received some form of compensation ex post at public expenses. This is however an element that cannot be anticipated at the time a resolution authority needs to assess the public interest and that rather pertains to the domain political considerations.

to the failing bank (e.g. in the case of a bank owned by a Member State). Under this profile, public sector entities are considered as any other creditors.

With regard to the protection of covered depositors, the public interest assessment will concentrate on the resources available after liquidation. To give a concrete example, for the protection of covered depositors the resolution authority will compare the amount of covered deposits to be repaid also in case of liquidation with the financial means of the relevant deposit protection schemes. Should the covered deposits significantly offset the repayment capacity of the protection scheme, it should be concluded that liquidation would hardly meet this objective. For covered investors and the protection of client assets and client funds (segregated from the assets of the bank), the assessment is based on the legislative framework of each specific jurisdiction. Nevertheless, for these objectives, it is hard to detect specific differences between liquidation and resolution on a general level, as the same legal provisions would apply in both cases. At most, there could be differences on a bank-specific level, in case specific deficiencies – for example on the ability to segregate and identify client asset and funds – are known in advance to the resolution authority.

By far, the most complex assessment pertains to the objective on financial stability and market discipline. The SRB PIA Approach considers three main risk dimensions, which are (1) the direct contagion (or the first round effects due to direct financial linkages to other institutions), (2) the indirect contagion, and (3) the potential impacts on real economy. Resolution is considered to be in the public interest, when liquidation is expected to produce negative consequences in any of these three areas.

For each of the three, the SRB has selected a set of indicators. For example, the risk of direct contagion will be assessed considering the data on interbank exposures and the own funds and debt instruments issued by the failing bank and held by other actors of the financial sector. Material exposures of other financial institution to the failing bank would produce direct contagion effects in case of liquidation. To be clear, in the same way clients are affected, if a financial institution is a creditor of a failing bank, in liquidation it will probably not be able to recover its claims in their integrity. The direct contagion is quantifiable based on observed data: the magnitude of direct contagion will correspond to the claims of financial institutions minus the net asset value (i.e. the resources available in the insolvency estate) and the other claims to be repaid before in the insolvency hierarchy.

Indirect contagion risks may arise due to the market reactions to the distressed situation of the failing bank or due to indirect exposures of other financial institutions (i.e. second and third round effects due to exposures to an institution that would be affected by the failure). The indirect contagion is an area of less definite borders and, as the reader may easily guess, also more difficult to assess. To visualise the differences in the assessment of direct and indirect contagion, we may think about a small basket of raspberries unduly forgotten on the dining table. After one day or two out of the fridge, we could probably observe a berry that is badly spoiling, spreading mould around. Now, the mould that we see passing from a berry to another is like the direct contagion: The proximity with the rotten fruit makes it easier to spread and also visible to the unlucky holder of the basket. However, what can we say about the berries at the bottom of the basket that we cannot observe? They might have preserved due to lesser contact with air as compared to the superficial layers, but an alternative possibility is that fluids pouring from the rotten fruit have vectored bacteria and fungi also to the lower layers. This is the key difference between direct and indirect contagion: direct contagion is observable, and indirect contagion needs to be estimated. To do so, the SRB considers a wide set of quantitative and qualitative indicators that are instead observable. On the quantitative side, an indication of indirect contagion can be seen through the bond spreads (i.e. the difference in the yields of bonds issued by different institutions). Similar trends between even unrelated banks, which in turn may further differ from the average registered on the markets, might indicate some contagion effects due to phenomena of panic selling on the market (for more details on methodologies to estimate indirect contagion, see Brunnermeier, 2009; Iyer et al., 2014; Clerc et al., 2016; Avdjiev et al., 2019; Cont & Schaanning, 2019; Foglia et al., 2020).

Another way of estimating indirect contagion effects is through the common exposure method. Without entering in excessively technical details, the idea behind this method is that two financial institutions (it does not matter whether related between themselves or not) are exposed to same counterparties. A sudden and extensive deleveraging or risk reduction by a failing bank might then indirectly affect another bank exposed to the same counterparties. For example, on the interbank market a failing bank might try to reduce its exposures on other banks, anticipating problems in borrowing and lending liquidity at the same prices. Following a single partial exit from the interbank channel, rumours may spread very quickly on the liquidity market and dry it up in a very short time (this was observed for example in Müller, 2006; Goldsmith-Pinkham & Yorulmazer, 2010; Baglioni, 2009).

Operationally, the SRB considers entire types of exposures grouped by sector, for the banks under its remit (e.g. loans to other banks, loans to firms, consumer loans and mortgages, private deposits, interbank liabilities, etc.). For all banks in scope, the SRB then calculates the Euclidean distance (i.e. the standard deviation) from the failing bank in terms of exposures, considering on an aggregate level the sum of all exposures by sector, normalised by the total exposures of the failing bank. A low standard deviation between two banks will indicate a high exposure to the same counterparties or sector, which in turn denotes a higher risk of indirect contagion.

On the qualitative side, the analysis of the business model of a bank can also provide some insights on the potential indirect contagion risk. Banks with similar business models will be exposed to similar counterparties and sectors. For example, medium-size commercial banks will have a rather traditional business model based on deposit taking and lending. They will therefore be exposed to the same market, which might be jeopardised by the troubles faced by one of its players.

In addition to direct and indirect contagion, we mentioned above the impact on real economy as the third element factored in the SRB PIA Approach for the second resolution objective. In this case, part of the assessment overlaps with the analysis of the critical functions of the bank, as they represent by definition the importance of the activities carried by the bank for society at large. Next to critical functions, the SRB may consider other macroeconomic indicators to assess the impact that the liquidation would have on real economy. For this part, timing has a certain relevance. To give a concrete example, during the recent Covid-19 pandemic, in many countries banks were important actors of the measures implemented by their governments (Crosetti & Di Gaspare, 2020; Li et al., 2020). If a PIA had to be carried in those circumstances, this is an element that would have probably been taken into consideration in addition to critical functions, since a liquidation would have interrupted the support provided through the credit channel to households and corporates.

From the example of the SRB PIA Approach, the assessment of public interest as decisive condition for triggering a resolution action is far from being a simple task. Certainly, it would be very challenging to apply all the methodology 'out of the blue' in a timeframe that conciliates with the needs of a swift course of action to be taken by resolution authorities. This is the reason why the SRB PIA Approach[23] also includes a preliminary PIA, to be carried and updated in each resolution planning cycle. When we say preliminary, we should not interpret it as an indication that the PIA is incomplete or partial. Actually, the methodology to be followed – mutatis mutandis – is the same we explained above. Preliminary however indicates that in any case the resolution authority will need to perform a final PIA at the time an institution is declared failing or likely to fail. At this point in time, the resolution authority will be able to leverage an existing PIA, which will need to be updated rather than being performed from scratch.

If anything, the preliminary PIA will be wider than the final one, as it will include additional scenarios that may facilitate the re-usability of the assessment in different situations. In this respect, both the preliminary and the final PIA need to be based on current circumstances, which mean the market conditions at the time when they are performed. However, in the preliminary PIA the resolution authorities can also factor other situations, such as a stressed environment due to a systemic crisis, or take into consideration historical data. This is because the preliminary PIA is carried to ease the final one, but the situation of today is not necessarily a good indication of the situation that will materialise in the future.

To conclude this section on the preconditions to resolution and the PIA, we need to pay attention to an important methodological remark, distinguishing the preliminary from the final PIA. Above we noted that the assessments of direct and indirect contagion will differ in nature, as the former can be measured while the latter only estimated. In the preliminary PIA, both the direct and indirect contagion can be only estimated. In fact, we cannot know in advance what will be the net asset value of a bank if it is failing. This will very much depend on the nature of the crisis and the circumstances that led to this failure. For the preliminary PIA, resolution

[23] We refer here to the PIA Approach, but this was already the case in the first wave of resolution plans (see SRB 2016).

authorities then need to make assumptions on the hypothetical asset side of a failing bank, to estimate how big would be direct contagion effects in liquidation.

The immediate practical consequence is that for the preliminary PIA resolution authorities will need to assess direct and indirect contagion against different hypothetical levels of losses. In fact, it is not possible to predict how big will be the losses a bank will suffer before being failed or likely to fail. Nor there are proxies that can provide an indication for that. In fact, when the preliminary PIA is performed in the annual planning cycles, the considered bank is healthy and well performing. Hence, based on the most recent reported balance sheet figures, resolution authorities need to assess how large the contagion effects would be in different situations.

The results obtained in the preliminary PIA on different level of hypothetical losses cannot be reused as such in an actual resolution case. In the meanwhile, the underlying metrics will have changed. Therefore, the contagion assessment will need to be repeated. However, there are at least two elements of continuity. First, although the quantification of the effective contagion risks will differ from its preliminary estimation, the conclusion of the assessment is likely to remain the same. The PIA – as we explained – is aimed to determine whether there is a public interest to resolve a bank, for which the quantification of risk is certainly a decisive factor, but not the decisive goal. The true aim of the preliminary PIA is to have an indication of whether an institution should be resolved or liquidated. This is a crucial question, because the preparation for resolution is a long process, which imposes costs on banks for developing and maintaining all the necessary capabilities for the implementation of a resolution procedure. If the preliminary PIA has earmarked a bank for resolution, for example due to the presence of critical functions and contagion risks, the same bank at distance of a few months[24] will not have changed too much to completely reverse the conclusions of the assessment.

As a second element of continuity – as we already mentioned above – the PIA is a data-driven complex assessment, which requires the sourcing of data coming from sources external to the resolution authority (e.g. statistical data of central banks). The processes to obtain these data as well as the methodologies to treat them is not something that can be developed ad hoc in the strict timeline of the preparation of a resolution scheme. Therefore, the completion of a preliminary PIA is also a way to ensure that all the elements needed for the final one are readily available.

5 The Resolution Tools

When meeting the pre-conditions for resolution, a bank will enter the resolution procedure, in which the resolution authority will apply one or more resolution tools. When we refer to resolution tools, we do not use a generic expression.

[24] Note that the preliminary PIA is performed annually. Hence, whatever it is the timing at which a bank fails, this failure will happen no later than one year after the last preliminary PIA.

This is a specific concept, derived from the language of the KA. The legal frameworks transposing the KA have welcomed this term, giving it a precise juridical connotation. Resolution tools are the implementing powers conferred to resolution authorities that are used in the context of a resolution procedure and that are directed to resolve a crisis case in line with the resolution objectives. By being strictly linked to a resolution procedure, these tools are distinguished from the rest of the powers of resolution authorities, which depending on the type might be used in going concern (e.g. information and inspection powers) or in the lead up to resolution (as some of the early intervention measures of the BRRD described above in Sect. 4). The choice on the type of tool to use will depend on the characteristics of the bank to resolve as well as on the type of the crisis to address. Resolution authorities may apply them singularly or in combination or even to use different tools for different entities in the group (KA 3.8).

These tools are the object of Sect. 5 of the KA. For banks,[25] the resolution tools are:

i. The bail-in
ii. The sale of business
iii. The bridge bank
iv. The asset separation tool

The entities to which resolution tools are applied are defined resolution entities, whereas their subsidiaries are non-resolution entities. This does not mean however that the entities to which resolution powers are not applied directly will not bear any effects or will be left behind. When operationalising the tools, resolution plans often adopt a group perspective (see for example the statement in König, 2021), considering that other entities in the group may also concur from an organisation or operational point of view to the performance of critical function or to the profitability of the group. A resolution entity with its subsidiaries that are not themselves resolution entities forms a resolution group.

Although in most cases the resolution group will coincide with the entire group (and with the scope of consolidation used by supervision authorities), there might be cases in which resolution authorities design a specific perimeter. We may think for example to a very large banking group, established in multiple countries. In case of crisis, for resolving this group more effectively and efficiently, it might be necessary to apply resolution tools to different entities in the group (e.g. to the main operating entity in the home country and to one or more intermediate parent undertakings in host countries). This second case is referred to as a multiple point of entry approach, and it entails the coexistence in a single commercial group of multiple resolution groups that will be resolved with the application of a resolution tool to each one of them.

[25] The KA also outlines the resolution tools for insurance, which are not covered by this chapter.

5.1 Bail-In

Bail-In Functioning and Sequence

The bail-in tool is possibly the most 'iconic' feature of the resolution regimes. It is not surprising, considering that – as we outlined in the introduction to this chapter – it has been a driving concept in the academic and public debate preceding the adoption of resolution legislation.

Per se the idea behind this tool is very simple: Banks can be resolved by downsizing their balance sheet and using their debt to create new capital. Traditionally, failing banks were rescued by some forms of external interventions, such as special credit facilities or recapitalisation measures, very often at the expenses of taxpayers (see Sect. 1 above). The bail-in tool was then conceived as a great game-changer, aimed to achieve the same results of a recapitalisation but without the need of external intervention. As we explained above, the internalisation of the costs of resolution also functions as a way to prevent or limit moral hazard (specifically on the internalisation of costs see Hadjiemmanuil, 2015; Avgouleas & Goodhart, 2016; Barba Navaretti et al., 2016; Machado, 2016).

In essence, the bail-in tool has two functions: absorbing losses and recapitalising the bank. These two functions are covered by two distinct operations, which are i) the write down of capital instruments and (depending on the level of losses to absorb) other eligible debt instruments and ii) the conversion of debt instruments into new capital.

To understand the functioning of the bail-in tool, we can visualise the balance sheet of a bank as a real 'weighting balance', an old-style one, with a bar, two pans, and a set of weights (see this representation in Fig. 5.1 below). The two plates represent the assets and liabilities sides of a bank. Let us imagine that each asset or liability is a weight on the respective plate. In normal times, our balance will be in perfect equilibrium, with the sum of the weights on one side equalling the sum of those on the other one. If our scale effectively represented the balance sheet of a bank, weights would be added and removed on both sides continuously, but always leave the bar in equilibrium.

We can now consider that in troubled times a bank will face higher rates of defaults in its exposures. We experienced it in the last financial crisis, when in certain countries non-performing loans surged dramatically. Exposures that are no longer performing are like weights on our scale being removed: They do no longer contribute to the overall weight of the asset side. In normal conditions, there are also 'weights being suddenly removed' from the asset plate, but a bank knows how to manage these losses. For example, each year a bank put aside provisions, which in our example are some 'extra weights' that come to play to keep the bar in equilibrium. In a crisis case instead, the weights are removed in a quantity or at a speed so high that no remedial measure – including our extra weights – is sufficient to restore the equilibrium.

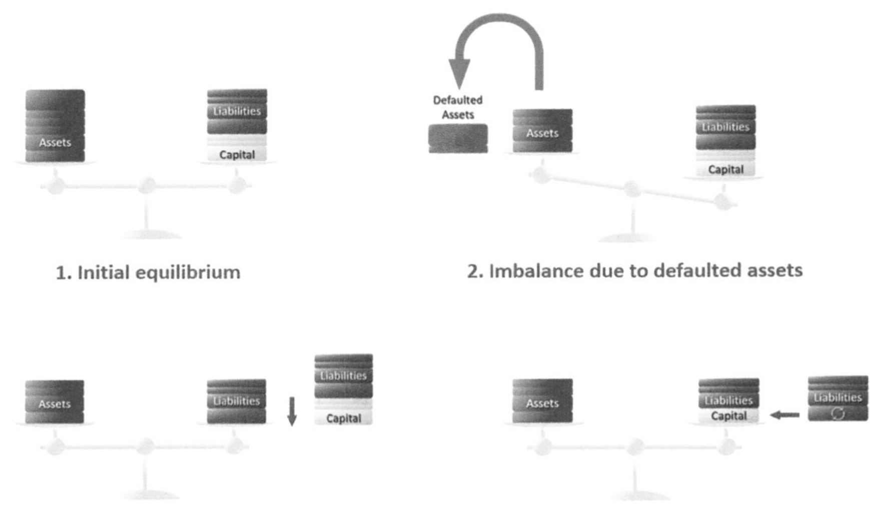

Fig. 5.1 Schematic representation of the bail-in tool (Source: Elaboration of the author)

A bank that as in our example is failing or likely to fail due to credit losses (e.g. due to the effects to material non-performing exposure) will therefore be in a condition of 'imbalance', with the asset side having fewer weights than the liability side. In other words, the missing weights (i.e. the losses) are so many that the assets are not sufficient to repay the debt.

It is at that point that the bail-in comes into play to restore the balance. What can be done if liabilities outweigh assets? The solution offered by the bail-in tool is a reduction of the liabilities, in a proportion sufficient to restore the equilibrium between assets and liabilities. This is the loss-absorbing function of the tool. We can represent it as a hand removing weights on the liability pan of our imaginary balance, up to the point at which the bar is horizontal again. In the real world, this action corresponds to a write down of capital and eligible debt instruments, in a measure that matches the amount of losses.

By doing so, we would therefore end up with the scale again in balance, but with less weight on both plates. This is effectively the situation in which a bank stands after a write down of capital and eligible debt instrument, with a balance sheet that is again viable but smaller as compared to the size before the failure. However, this is not likely to be the ending point of the application of the bail-in tool. After using capital instruments and – depending on the amount of losses – potentially also eligible debt instruments, the balance sheet would not yet be ready for the second life of the resolving bank. To continue to operate, a bank needs to hold capital in a measure sufficient to comply with the requirements for authorisation and any other prudential requirements. Being declared failing or likely to fail due to credit losses, it is equivalent to say that the capital even before the application of the bail-in tool was not sufficient to absorb losses and at the same time insure the compliance with capital requirements.

This is why the bail-in tool also entails a second aspect pertaining to the recapitalisation of the bank. After the write down, we would have a bank with little or no capital left. This is why debt is then converted into new capital up to a level that makes it possible for the bank after resolution to continue to operate by confidently meeting its capital requirements. To continue with our metaphor, this operation consists in replacing some of the weights; let us say some of the bronze ones ideally corresponding to debt, with other of equal mass but different nature, such as golden brass weights representing capital. The result of this operation is that the bar is still in the same equilibrium as after the write down, but on the liability plate where we before had bronze weights only or predominantly, we now have the right mix of metals required by legislation and investors.

To summarise, the bail-in is the resolution tool that through the write down and conversion of capital instruments and eligible liabilities can absorb the losses of a failing bank and recapitalise it. The way in which this write down and conversion takes place needs however to respect certain rules (for a more extensive description of these rule, see Wojcik, 2016). First of all, there is a sequence in which own funds and eligible liabilities can be subject to a bail-in. This sequence corresponds to the insolvency hierarchy in reverse order. The insolvency hierarchy is the order in which claims need to be repaid in liquidation. When an entity is liquidated, all the remaining assets are pooled together in the insolvency estate. However, as we have shown with our example of the weighting scale, when an entity is failing the sum of the assets is not sufficient to repay all liabilities. With what is left on the plate, it is not possible to repay in full the claims of all creditors. However, not all claims are born equal. Some of them rank senior than others. This means that when distributing the insolvency estate, the liquidator will start from repaying the most senior claims. Once (and if) the most senior rank is fully repaid, the liquidator will then move to the next lower rank in the insolvency hierarchy and continue with this process until the resources of the insolvency estate are completely exhausted.

The structure of the insolvency hierarchy and the number and composition of its ranks depend on the national insolvency legislation. However, with good approximation there are certain common rules that apply everywhere, which are rooted in the in international standards of the Basel Accords, currently in their third version (Basel III). The most senior ranks typically include tax liabilities, salaries due to the employees, rental costs, and bills, along with secured liabilities (i.e. debt instruments covered by a pledge or a mortgage) and covered deposits (i.e. deposits that always need to be repaid in liquidation and that normally benefit from a deposit guarantee scheme). Below this type of liabilities, insolvency hierarchies include senior unsecured liabilities, both in the type of issued instruments (e.g. bonds or derivatives) or not covered and not preferential deposits. In some jurisdiction senior unsecured liabilities might be further classified in different ranks, but in other cases they would simply rank pari passu.

Below senior unsecured liabilities but before capital instruments, insolvency hierarchies include subordinated liabilities, otherwise referred to as junior debt.

Subordinated bonds belong to this category. These instruments function in a similar way to senior bonds, but due to the fact that in case of insolvency they would be repaid later, they are associated with higher interests, corresponding to the higher risk taken by investors. Banks in turn issue this type of instruments because part of their amount – as we will soon see – can be accounted in own funds (i.e. capital), thus contributing to their compliance with capital requirements.

Own funds cover the last ranks in the insolvency hierarchy, and they are divided into three main category in order of priority in insolvency: Tier 2, Additional Tier 1 (AT1), and Common Equity Tier 1 (CET1). The last two when considered together can also be referred to as Tier 1 capital and they are the core capital of a bank. CET1 is composed of stock (or share capital) and cash, including retained earnings and other reserves, and it represents the regulatory capital of highest quality. Instruments falling in the category of AT1 do not meet all the criteria of CET1 but still provide loss absorption in a going concern (i.e. even ahead of resolution). Within this class, we would find instruments such as preferred shares or contingent convertible securities. Preferred shares are instruments that have characteristics in between ordinary shares and subordinated debt. The preference is on the payment of dividends, as they need to be paid before the dividends on ordinary shares, as well as on the insolvency hierarchy. By contrast, these shares are nonvoting, so they do not concur to the ownership of the bank, which is the key characteristic of ordinary shares. Typically, upon the activation of certain triggers, such as a predetermined low level of CET1 on risk-weighted assets (CET1 ratio), preferred shares can be converted into ordinary shares, hence contributing to the loss absorption and recapitalisation of the entity. While not all preferred shares are convertible, contingent convertible bonds are so by definition. These are fixed-income instruments of hybrid nature between capital and debt, which in case of a capital shortfall are automatically converted. They have been otherwise described as a guarantee that gives holders 'contractual right to seize the firm's assets (or its equity interest) whenever the value of assets is below the value of its guaranteed debt' (Merton, 1990). Compared to preferred shares, contingent convertible securities are actually closer to debt in nature rather than to capital.

Tier 2 represents a supplementary layer of regulatory capital, which includes among the others general provisions, revaluation reserves, hybrid capital instruments not qualifying as Tier 1, and part of the subordinated debt. A revaluation reserve is an additional value arising from the revaluation of an existing asset which can be booked to the Tier 2 capital. The classical example would be a building owned by a bank whose market price has increased over time. General provisions are amounts that a bank needs to put aside in relation to its risk-taking activities (e.g. to cover for the expected defaults on the loan portfolio). General provisions can account in Tier 2 up to 1.25% of the bank's risk-weighted assets. Within the hybrid instruments falling in the Tier 2 class, we would normally find again preferred shares, provided that they would present some additional features distancing them from core capital and making them more similar to debt. These features include the possibility by the issuing entity to redeem these instruments after a predetermined maturity or the right of the holders to the retroactive payment of dividends in case one or more distributions of dividends are skipped and before any distribution of dividends to shareholders (cumulative preferred shares). Finally, subordinated bonds, under certain conditions, can qualify as Tier 2 provided that the remaining maturity is above 5 years. When the maturity falls below 5 years, banks will need to apply a regulatory amortisation of 20% per year and discount it from the amount included in Tier 2. We refer to regulatory amortisation because this is the discount factor applied under the Basel framework. However, many Tier 2 notes are not repaid until maturity. This means that on its balance sheet the bank will book an additional liability – for the amortised part – which will rank senior to the non-amortised Tier 2 and thus fall into the category of subordinated debt. Depending on the features and the residual maturity of the instrument, this liability although not being regulatory capital may still count towards the requirements on loss absorption imposed by resolution authorities.

To the aims of the present chapter and as a background introduction to the bail-in tool, this description of the insolvency hierarchy can be considered sufficient, with the obvious disclaimer that – as already stated above – the exact definition of the hierarchy and the various ranks will depend on national legislation. A specificity that we deem worth flagging is that the BRRD2 has introduced in the EU framework an additional layer of debt, which is defined as senior non-preferred (SNP). SNP instruments rank junior to senior debt, but senior to subordinated debt. Along with subordinated debt and regulatory capital, SNP instruments that meet the opportune eligibility conditions can count towards the subordination capacity of a bank, which is a part of the minimum requirement of own funds and eligible liabilities, i.e. the European version of the total loss absorption requirements (for more details please refer to Sect. 6).

As we said, a bail-in is performed in a precise sequence, which follows the insolvency hierarchy in reverse order. If in liquidation the question is ‘who is going to be repaid first?’ with the application of the bail-in tool, it becomes ‘who is going to take losses first?’. In reality, the two questions are specular: In both the cases, with resources insufficient to cover all the creditors and shareholders’ claims, somebody will see their value preserved and somebody else will need to bear a loss. With the application of the bail-in tool, capital instruments are first written down, starting from CET1 and gradually moving to AT1 and Tier2, up to the point at which losses are completely absorbed. In case capital instruments are not sufficient to absorb all the losses, the write down will then continue on other liabilities, always following the insolvency hierarchy in reverse order. Once losses are completely absorbed, the resolving institution will be in the situation described above of being again in equilibrium between assets and liabilities, bit with insufficient or no capital to comply with prudential requirements. At this point, residual eligible instruments will start to be converted into new CET1 capital, to recapitalise the resolving institution. The recapitalisation follows the same sequence of the write down. The write down and the conversion are actually a single process, where the second phase takes it over from where the first one ends.

In the sequence of write down and conversion, there is a rule to respect: Considered any given rank, it is not possible to move to the one above, until all eligible instruments have been used. To give two practical examples, it is not possible to write down AT1 instruments if there is still CET1 capital to use, and equally it is not admitted to start converting senior debt if there are still subordinated liabilities that can be subject to bail-in. The only partial exception to this rule can happen when after absorbing all losses there is still CET1 capital available. In order to recapitalise the bank, it will in any case be necessary to start converting instruments of higher rank.

At this point, an obvious question may arise. What does it mean in concrete that there is CET1 capital left? Let us assume for simplicity that the whole CET1 is composed of ordinary share capital. Does it mean that some shareholders will see their claims repaid and some others not? Of course, such an approach will not be justifiable under any terms. What happens in reality is that for each liability class the write down takes place on all eligible instruments on a pro rata basis (i.e. on a given percentage) until that class of liabilities is completely exhausted (write down of 100%) and it is necessary to move to the following rank. In our example, in case all losses are absorbed before the exhaustion of CET1, all the existing shareholders will remain so throughout the bail-in implementation, but their holdings will be diluted by the conversion of other instruments into new equity. To better understand this concept, let us reason with some fictional numbers (see the full representation of this example in Fig. 5.2) and imagine that the initial CET1, which we assume being completely made of equity, is equal to 10 billion[26] or 10,000 million. Let us now assume that the bank enters resolution after losses on the asset side that are equivalent to 6000 million. The amount of these losses is equivalent to 60% of our CET1. We therefore do not need to write down the full 10,000 million (actually, as we will see further below in this section, it is not even possible). To have again our balance in equilibrium, it will only be necessary to write down CET1 for an equivalent amount of 6000 million, which is 60% of the original CET1. This means that all existing shareholders see their holdings reduced by 60% in value and retain a 40% of them. Before the conversion of other instruments in new capital, although the existing CET1 has been written down by 60% the ownership has not yet changed. Let us imagine that the bank had three shareholders owning, respectively, 52%, 30%, and 18% of the share capital of 10,000 million (i.e. 5200 million, 3000 million, and 1800 million). After the write down the original shareholders would still maintain the 52%, 30%, and 18% of 4000 million (i.e. 2080 million, 1200 million, and 720 million). This means that shareholders have to bear different amounts of losses (i.e. −3120 million, −1800 million, and −1080 million), but that in proportion they all suffered a loss of 60% of their holdings. Applying the same write down ratio across all the creditors in the same class does not alter the respective proportions among creditors. Therefore, the write down per se, although affecting the share value, would not determine a change in the ownership structure of the bank.

[26] For this fictional example, we do not express any currencies, as it does not matter. The reader is free to assume that we reason in the currency he prefers. Oranges or apples would work equally well.

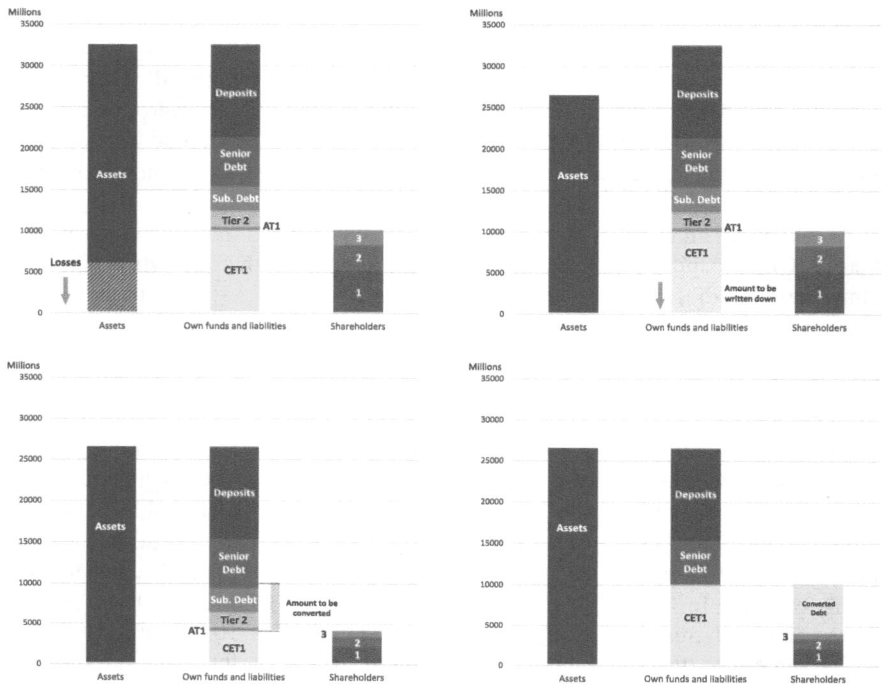

Fig. 5.2 Fictional example of application of the bail-in tool (Source: Elaboration of the author)

This effect is instead produced by the conversion of eligible instruments into new capital. After the write down, the bank is left with 4000 million of residual CET1. To rebuild the initial 10,000 million of CET1,[27] it will be necessary to convert 6000 million of other eligible instruments into new CET1. Through this process, the three original shareholders will be diluted along with former creditors now transformed into new shareholders. Looking at the numbers in our example, the original shareholders will have 20.8% (2080/10,000), 12.8% (1280/10,000), and 7.2% (720/10,000). Compared to the write down, the conversion does not affect the value of the claims in a given class, but it changes the composition of the class itself.

For the conversion, the same rules of sequence and pro rata effects apply. To continue with our fictional example, let us assume that the bank originally had 400 million of AT1 instruments, 2000 million of Tier 2, 3000 million of subordinated debt, and 6000 million of senior debt, and the other liabilities are deposits. As it is necessary to replenish 6000 million of capital written down, the AT1, Tier 2,

[27] For this fictional example, we do not express any currencies, as it does not matter. The reader is free to assume that we reason in the currency he prefers. Oranges or apples would work equally well.

and subordinated instruments will be converted in full. This would leave us with a remaining capital gap of 600 million. Senior debt instruments will be then converted to replenish this gap, where 600 million represents 10% of these bonds. Therefore, a proportional conversion rate of 10% will be applied to all outstanding senior bonds.

Some additional clarifications might at this point be needed in relation to the terminology used in this section. When discussing about the bail-in, we often referred to the eligible instruments or liabilities.[28] Although the bail-in sequence is based on the insolvency hierarchy, not all the liabilities considered in this hierarchy are eligible to the bail-in tool. As we will see in more detail further below, there are liabilities that cannot be admitted to the bail-in and others that to ease the resolution process or meet the resolution objectives might be discretionally excluded by the resolution authority (although on the basis on an explicit legal mandate to do so and with some predefined criteria).

Second, the write down and conversion applies to the outstanding amount of capital instruments and eligible liabilities. This amount corresponds to the sum of outstanding principal amount and the accrued interests. The outstanding principal amount is the part of the amount of a liability or capital instrument that is still to be re-paid and it will be determined in a different way depending on its type.[29] For equity, it will correspond to the share price multiplied by the number of issued shares. For debt instruments, the outstanding amount is the original (or principal) nominal amount issued minus any portions of this debt that have been repaid over time. For deposits, it will simply correspond to the integrity of the deposits held at the date of resolution. However, over time the creditors of a bank have also matured interests on their claims. A bank does not only need to re-pay debt but also interests on the money it borrowed. Accrued interests are those interests that had matured before the start of resolution, but those on the same date are still to be paid.

Furthermore, we described the bail-in tool as a combination of write down and conversion of capital and eligible liabilities. However, the reader should be made aware that in some jurisdictions resolution authorities may have the general powers to write down and convert certain instruments even outside resolution. This possibility is again rooted in the KA, which recommends that resolution authorities are endowed with general write down and conversion powers (3.2). These powers, although exercised independently from resolution, are often operationalised as additional measures to prepare for resolution. We already referred above to the write and conversion powers in the EU framework (BRRD Chapter V, see also Sect. 4 above). In this case, the write down and conversion powers have been differentiated from the bail-in tool in the sense that it is framed as a measure affecting only the resolution group internally, without consequences for external shareholders and

[28] Furthermore, the difference between liability and instrument consists in the fact that a bank holds liabilities that are not necessarily issued financial instruments (e.g. deposits).

[29] We give in this subsection some examples of what is considered within the outstanding amount for explanatory purposes. However, for the exact definition of outstanding amount, we recommend the reader to refer to the applicable legal framework and guidance by resolution authorities.

creditors. In practice, the write down and conversion measure is used to concentrate the losses on the resolution entity (i.e. the entity to which resolution tools will be applied) and recapitalise the other entities in the group. This measure can be conceived both under a single and a multiple point of entry approach, but the mechanics do not change: There are losses that need to be up-streamed to the resolution entities and capital to be down-streamed to subsidiaries otherwise also failing or likely to fail.

In terms of functioning, the equity of a subsidiary is written down, thus transferring a loss onto the balance sheet of the parent (our resolution entity), whose amount will therefore be accounted in the whole loss amount for the application of a resolution tool. The internal liabilities issued by the subsidiaries to the parent company (i.e. the money landed by the parent to the subsidiary) are converted into new capital, whose owner will again be the same parent company. In fact, while the initial shares are written down, the new share capital of the subsidiary is made of converted debt owned by the parent. This way, at the end of the write down and conversion, all losses will be concentrated in a single entity to be resolved and the affected subsidiaries will have been recapitalise, while keeping the same ownership structure.

However, in order to remain internal, the write down and conversion powers can only be applied to eligible internal liabilities that rank junior to any external liabilities. If this was not the case, it would be possible that external creditors would be converted into new bondholders, thus questioning the persistence of the subsidiary in the group. Also, the measure would fail to concentrate all the losses in a single entity, making its exercise rather pointless.

Now, the reader may wonder why it is advantageous to exercise write down and conversion powers to a subsidiary before applying the bail-in tool to the parent company instead of for example applying separately the bail-in tool to each one of the entities bearing losses, making each one of them a resolution entity. The first and most obvious reason is that in most of large groups, subsidiaries normally do not have their own access to wholesale funding and do not issue financial instruments. In many instances, the only eligible external liabilities of these subsidiaries are deposits exceeding the coverage limit. Subsidiaries issuing their own instruments are normally sizeable entities belonging to a very large group. We may think of the parent undertakings of a G-SIB in different countries, each one of them raising their own funding in the regional or national markets in which they operate. For G-SIBs in fact a multiple point of entry is more likely to be the preferred resolution strategy, but still this would not at all rule out the possibility of applying write down and conversion powers to smaller entities in daisy chains (i.e. 'subsidiaries of a subsidiary') should it be the case. Furthermore, some subsidiaries on top of not issuing any external debt might not even be licensed as credit institutions, hence not holding any deposits and being fully funded by the parent. Therefore there are cases in which it is materially not possible to apply a bail-in at different levels of the group.

There are other reasons that go beyond the financial aspects of the bail-in tool. We should not forget that the aim of resolution is to meet the resolution objectives, in particular the continuation of the critical functions, while ensuring that the entities coming out of resolution are able to stand and continue to operate. In the EU framework in particular where the write down and conversion powers are framed in this way, the bail-in tool is applied with an open-bank approach, which means that the resolution entity will be preserved through resolution. The entity after resolution will need to be able to thrive in the market and doing so is not just a matter of compliance with capital requirements. The long-term viability of a banking business, which the European bail-in is aimed to restore, is deeply interlinked with the business model and profitability of the whole group. Now, some of the subsidiaries might have a very specialised business model, often consisting in a single line of activities. Think for example of an entity performing leasing. While contributing even materially to the profitability of the group (and perhaps also to its critical functions), singularly taken these entities might have little chances to survive. Similarly, the parent entity once resolved would risk to find itself unable to stand on an amputated leg. There is therefore a necessity to keep together groups (or at least subgroups of a much larger groups) and resolve them through the application of resolution tools to the parent company.

Exclusions from Bail-In

The scope of the bail-in tool in terms of eligible liabilities is narrower compared to liquidation. In fact, not all liabilities of a bank can be subject to bail-in. Liabilities that can be subject to bail-in are defined bail-in eligible or simply bail-in-able, whereas those falling outside of the scope are referred to as exclusions.

There are two types of exclusions: mandatory (or statutory) and discretionary. The KAs do not provide the exact perimeter of the eligible liabilities. In the Principle for Bail-In Execution (FSB, 2018b), a policy guidance document addressed to resolution authorities, and with a focus on the bail-in of G-SIBs, it is recommended that resolution regimes set out clearly which liabilities are mandatorily excluded (Principle 1) and that to the extent of possible resolution authorities communicate in advance their approach to discretionary exclusions (Principle 2).

However, if we limited ourselves to the KA and the related guidance we would not find any precise indications about what is in and what is out of a bail-in. This is understandable, because the exact definition of the insolvency ranking as well as the type of bank liabilities may differ greatly across jurisdictions. We would therefore recommend the reader interested to find out more about the exclusions from bail-in to further check into the legislation applicable in its jurisdiction of interest. Nevertheless, we may still try to build a high-level categorisation based on largely accepted principles reflected in the majority of resolution regimes. Within the mandatory exclusions, an obvious case is constituted by covered deposits or secured liabilities. Many jurisdictions in fact provide special protection for deposits of households and small and medium enterprises (sometimes also of pension funds and local authorities) up to a certain level. In the EU the level is fixed in a minimum of EUR 100,000 per depositor considering all its deposits on a given institution on an aggregate basis. The UK has an analogous protection of GBP 85,000 per depositor. In the Unites States rules may vary depending on the type of bank (for example it is still in existence a private insurance for deposits of cooperative banks, as noted in Crosetti et al., 2021), but for all the banks covered by the Federal Deposit Insurance Corporation is USD 250,000 per depositor. In case in liquidation there would not be enough resources to compensate protected depositors up to the protected level, deposit guarantee schemes would intervene to compensate the difference. It would be illogical if the bail-in could affect these deposits that are in any case protected against the insolvency of the bank. Also from the point of view of the resolution objectives and financial stability, deposits from households and small and medium enterprises appear to be a category that is worth protecting in order to avoid the effects of a banking crisis hitting hard also on real economy.[30] In some resolution regimes, should the bail-in be extended to deposits, the deposit guarantee schemes can be requested to contribute to the financing of resolution, by paying the amount corresponding to the ratio at which covered deposits should be written down or converted, but without exceeding what they would need to pay in liquidation (see for example Art. 109 BRRD).

Secured liabilities are built in a way to give the investor the guarantee that the borrowed amount will be repaid or at least compensated by collateral of equivalent value. Making these liabilities subject to bail-in would mean circumventing the purpose itself of securing a liability to protect the investor against the risk of insolvency of the borrower.

Another type of mandatory exclusion has to do with the need to preserve financial stability throughout a resolution action. For this reason, resolution regimes might exclude from bail-in short-term interbank transaction or liabilities to central counterparties due to mature in a few days from the start of resolution. If this was not the case, an idiosyncratic shock might easily escalate through contagion and panic reactions and quickly dry out the market.

Other mandatory exclusions may pertain to the custody or fiduciary duties of a bank, as long as the counterparty is protected under national insolvency law. The typical example is a liability arising from the custody services of a bank on behalf of a collective investment company. Writing down or converting liabilities arising from assets or cash conferred in custody would mean sharing the burden with people who did not invest in that specific bank and that – especially in case of collective bodies – might not be even aware of that bank acting as a custodian for their savings.

An additional and rather broad category normally involves all those liabilities that do not pertain to the funding of a bank to be used in financial activities. For example,

[30] There is an extensive literature concerning the need for deposit guarantee, which spans over multiple decades starting from the debate of the adoption of the Glass-Stegall Act. The reader interested to get a better view on this topic may refer to the by now classical contributions by Diamond and Dybvig (1983), Diamond and Dybvig (1986), outlining an economic model of bank runs and discussing the role of deposit insurance in mitigating their effects. Costs and benefits of deposit insurance have been analysed for example by Carlstrom (1988), Hein (1992), Blair et al. (2006), or Anginer and Demirgüç-Kunt (2018).

salaries of the employees are also normally excluded from bail-in, except for the variable remuneration part. Any other liabilities arising from contracts concerning the provision of goods, services, or utilities are also likely to be a mandatory exclusion. How would you otherwise explain to the phone company that they will not get paid for their services but that they are now shareholders of a bank? Tax liabilities and social security liabilities, as well as contributions to deposit guarantee schemes, are also typical mandatory exclusions. These liabilities are related to the financial activities of a bank, in the sense that their amount depends on the business volume, but they are not themselves part of the business.

Finally, the last category that is likely to be mandatorily excluded is represented by intragroup liabilities. We explained above that a write down and conversion of capital instruments and internal eligible liabilities may be applied to entities that are not themselves resolution entities in order to upstream losses and downstream capital. Vice versa, if we applied the bail-in tool to the liabilities due by the resolution entities to other entities in the resolution group, we would actually go against the objective of centralising losses. Furthermore, from a financial point of view, losses would simply be passed to other entities, but from a group perspective, they would not be absorbed. If three entities A, B, and C in a group collectively (or in more technical terms on a consolidated basis) have 80 billion of assets and they need to repay 100 billion to external creditors, it does not matter if A owes 30 billion to C and those 30 billion are written down: C would have 30 billion of losses on its individual balance sheet, but there would still be a gap of 20 billion that together taken these three entities are not able to repay.

In summary, we can conclude that certain liabilities are normally mandatorily excluded from the scope of the bail-in tool, to achieve three main goals, which are the preservation of financial stability, the possibility to effectively absorbing the losses, and the limitation of the effects to protected creditors or creditors that have a claim that is not related to the funding of banking activities.

Now, for what concerns discretionary exclusions, it is more difficult to say if and how resolution authorities would exclude certain additional liabilities. However, the recalled Principles on Bail-In (FSB 2018) are clear in stating that liabilities can be discretionally excluded only in exceptional circumstances and that resolution regimes should clarify in advance what are the grounds for doing that. Some legal texts (the EU BRRD for example) have put forward some criteria. For example, certain liabilities might be discretionally excluded in order to continue the critical functions or preserve financial stability. It may be argued for example that for a retail bank mainly exposed to individuals and small and medium enterprises, it might not be the best idea to bail-in eligible deposits[31] if the goal is to preserve the critical function of deposit taking and if a large number of these enterprises had to slow down their activities due to part of their deposits being transformed into bank equity. There might be then reasons to exclude liabilities from the application of the bail-in tool due to the material impossibility to bail them in a reasonable timeframe or at a

[31] Eligible deposits are the part of deposit that is not covered by a deposit guarantee scheme.

reasonable cost. We may think for example to derivatives, who often belong to the same rank of senior debt, but whose value would be extremely difficult to determine in the context of resolution.

It is however to be noted that exclusions, discretionary in particular, are an exception to the rule according to which all the creditors in the same class should be treated in the same manner (pari passu rule), which applies both in liquidation and in resolution. While mandatory exclusions mirror to a large extent the forms of protection or superseniority given to certain creditors in liquidation, for discretionary exclusions the problem becomes more tangible. If we think about write down component of a bail-in, excluding on a discretional basis certain liabilities in a given rank means that the other creditors in the same rank will need to absorb also the losses that would be otherwise passed onto the excluded liabilities. Considering that in liquidation after loss absorption the net value from the sale of the assets is distributed proportionally to all claims without exceptions, it would be possible that following discretionary exclusions some creditors would receive in resolution less than they would in liquidation. This is the reason why the application of resolution tools is accompanied by the principle according to which no creditor in resolution should be treated less favourably than in liquidation, which goes under the name of 'no creditor worse off'.

'No Creditor Worse Off' Principle, Valuation and Financing Arrangements

A resolution procedure comes with certain operational risks regarding their implementation. In particular, it might be challenging to correctly estimate the net asset value after losses ahead of resolution, if raising from complex financial assets. Resolution has to deal with uncertainty and with the risk that preserving critical functions comes at costs that in some cases might end up being higher than liquidating the whole business. Without any form of guarantee and the possibility of financing resolution, this unpleasant outcome would entail questions. As we highlighted above, resolution is a derogatory procedure, whereas liquidation remains the default option. The derogatory power of resolution is motivated on the back of what we refer to as public interest. However, can a public interest be weighted more than the rights conferred to creditors of a failing bank?

The answer to this question has always been negative: The derogation to protect a public interest can be exercised in relation to the procedure to follow (resolution instead of liquidation), but it cannot be extended as much as violating the rights to which the creditors would be entitled in case of insolvency of a bank.

For this reason, resolution regimes have always been accompanied resolution with the guarantee of the above recalled no-creditor-worse-off principle. However, we have seen that there are at least two cases in which the risk of treating certain creditors worse than in liquidation is very tangible. In the resolution of a group of entities (either an entire commercial group or other subgroups of entities in a larger group), the prior use of write down and conversion powers implies that the creditors of the entity subject to bail-in would absorb losses otherwise passed to the creditors of the subsidiaries, which in insolvency would be liquidated separately. Depending on the amount of losses to be absorbed and the consequent extension of the bail-in write down, it may be possible that the creditors of the resolution entity would be treated better in liquidation.

Similarly, after discretionally excluding certain liabilities means that creditors, in case CET1 is not sufficient to absorb the integrity of losses and the write down part of the bail-in needs to extend to higher ranks in insolvency, would see their claims written down to an extent which also covers the losses not absorbed by excluded liabilities. In this case, the risk is that the write down ratio may be higher than the unrepaid portion of the claim in liquidation.

What can thus be done in those situations where the only way to implement a resolution tool would imply a pejorative treatment of certain creditors? Can a resolution scheme be adopted? And ultimately, can a public interest prevail on individual rights? The reader can easily guess that without a compromise solution these questions would be subject to an endless debate. If we had to decide whether a public interest is more or less worth of protection than an individual right, we could provide diametrically opposite answers, depending on where on the political spectrum we position ourselves.

Resolution regimes have found the compromise to avoid the endless dilemma of public interest and individual rights. In cases like this, where it is likely that some creditors would be treated worse in resolution than in liquidation, a resolution action can still be implemented to protect the public interest, but those 'worse off creditors' will be able to claim a compensation. This compensation will be measured as the difference between the loss in resolution and the hypothetical loss that the same creditor would have suffered in liquidation. The KAs are very clear in stating that (5.2) 'creditors should have a right to compensation where they do not receive at a minimum what they would have received in a liquidation of the firm under the applicable insolvency regime'.

In short, resolution can go ahead in pursuing the public interest. If some creditors find themselves in a position that is worse than in resolution, they will be entitled to a compensation. Such a solution, although offsetting the debate on the balance between public interest and creditors' rights, needs however to take into account two additional elements: how to finance the compensations and how to determine the hypothetical difference of treatment between liquidation and resolution.

In order to finance the compensation for creditors that would otherwise find themselves in resolution worse than in liquidation, resolution regimes dispose of financing arrangements (KA 6), entailing the intervention of deposit guarantee schemes or privately financed resolution funds (KA 6.3). An example of resolution financing mechanism is the Single Resolution Fund of the Single Resolution Board in the European Banking Union. This fund is financed by the contributions of credit institutions up to a level corresponding to 1% of covered deposits of all credit institutions established in Member States (Art. 69 Regulation EU 2014/806, Single Resolution Mechanism Regulation or 'SRMR'). The Single Resolution Fund can therefore provide compensations for creditors after exclusion of certain liabilities, at the condition of a prior bail-in or write down and conversion of an amount no less than 8% of the total liabilities and own funds of the bank or corresponding at least to 20% of risk-weighted assets. The intervention is normally capped at 5% of total liabilities and own funds of the bank in resolution unless its eligible liabilities and capital have been already written down in full and there are remaining funding gaps for resolution (Art. 44 BRRD).

There are other types of intervention by resolution financing arrangements, some of which will be examined in relation to other resolution tools. However, the concept we want to stress is that these financing arrangements are not intended as a surreptitious bailouts performed at the expenses of the whole banking system. If this were the case, resolution regimes would not be able to provide enough disincentive to the TBTF issue discussed in the introduction to this chapter. Instead, financing arrangements should be seen as a mean to facilitate the implementation of resolution tools, which would be otherwise hampered by obstacles of financial nature, such as the impossibility to compensate creditors who would receive a better treatment in liquidation.

Now, the obvious question is around how to ascertain whether a creditor would be treated better or worse in liquidation than in resolution. How can such conclusion be reached? Unavoidably, the exercise is somehow hypothetical, considered that there is no effective counterfactual against which the treatment in liquidation can be measured. However, based on the same financials, it should be possible to 'back-test' how things would have evolved applying a different set of rules. Let us clarify this point. Once a bank enters the resolution weekend, her operations minimised (or even completely blocked, should the resolution authorities have moratoria powers). The influence of external variables in that span of time is reduced to a minimum. Differently said, until the application of resolution tools, at that moment the balance sheet of the resolving bank cannot undergo major changes.

In a given jurisdiction, the rules applicable in normal insolvency proceedings (remember for example the insolvency hierarchy we referred to above) pre-exist the resolution case. It is known in advance that should a bank be wound down under these proceedings, the value recovered from the liquidation of the remaining assets would be distributed to creditors according to their rank. Therefore, on the basis of the net asset value in resolution, it is not unreasonable to estimate what the outcome in liquidation would be. To visualise this reasoning, we can think about having a fixed amount dough for cookies and two different stamps to use, and let us say a hearth and a star. If we opt for the 'resolution-hearth', when the cookie is in the oven we cannot reverse the process and decide to make a 'liquidation-star'. However, we would still have a say about how many cookies we would have done using the other stamp.

Since the stamps do not change, everything else being equal, the only thing that can affect the result is the quantity of dough, which in our example represents the net asset value of the institution under liquidation or resolution. If we move from the kitchen to the crisis room of a resolution authority, the quantity of the dough becomes the real problem. In our example, it is something that we can measure: It is in our hands and under our eyes. However, the net asset value of a failing bank needs to be evaluated.

We therefore need to spend at least few words on valuation processes in resolution and how they relate to the assessment of the no creditor worse off principle. We will not enter into the technicalities of the methods used for valuation, as this specialist knowledge would go far beyond the purposes of this chapter. The KAs themselves do not contain references to the valuation processes. However, valuation has always been an integral part of resolution regime, which has been later reflected in the principles on bail-in execution (FSB, 2018b) and the bail-in execution practices paper (FSB, 2011).

All valuation processes are carried by an external and independent valuer. Resolution authorities operationalise the legislative framework concerning valuation and guide credit institutions in developing sufficient capabilities – especially on the side of information systems and IT equipment – to support a swift and accurate valuation. The independence of the valuer is to be understood as an additional safeguard for shareholders and creditors. To be clear, independence works in two directions: as much as the valuer needs to provide a non-biased assessment to the supervision and resolution authorities, he should also be exempt from conflicts of interest with the institution on which a valuation process needs to be carried.

Valuation processes serve a wide range of purposes, which can be classified into three different categories concerning the entry into liquidation or resolution, the application of the resolution tools, and the assessment of the no creditor worse off principle. In order to distinguish between these three functions, we can use a now spread terminology (see Commission Delegated Regulation (EU) 2018/345 of 14 November 2017 as well as SRB, 2019a) designating them, respectively, as valuations 1, 2, and 3.

The aim of valuation 1 is to determine whether the preconditions (see Sect. 4 above) for triggering a resolution procedure or a write down and conversion are met. As the public interest assessment is performed by resolution authorities, valuation 1 will concentrate on whether the aggregate asset value of a bank exceeds liabilities and the conditions for authorisation are still met. In other words, it should be checked whether the bank is effectively failing or likely to fail. Valuation 1 will be therefore carried mainly on the basis of the accounting principles that the bank use in going concern to assess the compliance with prudential requirements, although the valuer may deviate from these principles should he conclude that the accounting practices used by the bank do not allow for a fair and realistic valuation.

Valuation 2 serves instead to inform the use of resolution tools. In relation to bail-in, this valuation will be the basis to determine the amount of losses to be covered and consequently the extension of the bail-in tool (i.e. how much to be written down and how much to be converted into new capital). As resolution procedures are performed under time pressure, it might be the case that valuation 2 is performed on a preliminary basis before the adoption of the resolution scheme. This could be the case in jurisdictions such as the EU countries where the bail-in tool is performed with a continuation of the legal entity to which the tool is applied (i.e. under an open-bank approach). In such a case, valuation 2 (as well as valuation 1 if also preliminary) will need to be confirmed by a definitive valuation after resolution.

This additional valuation may then result in final adjustments to the rates applied in the write down and conversion under the bail-in tool.

Finally, valuation 3, normally to be conducted after resolution when the outcome of the bail-in tool is already known, will assess the respect of the no-creditor worse off principle. On the basis of the financial situation of the entity at the entry into resolution, valuation 3 will estimate what would have been the treatment of shareholders and creditors if the entity had undergone normal insolvency proceedings. It is – as we said – a hypothetical exercise, considered that when valuation 3 is carried, the bank has already passed through resolution. Nevertheless, on the basis of the same starting point, valuation looks back to what would have happened in liquidation, to ensure shareholders and creditors that the decision taken was right and also in their best interest. In principle, the bail-in tool should not result in a worse treatment than liquidation: Shareholders are in both cases likely to be wiped out entirely, whereas most of the creditors would receive a higher protection of their claims, through the conversion of all or part of the amount they are due into new capital. When this is not the case, because to achieve the resolution objectives the authority had for example to discretionally exclude a wide range of liabilities or because the resolution entities had to bear significant losses from other entities in the group, creditors would receive a compensation to cover their claim up to what they would have theoretically received in resolution. This is to ensure that behind the achievement of the public interest, no physical or juridical person should be penalised bearing more losses than it should.

5.2 *Sale of Business*

Is It Possible to Sell a Failing Bank?

After having presented the main features of bail-in, we can now provide some elements on the other resolution tools. As they all entail in some forms the transfer of assets or liabilities of the failing bank, they often go under the collective definition of transfer tools.

The first of these tools is the sale of business.[32] The reader may be familiar with the concept of this tool, as to a certain extent it represents the formalisation in legal terms of crisis management strategies that for decades have been used by central banks and supervision authorities. In the past, although in lack of a formal sale of business tool, moral suasion was often used by public authorities to convince a large player to take over a smaller failing bank (see for example Lindgren, 1999).

[32] Please note that the term sale (or transfer) of business, now largely predominant in resolution regimes, is based on the EU BRRD language. American readers may instead be more familiar with the notion of purchase and assumption (see for example Giliberto & Varaiya, 1989; McGuire, 2012).

From the point of view of its functioning, if we put aside the technicalities and the operational steps to perform a sale in resolution, such a tool does not need specific explanations as to its meaning, given that it is to a large extent self-evident. The idea in fact is very simple: If the performing assets are not sufficient to repay the outstanding liabilities (remember the weighing scale metaphor used for the bail-in tool), the forced transfer of assets and liabilities to an acquirer can be a possible way out.

The obvious question is at which terms a healthy bank can be interested to take over an ailing business, where the liabilities offset the asset. In reality, at a sufficiently discounted price, a potential buyer can turn the acquisition of a resolving bank into a profitable opportunity (this is well documented for example in Cowan & Salotti, 2015; Dunn et al., 2016, although ground for adverse selection effects has been identified in Granja et al., 2017).

Let us look at some numbers to grasp the concept and imagine a bank of 100 billion of assets. In a going concern, the balance is in equilibrium. This means that own funds and liabilities will also equal 100 billion, in a proportion of – let us say – 10 billion of own funds (for simplicity let us assume entirely made of share capital at market price) and 90 billion of liabilities (including deposits, securities, tax, employees, and any other amount due to external creditors). In normal times, buying the 100% of this bank would cost at least the above 10 billion of share capital.[33]

Let us now imagine that the bank incurs 15 billion of losses. In other terms this would mean that out of the 100 billion of assets, only 85 are performing. Certainly the business does not look particularly attractive to potential investors at this stage. However, if the capital is written down to absorb losses, the balance sheet we would look at would have still the 85 billion performing assets and only 90 billion of claims to be repaid. Now, if the failing bank is transferred for free or at a symbolic consideration, the acquirer would only need to fund the gap of 5 billion, to get in exchange a business of 90 billion assets that is again in equilibrium.

Note that to buy the same bank in a going concern, the acquirer would have need to pay 10 billion, while now it has the possibility of taking it over for half the price. Certainly, out of those 85 billion of assets inherited from the failed bank, others may turn to be non-performing at a later stage. Similarly, a bank that fails has problems in its business model, which will need to be deeply reconsidered by the acquirer. However, all these difficulties are part of the normal activities of bank, which ultimately are risk managers. By contrast, for a bank interested to expand its operations in a given country, taking over a failing bank in resolution might be a good opportunity.

Furthermore, another element contributes to the advantage of the acquirer. Valuations 1 and 2 on a failing bank to be sold tend to be very conservative.

[33] In reality, to convince existing shareholders to sell, an acquirer must be ready to put more on the plate and offer an additional mark up, but to keep this example simple we assume all shareholders are ready to sell at the market price.

Naturally, an acquirer would also be prudent in making such a deal. However, it should not be excluded that in the end the effective asset value can be higher than what is valued in resolution, making the gap to fill a bit smaller.

The Roles Involved in a Sale

The answer to our main question is therefore that an acquisition under the sale of business tool can be a reasonable operation for an acquirer that desires to increase its business in one or more of the areas in which the failing bank had a relevant market share, especially in the presence of a well-established branch network, as found in Abedifar et al. (2022). It will of course very much depend on the situation and the liability gap the acquirer will need to take over, as we will explain further below.

However, what is the role of resolution authorities in such a sale? First, resolution authorities aim to maximise the proceeds, in order to repay existing claims as much as possible and avoid undue destruction of value. In practical terms, in case multiple potential acquirers are interested, the resolution authority will try to maximise the sale price or – in cases of the transfer of the whole institution for a symbolic price – negotiate the best possible conditions for the takeover. In case instead of a low interest for the entity in resolution, the resolution authority will engage itself in a real marketing process to tease potential acquirers.

With the sale of business tool, we face a modus operandi of the resolution authorities that mixes the use of authoritative powers with the adherence to market practices. In fact, a resolution authority can decide authoritatively to put an entity on sale, but at the same time it cannot impose anybody to buy it. As a consequence, after the initial decision to sell, the modalities, terms, and processes for the sale of an entity or an asset portfolio will not differ much from a private sell, especially from the point of view of the buyer. Any additional administrative burdens or obligations could only make potential buyers run away from the deal.

The specific nature of the sale of business tool has some precise consequences. First, if on the one side resolution authorities should try as much as possible to mirror an ordinary sale on the market, it is also true that the circumstances could not be more distant from business as usual. In particular, the urgency due to resolution may impose to shorten or cut some processes normally involved in an acquisition in the banking sector. For example, the non-binding offer phase might be skipped or the terms for the sale might not be subject to negotiation.

The key issue with the application of the sale of business tool is that resolution authorities need to fit in a very short timeframe a process that would otherwise require entire months to be finalised. It should therefore not be seen as a surprise that in cases for which the sale of business is seen as the preferred resolution strategy, the marketing phase may be triggered weeks or even months ahead of the formal failing or likely to fail declaration. At the same time, resolution authorities may prepare themselves and the bank for a sale in the resolution planning phase. As in most resolution regimes resolution plans are updated annually, they can already include up-to-date documentation for the sale and identify a preliminary list of potential buyers to be contacted in case of resolution (SRB, 2021a).

Although needing to adapt to market practices, no resolution authority is actually an expert on mergers and acquisition. The application of resolution tools, there including also the sale of business, is (luckily) rare events. It is not infrequent that two consecutive crises cases are years away. During this time, the resolution authority is only engaged in preparation and testing. It can of course recruit among its staff people that have already experience in investment banking and operations of mergers and acquisitions. However, building a true skill centre, let us say a full department of specialists on market practices for sales of business, would certainly be disproportional to the effective needs of the organisation. That is the reason why in the actual application of the sale of business tool resolution authorities are likely to be supported by teams of consultants, who will deal with the accounting, financial, and legal technicalities concerning a sale.

The reader should not be surprised by the use of external advisors for the application of the tool. He should be not, because indeed they are there to advise, not to replace the resolution authority in its decisions (e.g. when to sell and who to sell to). Specialists carry highly technical but time-consuming tasks with little or no discretion involved. Should these tasks be taken on board by the resolution authority itself, the timeline for the application of the sale of business would unduly expand, posing a risk for the swift and effective implementation of a resolution procedure.

Furthermore, the potential buyers will also be supported by external teams of equivalent nature. In reality in fact, there are very few banks who actually have a well-established internal expertise in house. Although we may perceive that merger and acquisitions are rather frequent on the market, if we consider instead a single credit institution, the sell or the acquisition of business would be actually events that do not occur with a high frequency. Under this perspective, the resolution authority and the buyer are the two main parties concluding the deal. However, both sides for this exceptional event will need external support from specialists.

And what we can tell about the failing bank? What is its role in the application of the sale of business? As for any of the resolution tools (although we did not concentrate on this aspect when discussing about the bail-in), the resolving bank needs to cooperate in good faith with the resolution authority and provide all the information that is relevant to a fair and realistic valuation and consequently to a correct calibration of the resolution tools.

The cooperation of the failing bank is an element of primary importance. As much as a resolution authority can have familiarised with the business through the planning process and as much as advisors may have gained experience through successive deals, nobody knows a bank as well as its own staff and management. The people in the company will be those who ultimately can explain what went wrong with their business and what instead they are really good at. The retained profitability drivers need to be preserved through resolution, in order to allow the entity or the entities continuing or taking over the business after resolution to ensure its long-term viability. These profitability drivers form the franchise value of an entity or business to be sold, i.e. they are what a buyer is paying for. In this process, the staff of the resolving bank is there to literally make sure that nothing is lost in translation. Although operating on the same market, two entities always come from different business histories. They will therefore both have their internal jargon and ways of presenting information. These differences can create a hiatus between the seller and the buyer that can even prevent the latter from going ahead in case he cannot well understand the details. Any potential acquirer will in fact want to gain deep intelligence on what they may intend to buy.

For the sale of business tool and along the same need for extensive information, the resolving bank also needs to be able to set up a virtual data room for the involved participants. A virtual data room is a centralised repository of information that can be used by all the parties involved to conclude a process, in this case the sale of an entity in resolution. The virtual data room will serve many purposes in a resolution context. It will provide the basis for the due diligence processes to be conducted by the specialists to review the business of the entity in resolution. The data there included will also be necessary for the performance of the valuations carried on the failing bank. Furthermore, the virtual data room is aimed at reducing the asymmetry of information between the seller and the buyer.

Different Sale Strategies for Different Circumstances

So far we have indistinctively referred to the sale of business or part of the business. However, this is a generic and to a certain extent imprecise distinction. It is necessary instead to well understand what may form the object of a sale of business. Using a terminology derived from market practices, the distinction we should make is between a share deal and an asset deal. A share deal corresponds to a situation in which an entity is taken over by an acquirer who becomes the new owner. It is the idea of selling a business that is probably closer to the common opinion about what a sale of business represents. The example we included above represents in fact a deal of this type. To be clear, when applying the sale of business tool under a share deal approach, the purchaser is buying a company. In general terms, the entire entity or group is the object of the sale. However, as we will see further below, in some circumstances part of the balance sheet items or the group entities are left behind, as their transfer could compromise the outcome of the deal.

Also, if the operating company (i.e. the largest entity in the group effectively operating as a bank) is owned by a clean holding (i.e. a company that does not perform any operational activities) owned by external shareholders, the holding will not likely be part of the deal. For a purchaser, it would in fact represent only an intermediary empty shell. The existing shareholders would in this case be left behind to absorb the losses (net of any NCWO compensations where relevant[34]) and the operating company would be transferred to the acquirer for a symbolic price

[34] In this case however the undepleted capital should be considered in the consideration paid by the buyer.

(referred to as consideration fee). An asset deal is instead the situation in which only certain assets are transferred. This would be the case of a bank for which there is little interest of the market for the acquisition of the whole company, while parts of its business (e.g. specific portfolios or segments of clients) still retain potentials for profitability (or maybe are even profitable, singularly considered). Such an approach would of course better function with a bank having a clear segmentation of their business in different lines.

To help us visualise this case, let us imagine a local (but large) regional bank in a developed country with three business segments. The first one entails retail banking for households and small and medium enterprises, with a predominant exposure to households and with local enterprises being concentrated in the construction sector. In this segment, the bank performs the traditional banking activities of collecting deposits and granting loans and mortgages. The second segment is represented by public administrations, to which the banks provide banking services, as for retail clients, as well as treasury services. The third business line is instead car leasing, a non-banking activity carried via a dedicated subsidiary. Before the shock the retail segment is moderately profitable. The public segment instead is not particularly profitable, but at least it has a very low default rate and regular cash flows. The car leasing activity has instead good profitability, with a positive outlook concerning the further growth of the business in the future.

The deposit taking and lending functions from households are considered critical due to a material market share, and let us say around 10% of the market. Deposit taking and lending from small and medium enterprises are instead not critical, because in spite of some rather material exposures to single clients, the bank does not retain a large market share. The activities carried for public administration are critical as well because there are actually few banks in that jurisdiction that are specialised in this business. Finally, the leasing segment does not entail critical functions, because although growing it has not yet reached a volume for which the disruption would endanger financial stability and substitutability is high.

Now let us imagine that the area in which our regional bank operates is hit by steep decline in house prices. What would happen next can easily be imagined by our reader, since on a regional scale it would mirror what happened on a global level in 2007 and 2008. For the non-performing loans, the bank now only rely on depreciated collateral, which is not sufficient to recover from the loss incurred in case the loans defaulted. At the same time, the enterprises in the portfolio of this bank were concentrated in the construction sector. Many of them would not be any longer able to honour their payments. At the same time, they would need to draw more credit to continue their activities.

Now let us imagine that the shock in the housing prices is so deep that the bank ends up being failing or likely to fail. Potential acquirers would be very reluctant to take over exposures to the construction business that are very hardly performing. At the same time, the resolution authority cannot let these exposures prevent a deal to continue the banking services to households and public administration. The asset deal could therefore represent a solution to this dilemma. An acquirer would probably be interested to get the mildly profitable but safe public segment as well as the profitable and growing business of leasing, while it would be scared to take on board also the retail segment, due to the exposures to the construction sector and households defaulting on their loans with insufficient collateral. The compromise between the continuation of the critical function and a feasible deal would be the transfer of the whole public and leasing segments, along with most of the retail one, net of the most problematic exposures, which could be left behind in the failing bank. This in turn would be gradually liquidated, with the intention of recovering over time as much as possible from defaulted exposures. Conversely, the critical functions would be continued under a different company, after the transfer to a purchaser. The purchaser will probably need to pay a consideration for the assets transferred or – in case they are transferred for a symbolic price in block with liabilities – finance the gap between performing assets and claims to be repaid.

It is also not to be excluded, under an asset deal approach, that the sale will be concluded with multiple purchasers. In our example we can imagine to have two different acquirers for the public and the leasing segments, sharing in equal proportions the part of the retail segment that is transferred along with the sale. For the purchasers, this would mean making a 'smaller step' in taking over the activities of a failed bank, each one of them purchasing just one profitable segment (the one in which they are already specialised or they want to expand) and only a half of the problematic portfolio for sale.

The asset deal can also be combined with a share deal. In our example above, if a potential buyer can be found for the main operating company (covering retail and public segments), the largely independent leasing business could be sold separately at a positive market price, whose proceedings in turn would alleviate the gap at the level of the parent.

The choice between a sale and an asset deal will depend on a number of factors. We already mentioned in our example the split of the business in well-defined segments as one of the factors facilitating an asset deal. We also noted that the asset deal can be a potential alternative in case of lack of interest for the whole company. In addition we can also consider the dimension of a bank: The bigger it is, the more difficult it will be to sell it under a share deal. In the end, the concrete approach to follow will be determined by the precise circumstances in which a bank becomes failing or likely to fail and in particular on how much the purchasers will need to put in the deal. As a matter of fact, in the planning phase resolution authorities and banks will normally prepare for different alternative sale approaches.

Nevertheless, this brings us to an obvious question. We started from an example in which after the write down of the shareholders the liability gap left would still make a share deal attractive. We continued with an example of losses concentrated in a single segment, with other business segments still in good financial health. But what would happen in all those circumstances when losses are more pronounced or there is no sufficient clarity on the retained franchise value? Shall resolution authorities give up on the possibility of using a transfer tool? And if so, what would happen if the bail-in tool could not be used effectively (i.e. face to losses being so high that or issued instruments so low that it would be needed to convert a large amount of deposits while deposits themselves are considered a critical function)?

In reality, resolution authorities would still have some bullets in their cartridges. Let us first concentrate on the uncertainty regarding the value of the company or the assets to be sold. In some cases in fact, it might be rather difficult to predict how much of the transferred assets will continue to perform in the future. Left aside the losses that brought a bank to be failing or likely to fail, the remaining assets may take alternative paths. Some of them will be performing, while some others will not. In some cases it is very high to predict how a portfolio will perform. Also, in a case like the one we described in our second example, after the depreciation of the collateral (i.e. the houses), there would be less coverage for future defaults.

These are elements that may discourage a potential buyer from agreeing to the deal. A possibility in this case would be to call into play the resolution financing mechanisms for what is called an asset protection scheme. The way in which these schemes are built is highly technical and entail the segmentation of the problematic assets in different tranches, which will receive a different degree of protection by the guarantor. In its essential terms however, the idea is that the financing arrangements (typically a resolution fund) will provide a guarantee on part of the assets being transferred to a purchaser, posting financial collateral as coverage. The financing mechanism will then pay for the loss events triggered by the terms stipulated in the asset protection scheme and receive fees for the service provided. Part of the risk will remain within the portfolio being transferred. However, this at least partial risk hedging can constitute the clincher to convince a potential buyer to close the deal.

Although not explicitly mentioned in resolution legal frameworks, asset protection schemes are to be seen as an element facilitating the conclusion of a share deal. In case of limited interest for the whole company, instead of transferring segments of business separately with the risk of leaving an excessive portion behind, the asset protection scheme can facilitate the acquisition of the entire company, which – ça va sans dire – would be a preferable outcome in terms of efficiency. It appears instead less realistic to use an asset protection scheme for an asset deal. First of all, derisking a subset of assets to be transferred separately would simply mean deliver a gift to an acquirer. At those terms, one can bet any bank would agree to take over. However, the asset protection scheme has a cost, which is born by the resolution financing mechanisms. In most jurisdictions resolution financing mechanisms are financed by banks themselves. This means that packing a group of substantially safe assets to be transferred to an acquirer would result in an undue competitive advantage. By contrast, in a share deal (where in any case the APS can only concern a limited portion of the assets) substantial business risk would in any case be passed to the acquirer.

Nevertheless, let us put aside these criticisms based on principles, and let us concentrate on why an APS is either not needed or not doable under an asset deal approach. We can face two alternative situations. The first one is when in lack of interests for the whole company, parts of its activities are still profitable. In this case, the asset deal itself is cornered around the idea that the non-performing part of the assets would be packed along a more generous part of profitable activities. Hence, in this situation an asset protection scheme would not be necessary to close the deal. More precisely, the resolution authority would be prevented from moving down that line for the cost efficiency of resolution. In short, why to spend additional money when the same result can be achieved without spending anything?

The second situation is when instead it is very difficult to identify profitable parts of the business and before selling the balance sheet would need an extensive restructuring. In a such a case, not even a share deal would have a chance alone to be concluded. Forcing it through an extensive asset protection scheme would in substance correspond to bailing out the bank. To achieve the goal of restructuring the balance sheet, the resolution authority may instead resort to other resolution tools: the asset separation and the bridge bank.

5.3 Asset Separation

A key feature of resolution tools, as the reader may have noticed from previous sections, is their interoperability. Resolution authorities may in fact apply them in different combinations and at different levels of the bank to be resolved. Thanks to this characteristic, resolution tools are potentially adaptable to a wide range of business models and crisis situations. There is however a tool that will always need to be used in association with another resolution tool.[35] This tool is the asset separation, better known to the general public as the bad bank. With this tool, particularly problematic assets are transferred to a separate vehicle, which in turn can face two possible outcomes. As the first outcome, the entity may be sold separately – under market terms – to an acquirer interested in the troubled portfolio. Such a sale should not be seen as something unrealistic, since in recent years there has been a development of intermediaries specialised in the business of non-performing assets (for better grasping this phenomenon, refer to Fell et al., 2016, 2017; Miglionico, 2019; Qian, 2023). By acquiring them at a discounted price, these intermediaries may generate a profit should they be able to recover more than they paid for. It should not be forgotten that up until these intermediaries kick in, the obligations related to non-performing assets have not been renegotiated. In practical terms, this means that if a defaulted debtor owed 100 to the bank and did not pay, he will still owe 100 to the asset management vehicle after the first transfer and continuing down the line he will owe 100 to the specialised intermediary after the second transfer.

The intermediary will have not paid 100 to get this defaulted credit of 100. Following the valuation processes, if it was estimated that from that defaulted asset the creditor could recover up to around 30%, the intermediary will pay a price lower than or equal to 30. Now, up until this point we have left the debtor aside, but in reality nobody has cancelled his debt. Note that for the debtor being insolvent entails very unpleasant consequences. We should not think about people running away with

[35] This limitation is made explicit in the EU BRRD framework. However, as the reader will see from its functioning, common sense would also arrive to the same conclusion.

the bank money. For a wide number of reasons – not depending on the debtor – the amount lent cannot be repaid. For an enterprise this could mean being in serious troubles with the continuation of the business. What if at this point the intermediary that now owns the claim shows up and tells the debtor 'give me 36 over a longer time horizon and let us close this issue once and for all'? The reader can rest assured that the debtor will be very willing to see the debt reduced from 100 down to 36 with a longer maturity and he may be also able to settle it under the new terms, even if the financial position of the debtor has deteriorated over time. By contrast, the intermediary will have earned a margin of 20% (6/30) on the operation.

In reality, things may be a little more complicated. A good part of the troubled assets will be defaulted for good, which means that on a good portion of the assets acquired from the bad bank the intermediary is losing money. The good results of the operation will depend on the amounts recovered from the other troubled assets. This is why the intermediary will need to table individual negotiations with all the debtors involved, trying to recover as much as possible. In conclusion, the operation will be profitable if the sum of the amount recovered from all the assets is higher than the price paid for it. However, this individual screening is a task that neither the failing bank itself nor the bad bank could do.

For the bank, settling individual non-performing exposures at this discount rates individual exposures would be equivalent to take on losses. As long as possible, a bank would deploy its resources to work around defaulting exposures rather than to take them on board. It would not make sense to start thinking about what you can save from a burning house if you can still prevent the house from burning. When instead the house is burning, what you can recover would in any case appear as a second-level concern. The bad bank is a slim ad hoc entity staffed to a minimum[36] with the only goal to manage the separation transaction. Normally it does not have the capacity to perform this role, unless if forced by the circumstances.

In some cases in fact the portfolio transferred to a bad bank – and this is the second outcome – might be deteriorated at the point that it will not be possible to resell it on the market. In these situations, the bad bank will operate as a run-off manager. It may of course try to act in a similar way to what the intermediary specialised in troubled portfolios would do. However, if even professional actors have declined to take over this task, it should not be expected to see encouraging results in terms of recoveries. In this hypothesis, the bad bank will rather concentrate on the orderly liquidation of the assets in the shortest possible time.

Having outlined the functioning of the asset separation tool, we still need to explain why it cannot be applied on a standalone basis. There are at least two orders of reasons, pertaining to the financing of the tool and the overarching goals of resolution.

---

36 It is worth noting that in most resolution regimes the staff members of the failing bank cannot be appointed in the bad bank, under the assumption that they (or at least those of them who remain) will need to keep the critical functions alive. For the record, given the limited life span of a bad bank, it should be expected that it would be rather hard to staff it, unless generous salaries are paid. This comes as an additional reason to use caution in recurring to this resolution tool.

The financial argument goes in the same line of the considerations made above for the use of the asset protection scheme. The bad bank for the asset separation is set up at the expenses of the resolution financing arrangements. The greater will be the transferred portfolio, the greater will be the bill. As long as the gap between asset and liabilities could be closed by the bail-in or the sale of business tools, these ways should be clearly preferred.

Furthermore, we noted in the introductory remarks to this chapter that resolution regimes are conceived to reduce moral hazard. Cleaning the balance sheet of a troubled bank might easily turn into the expectation that an asset separation will be performed at an early stage of the deterioration, when a bank can still recover from the losses recorded in the balance sheet after the transfer. Such an expectation could incentivise excessive risk-taking behaviours going against the objectives themselves of resolution and turning what is to be conceived as a procedure to protect public interest into a life vest to rescue from mismanagement.

The need to accompany the asset separation tool with another resolution tool also automatically disqualifies its use as a sufficient mean to address the failure. In fact, if hypothetically the asset separation tool were used alone, it would only result in the booking losses to the balance sheet (unless of course for the transfer the bad bank paid a consideration well above the retained value of the assets, but that would be practically a bailout).

If it is clear what not to use the asset separation for (i.e. bailing out a bank), what will be its function in resolution? In essence, the asset separation should be understood as a mean to support the long-term viability of the business resulting from resolution and in turn the continuation of the critical functions. After the application of the bail-in tool, the resized bank will need to be able to operate. Retaining highly risky assets in its balance sheet would endanger the possibility of doing so, undermining the market confidence towards the resolved institution. In a sale of business, particularly a share deal, the intention is of course to have the buyer funding a good part of the imbalance. However, the transfer should not become itself a source of contagion. The asset separation can hence be used as a way of normalising the risk of the transferred portfolio to a manageable level.

To understand this function of risk normalisation of the asset separation tool, we may think of a small portfolio characterised by very high legal or reputational risk. Recent cases (such as the Anglo-Austrian Bank or the Amsterdam Trade Bank) highlighted that an otherwise solvent bank can very quickly become failing due to the loss of market confidence and the material impossibility of continuing its operational due to single losses correlated with a high reputational impact. Money laundry issues or capitals tied with the proceedings of criminal activities would be a key example of a problematic portfolio.

Now, the amount of these exposures may be very low, but it would anyhow be extremely dangerous after resolution (one additional reason to pay extra attention to valuation and due diligence processes). Applying a bail-in tool without removing them would be equivalent to repairing a house and leaving the site with a gas valve open: Although everything is ready to function well, a single sparkle can easily turn the new building into ashes. Similarly, it does not matter how little in value these exposures might be: A potential buyer will always refuse to take them on board. And – we add – he would be right in doing so, because bank is excellent risk managers, but these assets would entail risks that a bank cannot (and is not allowed to) manage.

5.4 *Bridge Bank*

The fourth of the tools a resolution authority has in store is the bridge bank (KA 3.4). In this case as well the name can pretty much suggest what such a tool entails. All or part of the assets and liabilities of the bank under resolution are transferred to an entity devoted to the management of that portfolio under the oversight of the resolution authority. The bridge bank would be normally constituted on purpose, with the resolution financing arrangements providing the initial capital. Some resolution authorities, especially if they already made use of bridge banks, might already have empty shells ready to become a bridge bank. However, this would be an exception rather than the rule.

Unlike the asset separation tool, the staff of the entity under resolution can be transferred to the bridge bank. This is understandable, considering that the aim of the tool is not to 'liquidate' high-risk activities, but to migrate a business that needs to be continued. The people who run that business – not the management responsible for decisions leading to the failure, but rank and file employees devoted to daily operations – are those who retain the knowledge that can ensure substantial continuity in the activities.

The distinctive trait of the bridge bank is its temporary nature. Although the transfer of assets and liabilities to such a bank prevents them from ending up in liquidation, the tool needs to incorporate a thorough planning for a return to the market. In fact, if the bridge bank could continue to manage the business received from a bank under resolution for an indefinite period of time, this resolution tool would achieve results substantially symmetrical to a bailout.

Therefore, resolution authorities, as soon as the bridge bank receives the transferred assets, need to start working on their marketing. The EU framework fixes a limit of 2 years, which can be further extended by 1 year only under the condition that this is necessary to continue critical functions and to facilitate the end of the bridge bank operations. The continuation of critical function alone would not be a sufficient motivation, as otherwise the life span of a bridge bank could be extended indefinitely.

Resolution authorities therefore need to act quickly to pave a way for this return to the market. The ideal (and so far most frequent) outcome of the bridge bank tool is a sale to a private purchaser. In this case, differently from the application of the sale of business tool where the procedure is governed by public law, the sale of the bridge bank needs to be entirely carried under market terms. In fact, the sale of business tool is conceived for being applied to a failing or likely to fail bank, not to a bank that is already the result of a resolution procedure.

Another possibility is that in lack of an acquirer the resolution authority dismisses the activities of the bridge bank through an orderly wind down. In reality, this would be far from being an excellent outcome, because creditors may incur the risk of seeing their claims not repaid in full. For a resolution authority, this might increase the costs of resolution, because in addition to the capital provided for opening the bridge bank the resolution financing arrangements might be called to provide compensations for breaches of the no-creditor-worse-off principle.

To protect the resolution financing arrangements from excessive payout events in the use of the bridge bank tool, many legal frameworks stipulate that the liabilities transferred from the institution under resolution should not exceed the net value of assets and rights of the bridge bank. Therefore, who will cover the gap between assets and liabilities that made the bank fail? In general terms, what we should expect to see is that the gap (or most of it) will be covered by the write down of shareholders. Furthermore, the capital paid by the financing arrangements to set up the bridge bank will constitute additional cash on the asset side, which will help closing the equation.

If the bridge bank ceases to exist with a return to the market, hopefully through the acquisition by another market player, what happens to the institution under resolution? Actually the transfer will tend to be 'in block'. All assets and liabilities of the institution are transferred to the bridge bank, except the capital written down, defaulted assets that are left behind. If the institution under resolution retains some high-risk assets, also in the case of the bridge bank it might be advisable to transfer them to a bad bank or leave them behind, in order to prevent that these assets at a later stage may prevent the sale of the bridge bank. The institution under resolution after the application of the bridge bank tool is therefore an empty or almost empty company that will be wound down in liquidation.

After resolution, while the original entity is due to be liquidated, the fate of the bridge bank remains to be decided. Furthermore, at the time assets and liabilities are transferred to the bridge bank, there is also a risk that due to a deterioration of the market or unforeseeable circumstances in the 2-year horizons the appetite of potential acquirers may decrease, making the 'liquidation outcome' more probable. In short, if a failing entity can be sold immediately better not wait to sell its assets at a later stage. Similarly, if the company can be put in the conditions of sustaining itself by a bail-in, there would be no reason to put it on hold for a couple of years and wait for a buyer. It appears therefore clear that this tool should be used as a last resort, when neither the bail-in nor the sale of business could be an effective remedy to the crisis. Note that this has important implications also for resolution planning. Resolution authorities have to prepare and operationalise a presumptive path they would follow in resolution, which is referred to as a preferred resolution strategy. In that respect, the bridge bank qualifies as a second best solution. This does not mean that there are no situations in which the bridge bank can be an effective resolution tool (quite the contrary, based on historical experience); however, if resolution authorities and banks need to invest time and resources in operationalising a preferred course of action to be followed in resolution, it is rational to expect they will orient themselves towards a tool that is sufficient to resolve the failure, without further steps needed at a later stage. At most, the bridge bank tool can be considered as an alternative resolution strategy (or variant strategy) as soon as the preferred one has reached a sufficient degree of operationalisation.

Nevertheless, as noted above, there might be cases in which in an actual resolution it will be necessary to make use of the bridge bank. We may think for example of a medium–large bank characterised by a very complex business organisation and losses on the subsidiaries high at the point that an internal write down and conversion processes would not be sufficient to centralise the losses to one or a limited number of entities. A bail-in in that context would not reach a definitive outcome. Since the bank is sizeable, it is not possible to think about potential buyer to step in at the time of resolution. In such a situation, a bridge bank would be a valid solution to simplify the organisation by concentrating assets and liabilities in a single entity, i.e. the bridge bank. More importantly, the tool would give more time to the resolution authority for marketing a rather large business, for which it is not to be excluded that the assets can be sold in different blocks to multiple acquirers.

Another case in which the application of the bridge bank tool can be a good solution is when a medium to small bank is earmarked for sale, but due to market turmoil it is not possible to find an acquirer to sign off the deal. This can happen for example when a bank fails as a consequence of a very bad performance, in a year in which the average performance is also rather poor. Most of the peers will be themselves trying to recover from a bad year and not certainly in the position to take over any additional business to reorganise. The same situation can also materialise after a first large bank failure. Although the failing bank is limitedly exposed or not exposed at all to the first failure, the market players will tend to turn into a wait and see mode. In such a situation, a bidding would likely go desert or result in very low bids. However, in both the cases the bank is fit for sale and actually prepared to undergo it, while the problem is just about bad timing. In this context, the bridge bank is the best solution to buy that additional time needed to sell the entity at a fair price.

6 The Loss Absorption Requirements

6.1 The Total Loss-Absorbing Capacity for G-SIBs

From the sections above it should be rather clear that resolution procedures come at certain costs. Resolution financing arrangements might provide additional resources for specific purposes (e.g. no creditor worse off compensations or asset protection schemes). However, most of the resolution funding needs to come from elsewhere. We have also examined that one of the resolution objectives is to avoid the recourse to taxpayers' money to rescue banks. If resolution financing arrangements can only provide a 'top-up' coverage and the option of public funds is out of table, the inherent consequence is that the costs will need to be internalised to the market.

This conclusion should not come as a surprise. When we presented the functioning of the bail-in tool, we demonstrated that most of the costs are confined to the bank and its investors, shareholders first, and then creditors. When we described the sale of business tool, we considered a likely write down of its capital followed by a downstream of cash from the acquirer. In this case also, losses are absorbed by shareholders, and potentially other creditors, should the write down be particularly extensive. Even more in the case of a bail-in, losses will be borne by shareholders and potentially other creditors, while some debt will be converted in new capital.

The reasoning seems to work very well: Public finances are saved from undue bailouts, the critical functions are continued, and most importantly the resolution tools come with a deterrent component and a clear disincentive to moral hazard. However, we cannot keep ignoring the elephant in the room. What if the liabilities to perform a write down or a bail-in are not there? Is this the weak spot of all our resolution regimes?

This question – far from being purely rhetoric – is supported by very basic considerations linked to the nature itself of certain banks' funding (i.e. its liabilities). First we need to observe that capital requirements – the ratios imposed by bank supervisors – have to do with exposures. However, write downs and bail-ins are performed not just on capital but also on liabilities. Are we sure that the 'right' liabilities will be there, ready to be written down or converted? We described above that the scope of bail-in and write down and conversion powers mandatorily excludes certain liabilities, such as retail deposits up to the level of protection. A bank with the most traditional business model we can imagine will collect deposits from retail clients and grant loans and mortgages. Deposits are a cheap and relatively stable source of funding.[37] For medium to small banks, it might be even unprofitable to seek additional funding by issuing tradable securities on financial markets, and they would prefer to rely on deposits only. However, should it be necessary to perform a resolution action on a medium-sized bank of this type, let us say to continue a critical function of deposit taking in the domestic economy, once written down the capital, the costs would be entirely shifted to deposit guarantee schemes, replacing covered depositors in the amount by which they would contribute to resolution. This outcome would be undesirable, as it would be too close to a bailout, as although formally in line with the rules of resolution, would substantially shift the costs outside the bank.

---

[37] This is a commonly accepted conclusion based on the fact (a) that deposits are remunerated at a lower interest than securities, (b) that their remuneration rates adapt more slowly to changes in market interest rates (Driscoll & Judson, 2013; Duquerroy et al., 2020), and (c) that they have been observed to display a relative stability in the medium-to-long term, with covered deposits also being relatively stable in times of crisis (Martin et al., 2016). For a descriptive comparison of deposits with other sources of funding, see also (Beau et al., 2014).

This is the reason why resolution regimes would be incomplete if they did not include requirements on the liability and funding structure banks should have in place as a cushion of resources ready for resolution. Furthermore, these requirements disincentivise too-big-to-fail behaviours, by requesting banks to have in place liabilities to be used in resolution, which is equivalent to offsetting the argument that a gap between assets and liabilities cannot be covered by a write down and conversion (Salleo, 2015; Brierley, 2017; Kazandjieva-Yordanova, 2017; Furukawa et al., 2021).

The idea is that considering all the uncertainties relating to the operational difficulties of applying write down and conversion powers or the bail-in tool to certain liability items as well as the presence of mandatorily excluded liabilities, banks should hold a subset of 'high quality' liabilities, which are ready at any times to contribute along with the own funds to absorb the losses and recapitalise the institution (on the point, see also Laboureix & Decroocq, 2016; Schiavo, 2016; Crosetti, 2018).

This is the rationale behind the publication in November 2015 of the Total Loss-Absorbing and Recapitalisation Capacity (TLAC) Term Sheet by the Financial Stability Board (FSB, 2015). The soft law principles included in this document are conceived for G-SIBs only, as long as in case of failure they pose the highest risks in terms of systemic stability and the difficulties with the coordination of resolution procedures across different jurisdictions globally, with multiple resolution authorities involved (Quaglia & Spendzharova, 2019). The TLAC requirements imposed in force of the legislation reflecting the 2015 Term Sheet are therefore limited to this subset of very large banks. In this paragraph we will outline the main features of these requirements, with the obvious caveat that the exact calibration for each institution will depend on bank-specific considerations as well as on the local legislation and policy operationalising the requirements.

A first important distinction is to be made between external and internal TLAC requirements. The external requirements are those imposed at the level of resolution group and they are aimed to ensure that the bank holds a sufficient amount of own funds and externally issued liabilities, which can be used for a write down or a bail-in. Internal requirements are instead imposed on non-resolution entities, and they concern their own funds and internally issued liabilities (i.e. liabilities of the non-resolution entities towards the resolution entity). The idea for internal requirements is that with the write down of capital instruments losses are transferred to the resolution entity, while the conversion of internally issued liabilities will provide for recapitalisation, without changes in the ownership structure (external creditors of the subsidiary are not affected by the internal write down and conversion).

External TLAC requirements are imposed on resolution entities at a consolidated level. The consolidation refers to the aggregate position in terms of assets and liabilities of the resolution entities and their subsidiaries or in other terms to the balance sheet and relevant metrics net of intragroup positions. You will remember the example made on the implementation of the bail-in tool for three entities in the same group. Consolidating means the same thing: looking at all the entities together as if they were one. The difference here is that we consider the resolution group as the level of consolidation, which may be only a part of the G-SIB (or the group in the commercial sense).

Internal TLAC requirements are imposed on material subsidiaries at a solo level or – if considered together with their own subsidiaries – on a sub-consolidated level. The sub-consolidation is equivalent in most aspects to the consolidation, with the difference that the intragroup positions of the entity or group of entities in respect of the parent are in this case not netted out. The non-resolution entity will therefore be treated as a single economic agent along with its own subsidiaries, but it will still have assets and liabilities on its balance sheet in respect of the parent.

A non-resolution entity and its subsidiaries, when considered together for the purposes of the internal TLAC, are referred to as a subgroup. To qualify for internal TLAC, non-resolution entities and subgroups need to meet at least one of the minimum thresholds. The FSB Term Sheet suggests four criteria. For being considered material from a group perspective, non-resolution entities or subgroups need to contribute for at least 5% to either the consolidated risk-weighted assets, the consolidated leverage exposures, or the consolidated operating income. Alternatively, they can still be considered material if they are assessed to decisively contribute to the provision of critical functions.

The Term Sheet also lays out minimum levels at which the TLAC requirements should be calibrated. External TLAC requirements need to be imposed at a minimum level of 18% of the consolidated risk-weighted assets and 6.75% of leverage ratio exposures (i.e. the exposures used as a denominator in the calculation of the leverage ratio under the Basel III framework). For the internal TLAC requirements, resolution authorities should instead consider values ranging from the 75% and the 90% of hypothetical external requirement material non-resolution entities and subgroups would be imposed if they were themselves resolution entities or groups.

In the consolidation for TLAC requirements, exposures to other resolution groups or entities are retained, as if the other resolution group or entity was an external actor. They will therefore be included in risk-weighted assets and leverage ratio exposures. Note that an asset on the balance sheet of an entity corresponds to a liability for the entity to which the former is exposed. Should this exposure correspond to an instrument which would be otherwise eligible to the TLAC of the issuer (e.g. a subordinated bond with sufficient residual maturity), the issuer, which is the other resolution entity or group, will need to deduct it from its TLAC resources. This is clear, because if written down these liabilities would pass losses across resolution groups without absorbing them.

A specific case is the deduction corresponding to instruments issued by a resolution entity to a parent which is also a resolution entity. Here the Term Sheet requires the relevant resolution authorities to decide together on the amount of the deduction from the external TLAC resources of the parent and the subsidiary, fixing however a minimum floor. For the parent, the deduction will correspond to the entire amount of these instruments otherwise meeting the TLAC eligibility conditions for the subsidiary minus the portion of the subsidiary's surplus against its minimum

TLAC requirement attributable to the parent.[38] The reason is that resources issued by a resolution entity to a parent that is also a resolution entity cannot be used to absorb the losses at the level of the former. Here again, losses would simply be passed between different resolution entities and the parent may need to provide additional resources for the subsidiary. However, if net of these liabilities issued to the parent, the subsidiary is still in surplus of its minimum external TLAC requirement, it would be disproportionate to make the parent discount from its TLAC capacity an extra coverage for the subsidiary. If the externally issued TLAC instruments of the subsidiary are above the external TLAC requirement for an amount that is greater than the sum of TLAC-eligible liabilities issued to the parent, it would mean that the subsidiary would not need to rely on these internal liabilities for meeting the requirement. Therefore, also at the parent's level there should be no deduction in the resources used to comply with external TLAC.

The Term Sheet also designed a phase-in for the TLAC requirements, also factoring changes in the population of G-SIBs. The general phase-in is now obsolete, as the fully phased-in requirements mentioned above were to be met by 1 January 2022.[39] One exception was considered to this timeline: G-SIBs headquartered in emerging market economies will need to meet their final minimum TLAC requirements by 1 January 2028.[40] In addition to that, the Term Sheet includes also 'grace periods' for specific situation. A bank designated as G-SIB for the first time will have 3 years to comply with the minimum TLAC requirements. This is because issuing instruments require a financial planning, which can only be performed over a reasonable time horizon. Instead, G-SIB that has undergone a conversion of liabilities as a recovery measure outside of resolution or has been subject to a resolution procedure (including possibly also a bridge bank resulting from the transfer of the G-SIB's assets and liabilities) will have a grace of period of 2 years from TLAC compliance, provided of course that they are still designated as a G-SIB. This is reasonable, as a conversion or resolution has already depleted TLAC resources to recapitalise the bank, and on the other hand a resolution procedure is not performed under the assumption that a second one will be needed 1 week later.

If what we described are the minimum amounts that G-SIBs need to hold in terms of TLAC, what are the instruments they can use to comply with them? As we

[38] Attributable to the parent means in proportion to the percentage ownership of the parent. For example, if the parent owns the 75% of the resolution entity, only the 75% of surplus will be considered in this calculation.

[39] To complement, lower intermediate requirements were set for 1 January 2019, corresponding to 16% of risk-weighted assets and 6% of leverage ratio exposures.

[40] In this case also the Term Sheet considers lower intermediate targets, to be met by 1 January 2025. The intermediate minimum target levels are the same as for the rest of G-SIBs in 2019. The Term Sheet also included a clause on the anticipation of the timeline if the outstanding bonds of corporates and financial institutions reached an amount corresponding to the 55% of the GDP of the relevant jurisdiction. As of 2019 the threshold was not met. However, the FSB did not undergo an extensive review, considering the commitments of the Chinese G-SIBs to meet their minimum TLAC requirements ahead of 2025 (FSB, 2019).

said above in this paragraph, the TLAC requirements are intended to constitute a buffer of high-quality resources that will be there ready to be used in resolution. To be a bit more precise, TLAC resources are made of own funds, which are with limited exceptions the same capital instruments used to comply with prudential requirements, and a large portion of debt instruments.

The capital instruments are considered on a consolidated or sub-consolidated basis, which means the overall capital of the externally issued capital instruments of the entity on which TLAC requirements are imposed and its subsidiaries. However, Additional Tier 1 and Tier 2 capital instruments issued by subsidiaries can count towards the external TLAC of the parent only if the resolution authorities conclude that they can effectively absorb the losses.

Debt instruments are instead considered at the level of the resolution entity, and they must be issued by the entity on which the requirements are imposed.[41] The debt instruments must be unsecured, fully paid in, not subject to set off or netting rights and should not be directly or indirectly funded by the resolution entity itself or any other entity of the same G-SIB (with the exception of the hypothesis of the instruments issued to a parent resolution entity discussed above).

TLAC instruments also need to be sufficiently stable. Hence the Term Sheet prescribes a minimum residual maturity of 1 year, unless of course the instrument is perpetual. When falling below this minimum maturity, the TLAC instruments should be in principle refunded or replaced by new instruments, in order not to deplete the TLAC resources. In principle, instruments used to meet the TLAC should not be redeemed before maturity. In many resolution regimes, should a G-SIB intend to redeem a TLAC-eligible instruments or perform operations of market making (i.e. buy and sell individual positions on their instruments), they would need to apply for a permission by resolution authorities.

Furthermore, capital or debt instruments issued in a country different from the country of incorporation[42] of the resolution entity can be accounted for the compliance with TLAC only as long as the resolution authorities conclude that they can effectively absorb the losses. As a matter of fact, to reach this conclusion, resolution authorities often ask resolution entities to produce an independent legal opinion on the enforceability of resolution powers and tools on the instruments at stake.

The instruments used to comply with TLAC should normally rank lower than the instruments that can be discretionary excluded from the application of the bail-in tool.[43] This subordination needs to be reflected in the contractual terms of the instruments and also in the balance sheet structure of the resolution entity issuing

---

[41] An exception exists for debt instruments issued by a directly and fully owned funding entity prior to 1 January 2022, should resolution authorities conclude that they are fit to absorb losses.

[42] Note however that in EU on the back of a common legal framework to be considered as instruments issued in a different jurisdiction are only those issued in a country that is not a Member State of the Union (i.e. third countries).

[43] More correctly, to the instruments that the Term Sheet itself identifies as exclusions, which are covered deposits, sight and short -erm deposits, derivatives, derivative-linked debt instruments,

them. As we have already clarified, the key goal of TLAC is to create a buffer of resources to be used in resolution. If they overlapped with excluded liabilities, they could not be effectively used because after a certain critical point they would give raise to breaches of the no-creditor-worse-off principle. However, the subordination is not considered mandatory if cumulatively the excluded liabilities do not exceed TLAC instruments by 5% and the resolution authorities conclude that this does not negatively impact resolvability and there is no material risk of compensations due to the no-creditor-worse-off principle. Another hypothesis in which the subordination is not required is when the instruments that the Term Sheet excludes from TLAC are also mandatorily excluded from bail-in. This is rarely the case, because among those instruments we find derivatives and derivative-linked instruments. In most resolution regimes they are indicated as subject to discretional exclusion, but not mandatorily excluded, and they rank along other unsecured senior debt instruments. In these cases, the Term Sheet foresees an allowance for instruments ranking pari passu with instruments subject to discretionary exclusions for an amount corresponding to up to 3.5% of consolidated risk-weighted assets. Finally, a resolution entity should deduct from their TLAC resources any amounts of otherwise eligible instruments, corresponding to the holding of another G-SIB. To say it more simply, if a resolution entity of a G-SIB has 150bn of eligible subordinated and out of these 20bn are hold by other G-SIBs, only 130bn will qualify for TLAC.

In short and to facilitate the understanding of our reader, the instruments likely to be eligible to TLAC are CET1 instruments, Additional Tier 1 and Tier 2 instruments, subordinated bonds, and senior instruments up to the maximum allowance. To alleviate the issue of unsecured senior debt ranking pari passu with instruments that might be discretionally excluded from the application of the bail-in tool, in many countries an additional layer of debt has been created in recent years, with the so-called senior non-preferred bonds, which rank senior to traditional subordinated bonds but junior to senior bonds. The instruments eligible to the internal TLAC requirements have the same characteristics of those eligible for the eternal TLAC, with the difference that the debt component is issued towards the resolution entity and not externally. For the internal TLAC, the Term Sheet also provides for the option to meet the requirements with collateralised guarantees from the resolution entity concerning the recapitalisation of the subsidiary at stake. However, the use of guarantees to meet internal TLAC is subject to numerous conditions and the collateral posted for the guarantee cannot then be used again as collateral by the resolution entity. As a matter of fact, for the resolution entity it might be therefore easier and possibly more convenient to preposition the resources needed to comply with the internal requirements. This means that in addition to the capital instruments already owned, the parent will subscribe some additional debt issued by the non-resolution entity.

---

liabilities that do not arise from a contract, such as tax liabilities, secured liabilities, and any other liabilities to which a jurisdiction confers special protection in insolvency.

Regarding TLAC there is one last aspect to clarify. We explained above that prudential requirements imposed by supervision authorities concern capital, whereas TLAC requirements deal with both capital and debt instruments. If this is the case, what is the interplay between the two types of requirements, considering that capital instruments will in both cases be in scope? In general, capital instruments can at the same time count towards prudential and TLAC requirements, with a single notable exception. CET1 instruments used to meet capital buffers cannot be used to meet TLAC requirements. Capital buffers do not represent the integrity of prudential requirements; they are just one component of it. Many supervision authorities impose a combined buffer requirements, which in turns is made of different buffers, including the specific buffer for G-SIBs. We can therefore say that the TLAC requirements need to be met in addition to the combined buffer requirement, in the sense that effectively the TLAC capacity of a resolution entity, made as we said of CET1 and other instruments ranking senior to CET1, will need to be sufficient to cover at the same time the TLAC minimum requirements and the combined buffer requirements.

6.2 The MREL

If we talk about loss absorption requirements, we cannot avoid to make reference to the minimum requirement of eligible liabilities and own funds (MREL) provided under the EU BRRD framework and implemented also in country where the resolution regime is inspired by the BRRD.[44] The MREL requirements have been somehow a cornerstone in the development of resolution regimes, as in their first setting they appeared already 1 year before the publication of the FSB Term Sheet.

One of the key features of the MREL requirements is that they apply to all banks, not just to G-SIBs. Under this perspective, it is possible to say that the European Union has been particularly attentive in making sure that banks have sufficient resources to undergo a resolution or a liquidation procedure without the need of external support. Initially expressed as an amount to be maintained in capital and debt instruments in percentage of the total liabilities and own funds, the MREL has been subsequently revised in 2019 to have an overall implant symmetrical to the TLAC requirements. The current MREL requirements, in the same way as TLAC, are also expressed as percentages of risk-weighted assets and leverage ratio exposures. Similarly to TLAC, the MREL requirements are external if imposed to the resolution entity and internal if imposed on non-resolution entities.

---

[44] A key example is the United Kingdom, where the BRRD architecture was maintained in their legislation after the exit from the European Union. The United Kingdom also unilaterally implemented the update of the BRRD of 2019, which effectively concerned MREL mainly. On the developments of UK regulation after Brexit, refer to James and Quaglia (2020).

Considering the wide scope of entities subject to MREL requirements, the specific calibration for banks will depend on a number of specificities related to the organisation, business model, and the envisaged strategy upon failure. In this brief overview we will not pretend to be exhaustive as to the all possible outcomes and adjustments of the MREL requirements, but we will concentrate on the key features.[45]

The MREL has two main components: the loss absorption amount and the recapitalisation amount. After outlining the functioning of the bail-in tool and of the write down and conversion power, it will not be difficult for the reader to understand the reason behind this bi-fold structure. The first component is to provide for the write down, as losses are absorbed through the sequential cancellation of the outstanding amount of capital and debt instruments, up to a level at which assets and liabilities are again in equilibrium. The second component of the requirement is instead to make it possible to have instruments ready to be converted into new capital.

There is, however, an exception to this rule. For the banks that are envisaged to be liquidated upon failure, for example because none of their functions is material enough to be critical, the MREL will be limited to the loss absorption amount. This is logical, given that there is no need to recapitalise an entity that will be liquidated. One may think at first that the banks for which the preferred resolution strategy should have an MREL set in the same terms, considering that the recapitalisation function will be taken over by an acquirer or a bridge bank.

However, the BRRD foresees for these banks as well an MREL with the two components. The reason for that lays evidently in the need for resolution authorities to have the maximum possible flexibility in the actual decision concerning the application of resolution tools, despite the preferred resolution strategy designed in the resolution plans. When a bank is assessed to be a liquidation entity, it is likely that this assessment will not suddenly change upon resolution. The assessment of critical functions is performed annually, and it should not be expected to change from one day to the other when a bank becomes failing.[46] By contrast, the preferred resolution strategy is a presumptive path that does not bind resolution authorities in their decisions on the use of resolution tools. Differently from the provision of critical functions, which tends to be stable over time, the circumstances in which a bank fails may be often unexpected and not reflect the assumptions made in the planning phase. Hence the need to have a 'complete' MREL for all banks earmarked

[45] The reader interested to get a more in-depth knowledge of the MREL can refer directly to the BRRD or read the SRB MREL Policy, updated annually and available on the institutional website. At the time this chapter is drafted, we refer to the 2023 version, available at https://www.srb.europa.eu/en/content/mrel.

[46] Note however that this is only an expectation. In a real case, a bank earmarked for liquidation can ultimately be resolved in case new evidence appears to support this conclusion. A recent and notable example is the one of the UK subsidiary of Silicon Valley Bank. Although considered a liquidation entity in resolution planning, in March 2023 – when the parent entity failed – it was subject to resolution on a standalone basis and acquired by HSBC.

for resolution, regardless of the preferred strategy. The amounts at which the loss absorption and the recapitalisation amounts, as a baseline, are each of one set equal to the prudential requirements, excluding capital buffers. As for TLAC and with the same approach for CET1 instruments, the MREL requirement expressed as a percentage of TREA will need to be met in addition to capital buffers. Here also, the choice of the BRRD reflects a common sense approach. In fact, capital requirements and buffers are themselves designed to absorb losses. Banks need to hold capital instruments in a measure that the supervisor assesses as prudent. An institution will be in breach of them when after losses their capital falls below the minimum level. Now, a bank will be declared failed or likely to fail only if there is no prospect of returning viable, but hopefully not so late to completely deplete the capital used to absorb losses. Hence, capital requirements are a good reference level for a cushion of capital used to absorb losses.

With a recapitalisation, banks will need to comply again with the prudential requirements. So once again the amount to take into consideration is the one prescribed by prudential requirements. In short, the default calibration of MREL will correspond – net of the buffers – to twice the prudential requirements, but with the difference that the MREL will be complied with not only with capital but also with certain debt instruments. To give an idea of the levels we are talking about, under Basel III terms the minimum leverage ratio requirement is equivalent to the 3% of the leverage ratio exposures. The risk-weighted requirement has itself two components, denominated Pillar 1 and Pillar 2. The Pillar 1 requirement in the EU amounts to a value corresponding to the 8% of risk-weighted assets. The Pillar 2 requirement is bank-specific and reflects market conditions.

To give an order of magnitude, within the Eurozone, in 2023 the average Pillar 2 requirement of the institutions directly supervised by the European Central Bank was 2.24% of risk-weighted assets.[47] Given this average, a hypothetical baseline calibration of the MREL requirement corresponding to twice the capital requirements will be equivalent to 20.48% of risk-weighted assets and 6% of leverage ratio exposures.[48]

Now, what we have constantly repeated when describing the resolution tools is that the balance sheet post-resolution will be very different from the one of the banks before resolution. The metrics of today are only a proxy of what they will look like in the future. In particular, defaulted assets will no longer be there. As capital

[47] Pillar 2 requirements are disclosed by the European Central Bank on the institutional website. This average has been calculated by us based on the 8 February 2023 update.

[48] As a side note for the reader, we want to highlight that one should not be surprised by the difference in the percentages, almost 20.5% for the risk-based requirement in addition to buffers and 6% for the non-risk-based requirement. Risk-weighted assets are typically (and should be) very low compared to total assets, as some assets are accounted with weights lower than 100%, in some cases even equal to 0%, for exposures with very low credit risk. By contrast, leverage ratio exposures are roughly equivalent or a bit higher than total assets. In practical terms, except very specific cases, the absolute amounts of the risk-based and non-risk-based MREL requirements are typically not too far away one of the other.

requirements themselves are calibrated based on the exposures, risk-weighted and non-risk-weighted, it should be expected that even with an unchanged percentage their amount after resolution will be somehow lower.

This is the reason why the rules on the MREL contemplate possible adjustments to the recapitalisation amount. For example, they offer the possibility of performing an adjustment to the values of risk-weighted assets and leverage ratio exposures used in the calculation of the recapitalisation amount[49] to consider a balance sheet depletion effect. This adjustment is precisely meant to reflect a shrinking of the balance sheet after resolution to losses before resolution. However it will only be applied in cases of a net prevalence of credit risk in the overall amount of risk-weighted exposures. This condition reflects the fact that a total default of an asset will only follow the insolvency of their counterparty. By contrast, a depreciation will not affect too negatively the balance sheet if the assets are retained.[50] For changes in the balance sheet post-resolution due to the transfer of business segments or the entire activities after a write down of capital, the recapitalisation amount can instead factor a transfer strategies adjustment. Here also the risk-weighted assets and leverage ratio exposures are corrected by a scaling factor reflecting the effective scope of the transfer and ranging between 15 and 25%.[51] Differently from the balance sheet depletion effect, the adjustment for transfer strategies can only be applied to the external requirements. In principle there are other adjustments that may be applied to the risk-weighted assets and leverage ratio exposures used for the calculation of the recapitalisation amount. These adjustments pertain to the existence of restructuring plan or the possibility to implement recovery options before the entry into resolution. Under the EU State Aid Framework, where it is assessed that external support is provided to a bank, it will be necessary for the EU Commission to approve a restructuring plan[52] before granting the authorisation. Where this restructuring plan envisages a mandatory dismissal of certain activities,

---

[49] Note that the amount calculated based on prudential requirements and lower values of risk-weighted assets and leverage exposures will be added on top of the loss absorption amount and then expressed as a percentage of reported risk-weighted assets and leverage ratio exposures without adjustments.

[50] The reader will be familiar in these times with the depreciation of bonds following a rise in interest rates. As their market value decreases, an effective loss will materialise only if the holder is forced to sale. The sale of widely depreciated long-term US Treasury bonds to cover the withdrawn of deposits was the main cause of the failure of Silicon Valley Bank in the State of California. However, if a holder is not forced to sale a depreciated bond, this will maintain by contract its book value and will be repaid at maturity.

[51] Maintain by contract its book value and it will be repaid at maturity, which means that risk-based and non-risk-based exposures used for the calibration of the recapitalisation amount will be multiplied by (1 – the scaling factor), i.e. by a value between 75 and 85%.

[52] Pay attention to the terminology. Restructuring plan has a precise meaning in relation to the State Aid Framework. It is not a synonym of neither recovery plan, resolution plan, nor business reorganisation plan. The latter, in particular, is the plan prepared for the reorganisation after the implementation of a bail-in tool. In practice, restructuring and reorganisation may be often confused in the use by non-specialists or people not familiar with the EU legislative framework.

the relevant metrics will be subject to an adjustment to reflect this divestment. The assumption is that up to resolution the divestment might be delayed, with the consequent need to absorb losses, whereas in resolution the divestment process will be accelerated. As a matter of fact however, considering the clear disincentives posed by the BRRD to any form of State Aid and the fact that at the adoption of the new MREL in 2019 almost 10 years had passed from the last bailouts in the EU, this adjustment has never been applied.

Another hypothesis is to adjust the risk-weighted assets and leverage ratio exposures used to set the recapitalisation amount based on the recovery options that are likely to be used in the lead up to resolution. For example, if the bank in recovery implements de-risking and deleveraging strategies, the risk-based and non-risk-based exposures will decrease as an effect of these options. However, factoring this adjustment in the computation of the MREL requirements is very challenging, for two reasons at least. First, the use of recovery options must undergo a test of credibility and feasibility in all scenarios, both idiosyncratic and systemic. It is very hard indeed to conceive a measure that will be always implementable, regardless of the circumstances. Second, resolution authorities themselves have been very cautious in applying this adjustment, considering that reality often overcomes the human capabilities of scenario analysis. A failure might always occur in circumstances in which the expected measures to be implemented will not be any longer applicable.

The adjustments due to binding divestments or recovery options might be upwards or downwards depending on the expected impact of these operations on the relevant metrics. The balance sheet depletion and transfer strategies adjustments will instead always have a deflective effect. By contrast, resolution authorities may still apply two exclusively upward adjustments. Both of these adjustments concern only the external requirements and each one of them is applicable only to a single leg, either the risk-based or the non-risk-based requirement.[53]

On the risk-based side, resolution authorities may impose a so-called market confidence charge. We saw that the recapitalisation amount is proportional to the prudential requirements, although risk-weighted assets may be considered on a 'depleted' basis. However, if you think about it, prudential requirements fix a minimum level of capital instruments to be hold to continue to operate. However, a bank with the barely minimum capital would risk due to minimum changes in the underlying metrics to end up in breach of the requirements. Rather than being per se an issue (a temporary breach can still be remediated in a short-time horizons with minimum direct consequences for a bank), a breach of the requirements may trigger a loss of confidence towards the bank. We are talking in particular about a post-resolution bank. How would you react if you read that a bank that was resolved 1 month ago is in breach of the requirements? To avoid this unpleasant situation, the

[53] We omit in this section the specific adjustments due to strategies entailing multiple points of entry, given their inherent level of complexity. At a high level, we can however say that these adjustments reflect the same logic of the TLAC deductions.

adjustment adds a charge to make sure that the bank holds enough instruments to ensure a recapitalisation beyond the minimum levels set by prudential requirements. The market confidence charge is roughly equivalent in amount to the combined buffer requirement, calculated on the basis of the hypothetical post-resolution risk-weighted assets and further subject to marginal corrections.

On the non-risk-based leg, resolution authorities may increase the requirement up to a level corresponding to 8% of total liabilities and own funds (i.e. the whole balance sheet), where a level of 6% of leverage ratio exposures (balance sheet and off-balance sheet exposures) did not reach it already. This reference level is an echo of the first MREL, which as we said was imposed as a percentage of total liabilities and own funds. This adjustment needs to be grounded in reasons concerning financial stability and recapitalisation needs. The attentive eye will also recognise that an 8% of total liabilities and own funds is also the minimum level of write down or bail-in to be performed to allow the resolution financing mechanisms to contribute with their compensations. Second, as we will examine further below, certain banks also need to meet a subordination requirement corresponding to this reference level of 8% of total liabilities and own funds, which would not otherwise be effective without an overall MREL somewhere below that level.

In practical terms, when a bank is imposed MREL requirements, it will need to ensure to have MREL resources in excess of the highest between the risk-based (when considered in addition to capital buffers) and the non-risk-based requirements. However, one should bear in mind that both requirements remain applicable. It may well be possible – and it has been already the case – that risk-weighted assets and leverage exposures evolve in with different trends. Due to an asymmetrical evolution, after a certain critical point, one requirement may overcome the other as the biting leg. In any case, MREL requirements have been annually revised based on reported metrics and this will continue to be the case after their full phase-in as of 1 January 2024.[54]

In terms of eligibility, the rules do not differ much from those of TLAC, and we will not go through it in this section.[55] The main difference that we need to flag is that the overall external and internal MREL requirements can also be complied with senior instruments without a fixed limit. This means that senior unsecured bonds will in many cases be a material part of the MREL resources.[56]

There is however a part of the external MREL requirements that needs to be met with instruments of rank lower to senior unsecured debt. This part goes under the

[54] Lower intermediate requirements had to be met as of 1 January 2022. Resolution authorities have however faculty of deviating from the default transition period for specific reasons, mainly related to the timing for market access and the availability of MREL resources.

[55] The reader interested to have a precise view on MREL-eligible liabilities can refer to Article 45b BRRD.

[56] Note however that for the internal MREL, due to the need of performing an internal write down and conversion limiting potential no-creditor-worse-off issues, subordinated instruments are better placed to comply with the requirement.

name of subordination component and it is an integral part of the MREL requirement (hence the reason why it is also referred to as subordination requirement).

Subordination requirements will differ depending on the allocation of banks in three categories. The three categories are G-SIBs, Top-Tier, and Other banks. G-SIBs need to comply with a minimum level of subordination[57] equivalent to 18% of risk-weighted assets (in addition to the CBR) and 6.75% of leverage ratio exposures. It can be easily recognised that these targets are the same used for TLAC requirements. In addition to the minimum level of subordination, G-SIBs need to maintain an overall level of subordinated resources equivalent to the reference level of 8% of total liabilities and own funds. In this case, the BRRD allows the double-counting of CET1 instruments for capital buffers and the subordination at this reference level of 8%.[58]

Top-Tier banks are by default the banks having more than EUR 100bn of assets. All banks not being G-SIBs or Top-Tier are consequently classified as other banks. Top-Tier banks are subject to a minimum level of subordination corresponding to 13.5% of risk-weighted assets (in addition to capital buffers) and 5% of leverage ratio exposures. Top-Tier banks also need to ensure an overall level of subordinated resources at least equivalent to 8% of total liabilities and own funds. However, differently from G-SIBs, for Top-Tier banks this 8% reference level is capped at a second reference level corresponding to 27% of risk-weighted assets.

The 8% reference level for G-SIBs and Top-Tier banks can be further subject to adjustments upwards or downwards in line with formulas predefined in the legislation. The adjustments to the 8% reference level are linked to the progress on resolvability. However, these adjustments remain a discretionary option, which means that banks are not entitled to them. Also in the presence of a fully satisfactory progress on resolvability, the resolution authority may still impose a full 8% reference level unadjusted (provided of course that it is not capped for Top-Tiers by the above mentioned 27% reference level).

The Other banks are not subject in principle to a minimum level of subordination. However, resolution authorities may impose a subordination requirement should it be necessary to cover specific risks of breach of the no-creditor worse off principle (e.g. due to a material internal write down and conversion or due to a

[57] The minimum level of subordination is also referred to as Pillar 1 subordination, where Pillar 1 stands for G-SIBs and Top-Tier banks. We prefer however not to use this definition, as it may create confusion with Pillar 1 prudential requirement. Furthermore, the definition of Pillar 1 subordination has no legal relevance, but it is only a practice.

[58] As a practical consequence, the amount corresponding to 8% of total liabilities and own funds will be expressed in full as a percentage of leverage ratio exposures, but as a percentage of risk-weighted assets the same amount will be deducted of the amount corresponding to the combined buffer requirement. This way, also on the risk-weighted leg, it is possible to conciliate the provision of an overall level of subordination corresponding to 8% of total liabilities and own funds with the subordination being an integral part of the MREL requirement, to be met in addition to capital buffers.

material portion of liabilities that might be discretionally excluded). In this case, the subordination requirement will be proportional to the risks to cover.

Resolution authorities have also the possibility to treat a bank classified as Other as if it were a Top-Tier bank, should its failure entail substantial systemic risk. However, in making this decision resolution authorities need to be mindful of the funding model of the bank – if for example it is mainly funded through deposits with consequent need of performing several and material issuance to meet a full subordination requirement – the prevalence of CET1 capital in their MREL supply and the effective ability of the institution to access financial markets (on the optimal composition of loss-absorbing capacity see Mendicino, Nikolov and Suarez 2017). To alleviate the consequences of the passage to the Top-Tier treatment either in the change in the classification due to an asset increase or a decision of the resolution authority, a grace period of three years is provided for meeting the subordination component. This should give enough time to the concerned bank to gradually build up its subordination resources.

In terms of eligibility, we still need to complement with some options concerning the internal MREL requirements. As for internal TLAC, internal MREL requirements may be compiled with guarantees provided by the parent company. In addition, for internal MREL requirements there is also a possibility of waiving their application. However, both these options are based on a number of conditions (such as the parent and the subsidiaries being established in the same country, the absence of any material impediment to the prompter transfer of funds or specific features guarantees need to have), which made these two options an exception rather than the rule.

A specific treatment is also foreseen for cooperative groups. These groups are often organised in a structure with a central body and a number of entities affiliated to this central body. The affiliated entities have each their own local cooperative shareholders.[59] Within these groups, although the management functions are located at the central body, this one is owned by the affiliated entities. We therefore face

[59] We need to add that the shares of a cooperative bank are not profit-oriented, which means that profits are not distributed, and they are not listed. In principle, to be client of a cooperative bank, a person needs also to be a member of the bank, by the purchase of a share. The holdings of shares of cooperative banks are nominative and limited in number (in some cases even to a single share per client). Some jurisdictions also have (or had in the past) limitations as to the residence of the members, which should not be outside a certain maximum radius from the headquarters of the cooperative bank. This is because cooperative banks, in the tradition opened in the XIX by Friedrich Wilhelm Raiffeisen (cooperative rural and artisanal banks) and Franz Hermann Schulze-Delitzsch (people banks for the middle class), rather than profit-making organisation are treated by the legislation as a form of self-organisation of certain social classes to access credit services. In many EU countries people banks have been gradually assimilated by law to ordinary commercial banks and lost their cooperative corporate form. Cooperative banks coming from the rural and artisanal tradition are still in existence in many EU countries, with notable examples in Austria, France, Germany and Italy, although they have formed (or have been forced to form) large confederations at a national level. It is worth noting that the French Crédit Agricole is also classified as a G-SIB.

a sort of opposite ownership structure often referred to as 'inverted pyramid'. To further complicate the picture, affiliated entities normally would not access financial markets, with the debt instruments issued by the central body itself or dedicated entities. However, these groups have also solidarity mechanisms and cross-guarantee schemes in place, where each affiliated member is unlimitedly tied to the other companies. The BRRD foresees that in cases the solidarity bonds are so strong that the group as a whole can be considered as practically a 'single entity' from a financial standpoint, the external MREL – subject to a number of other conditions – will need to complied with all the eligible instruments issued by any of the group entities. This approach goes under the name of network eligibility. When this treatment is granted, the affiliated entities[60] will not be imposed an internal MREL requirement; however, their eligible instruments may concur to the MREL capacity of the group.[61] In concrete terms, the MREL capacity will be accounted including the cooperative shares at the level of all affiliated entities along with any eligible instrument at their level, along with the debt instruments centrally issued on behalf of the whole group.

Nevertheless, it should not be assumed that by default a cooperative group will be subject to a network eligibility treatment. The possibility of granting this treatment is assessed on a case by case basis, and ultimately conditioned by the establishment of a solidarity mechanism across the affiliated entities and the central body strongly enough that for real the whole group can be considered as a single debtor. This can be achieved by affiliation rules providing that all the group entities are jointly liable to external creditors (situation referred to as joint and several liability) or mutual guarantee schemes – often with a segregated fund – by which affiliated entities will automatically cover each other in case of imbalances. From a resolution point of view, the presence of this unlimited solidarity across entities has two practical consequences. First, the solvency and liquidity position of any of the entities will always correspond to the solvency and liquidity of the entire group, with losses automatically centralised, with no risk of no creditor worse off issues as in the case in which losses are centralised through a write down and conversion. Secondly, all the group entities jointly considered are either still solvent and liquid or they are not. In this second case, all the entities will be failing or likely to fail simultaneously. This is why for cooperative groups structured in this way the MREL is imposed as if the group was a single entity. However, in case the assessment of the conditions for granting this treatment does not go in this direction, a cooperative group will be subject to a 'default' MREL approach with external and internal requirements. In

[60] It should be noted that when this treatment is granted, it is applied strictly to affiliated entities. Subsidiaries of these entities that are not themselves directly affiliated to the cooperative group, will in any case need to comply with internal MREL requirements, should the minimum thresholds for a requirement be met.

[61] This goes hand in hand with the possibility of applying a coordinated bail-in simultaneously to all the entities in the cooperative group, where within each rank own funds or eligible liabilities are written down or converted on a pro rata basis throughout the whole group.

this case, it will still be possible to waive single relevant entities from the application of the internal MREL.

7 Ongoing Resolution Planning, Resolvability Assessment and Testing

A final important remark concerning the key concepts and tools of bank resolution concerns the ongoing work of banks and resolution authorities. In this chapter we have often anticipated that an extensive work takes place before the actual implementation of a resolution action. This preliminary work can be classified into three main areas:

(a) Resolution planning
(b) Resolvability assessment
(c) Resolution testing

These three main regular areas are in turn accompanied by a number of ad hoc activities, such as specific on-site inspections, deep dives, or thematic assessment, the details of which we do not enter in this chapter.

With resolution planning we refer to the preparation of resolution plans, i.e. the guiding documents describing the presumptive path to be followed in case of a crisis (see KA 11 and Annex 4 of Appendix I). With reference to the resolution plans, we need to mark a distinction between the United States and the jurisdictions subject or with a legal framework similar to the EU BRRD. In the United States resolution plans are prepared by banks themselves, with the resolution authority overseeing them. Under the BRRD instead, resolution authorities themselves draft and regularly update resolution plans. The update takes place at least annually or after any material change to the institution. Whatever is the approach followed, the preparation and update of resolution plans entails the continuous cooperation and exchange of information between banks and resolution authorities, which have also provided guidance about what they expect from banks for resolution planning, such as in the Resolution Handbook by the FDIC (FDIC, 2019) or the Introduction to Resolution Planning by the SRB (SRB, 2016, but see also the Resolution Planning Cycle booklets published annually on the SRB Website).

Resolution plans include all the bank-specific information necessary to implement a resolution tools as well as the envisaged process (normally complemented by separate playbooks). However, in order to allow for the implementation of the measures included in the plan, banks adapt their organisation and business and develop specific capabilities, in light of what we referred to in 3.c. as resolvability. In concrete, banks will take action on the policy guidance provided by resolution authorities (e.g. BoE, 2019, or SRB, 2020) and put in place a series of measures to ensure crisis readiness. Resolution authorities assess the progress made by banks on their guidance through the resolvability assessment (KA 10). As for resolution planning, the resolvability assessment is an annual task. Once again, with the legislation remaining on a high level for the resolvability assessment, resolution authorities themselves have developed their approaches to the assessment, such as the Resolvability Assessment Framework of the Bank of England (See SS4/19 and related policy documents.) or the Resolvability Assessment and Heat-map of the SRB (SRB 2022).

What would happen in case the progress of a bank is insufficient to deem it resolvable? In this case, mechanisms are in place allowing resolution authorities to adopt authoritative measures also in going concerns, which – where relevant and if provided for in the legislation – may be accompanied by sanctions or penalties. The BRRD for example, although in lack of sanction powers, confers to resolution authorities the power to remove substantive impediments to resolvability (for the concept of substantive impediments, see Bodellini 2019). In reality, a formal substantive impediment is rather rare. For example, in 8 years of existence the SRB has never adopted one. There are at least two motivations for the absence so far of these formal procedures. On the first level (see Gortsos 2021), developing policies and guidance documents has been up until recent times an ongoing process. The multi-annual transition period for the SRB Expectations for Banks – with additional pieces of guidance being published year by year – was concluded only at the end of 2023. It should be therefore considered that in the first place banks were given the opportunity to spontaneously comply with the SRB expectations. Opportunity that brings us to the second motivation, i.e. the simple fact that banks have generally spontaneously complied with the SRB expectations and disclosed – to various extents and with different levels of granularity – the progress made on resolvability in their annual report. It could be hypothesised the presence itself of a substantive impediment procedure and the potential stigma attached to it has been a sufficient deterrent against non-compliance. At this more mature stage however, especially in cases of delayed progress or unaddressed issues, it should not be excluded that substantive impediment procedures may be adopted. This is because the majority of banks by now have had the time to develop all the necessary capabilities in order to be resolvable.

The 'maturity' of the resolvability expectations has also another implication, pertaining to the third area of ongoing work of resolution authorities and banks. If banks and resolution plans are ready – or almost ready – for the implementation of a resolution scheme, would it not make sense to perform some sort of simulation? This is effectively the latest frontier of resolution regimes, which are increasingly oriented towards resolution testing. The SRB for example has disclosed in the Work Programmes for 2022 and 2023 (SRB, 2021b, 2023) its gradual approach towards resolution testing, with the first dry-runs taking place in the late 2022 to assess whether banks were effectively able to timely deliver accurate data for valuation purposes and for the implementation of a bail-in tool. Starting from data delivery, resolution testing should progressively extend to other areas, with the ultimate goal of completing a fully fledged simulation of a resolution weekend.

It goes without saying a complete simulation for large cross-border groups will be particularly challenging due to the necessary cooperation between authorities in different jurisdictions. However, forms of cooperation on an ongoing basis already exist for resolution planning purposes and for the adoption of the loss absorption requirements. These forms of cooperation go under the name of crisis management groups, and they are roughly the equivalent for bank resolution of supervisory colleges. In an actual crisis, the crisis management college will be called to coordinate the actual resolution action. It is therefore not too difficult to think that the mandate of these groups in the future could also entail resolution testing. And this future may not be too far away, considering that the FSB report on the best practices of crisis management groups (FSB 2021) indicates that effectively some of them 'are planning to carry out resolution readiness testing activities between authorities, including dry-runs and simulation exercises'.

Conclusively, resolution planning, resolvability assessment, and resolution testing are the three main areas of work of resolution authorities in regular times. After years of work on resolution plans and resolvability, times seem to be ready for a progressive shift of focus towards testing. This does not mean that resolution plans or resolvability assessments will not be updated (in the BRRD – as we said – there is a legal requirement for annual updates); however, more resources should be freed up for testing, which in turn has itself the preconditions for becoming a recurrent exercise. In analogy to what happens for stress tests for banking supervision, the natural changing of times will entail new scenarios and challenges not sufficiently catered for in previous exercises, but that would equally deserve testing as to the feasibility of a resolution action.

Conclusion

Banks are likely to continue playing a pivotal role in the financial system and the broader economy – at least in the short run. They will continue aggregating the savings of households and firms and lend to individuals, businesses, and governments. This function is crucial for economic output, as it would be significantly lower if businesses had to finance investments themselves or individuals had to rely on their savings alone.

As we have discussed in great detail, banks remain in essence intermediaries between depositors and borrowers. They take in funds – called deposits – from those with money, pool them, and lend them to those who need funds. This process involves maturity transformation – converting short-term liabilities (deposits) to long-term assets (loans).

However, the banking system is not without its failures. Banks can fail when they are unable to meet their obligations to their depositors or other creditors. This is where regulation comes in. Prudential regulation is designed to promote bank profitability and avoid bank failures, thereby protecting taxpayers and the stability of the financial system. In the event of a bank failure, regulators usually insure bank deposits up to a limit. By guaranteeing deposits, deposit insurance is intended to prevent bank runs and promote financial stability.

Despite these safeguards, bank failures can still occur. When they do, they can have significant impacts on the economy. Therefore, it is crucial for policymakers and regulators to continue monitoring the banking sector closely and take necessary actions to prevent such failures. Bank safety and soundness are a major public policy concern, and government policies have been designed to limit bank failures and the panic they can ignite.

In most countries, banks need a charter to carry out banking activities and to be eligible for government backstop facilities – such as emergency loans from the central bank and explicit guarantees to insure bank deposits up to a certain amount. Banks are regulated by the laws of their home country and are typically subject to regular supervision. If banks are active abroad, they may also be regulated by

N. Abidi et al., *Why Do Banks Fail and What to Do About It*, Contributions to Finance and Accounting, https://doi.org/10.1007/978-3-031-52311-3

the host country. Regulators have broad powers to intervene in troubled banks to minimize disruptions.

Regulations are generally designed to limit banks' exposures to credit, market, and liquidity risks and to overall solvency risk. Banks are now required to hold more and higher-quality equity – for example, in the form of retained earnings and paid-in capital – to buffer losses than they were before the GFC. Large global banks must hold even more capital to account for the potential impact of their failure on the stability of the global financial system (also known as systemic risk). Regulations also stipulate minimum levels of liquid assets for banks and prescribe stable, longer-term funding sources.

Regulators are reviewing the growing importance of institutions that provide bank-like functions but that are not regulated in the same fashion as banks – so-called shadow banks or FinTechs – and looking at options for regulating them. Over the last two decades, financial crises exposed the systemic importance of institutions, such as finance companies, investment banks, and money market mutual funds. Bearing this in mind, it is logical to consider that a significant climate event or cyber incident presents a considerable risk to financial stability. It is not about whether it will happen, but rather when.

References

Abedifar, P., Tarazi, A., & White, L. J. (2022). The sale of failed banks: The characteristics of acquirers—as well as of the acquired–matter. Available at SSRN 3983380.

Acharya, V., Drechsler, I., & Schnabl, P. (2014). A pyrrhic victory? Bank bailouts and sovereign credit risk. *The Journal of Finance, 69*(6), 2689–2739.

Acharya, V. V., Anginer, D., & Warburton, A. J. (2016). The end of market discipline? Investor expectations of implicit government guarantees. *Investor Expectations of Implicit Government Guarantees*. Available at SSRN: https://ssrn.com/abstract=1961656 or http://dx.doi.org/10.2139/ssrn.1961656.

Acharya, V. V., & Yorulmazer, T. (2007). Too many to fail—an analysis of time-inconsistency in bank closure policies. *Journal of Financial Intermediation, 16*(1), 1–31.

Acquisti, A., Grossklags, J., et al. (2007). What can behavioral economics teach us about privacy. *Digital Privacy: Theory, Technologies and Practices, 18*, 363–377.

Adrian, T., & Shin, H. S. (2010). The changing nature of financial intermediation and the financial crisis of 2007–2009. *Annual Review of Economics, 2*(1), 603–618.

Aghion, P., Akcigit, U., & Howitt, P. (2015). The Schumpeterian growth paradigm. *Economics, 7*(1), 557–575.

Alessandri, P., & Haldane, A. G. (2009). *Banking on the State* (Vol. 6). Bank of England London.

Allen, F., & Gale, D. (1997). Financial markets, intermediaries, and intertemporal smoothing. *Journal of Political Economy, 105*(3), 523–546.

Alogoskoufis, S., & Langfield, S. (2019). Regulating the doom loop. Available at SSRN 3453158.

Anand, K., Duley, C., & Gai, P. (2022). Cybersecurity and financial stability.

Anderson, R., & Moore, T. (2006). The economics of information security. *Science, 314*(5799), 610–613.

Angelini, P., Grande, G., & Panetta, F. (2014). The negative feedback loop between banks and sovereigns. Bank of Italy Occasional Paper (213).

Angeloni, I., Kashyap, A. K., & Mojon, B. (2003). *Monetary policy transmission in the euro area: A study by the eurosystem monetary transmission network*. Cambridge University Press.

Anginer, D., & Demirgüç-Kunt, A. (2018). Bank runs and moral hazard: A review of deposit insurance. World Bank Policy Research Working Paper (8589).

Anginer, D., & Warburton, A. J. (2011). The end of market discipline? Investor expectations of implicit state guarantees. Technical report, Syracuse University Working Paper.

Aramonte, S., Schrimpf, A., & Shin, H. S. (2022). Non-bank financial intermediaries and financial stability. In *The research handbook of financial markets*.

Arestis, P., Demetriades, P. O., & Luintel, K. B. (2001). Financial development and economic growth: The role of stock markets. *Journal of Money, Credit and Banking, 33*(1), 16–41.

N. Abidi et al., *Why Do Banks Fail and What to Do About It*, Contributions to Finance and Accounting, https://doi.org/10.1007/978-3-031-52311-3

Arrow, K. J., & Debreu, G. (1954). Existence of an equilibrium for a competitive economy. *Econometrica: Journal of the Econometric Society, 22*(3), 265–290. https://doi.org/10.2307/1907353.

Avdjiev, S., Giudici, P., & Spelta, A. (2019). Measuring contagion risk in international banking. *Journal of Financial Stability, 42*, 36–51.

Avgouleas, E., & Goodhart, C. (2015). Critical reflections on bank bail-ins. *Journal of Financial Regulation, 1*(1), 3–29.

Avgouleas, E., & Goodhart, C. (2016). An anatomy of bank bail-ins why the eurozone needs a fiscal backstop for the banking sector. *European Economy* (2), 75.

Baglioni, A. (2009). Liquidity crunch in the interbank market: Is it credit or liquidity risk. Technical report, or both.

Bains, P., Sugimoto, N., & Wilson, C. (2022). Bigtech in financial services: Regulatory approaches and architecture. international monetary fund.

Barba Navaretti, G., Calzolari, G., Pozzolo, A., et al. (2016). Bail-in, up to a point. *European Economy, 2016*(2), 9–32.

Barth, J. R., Caprio, G., & Levine, R. (2008). *Rethinking bank regulation: Till angels govern*. Cambridge University Press.

Battiston, S., Monasterolo, I., Riahi, K., & van Ruijven, B. J. (2021). Accounting for finance is key for climate mitigation pathways. *Science, 372*(6545), 918–920.

Beau, E., Hill, J., Hussain, T., & Nixon, D. (2014). Bank funding costs: What are they, what determines them and why do they matter? *Bank of England Quarterly Bulletin* Q4.

Bech, M. L., & Garratt, R. (2017). Central bank cryptocurrencies. *BIS Quarterly Review September*.

Ben Bouheni, F. (2014). Banking regulation and supervision: Can it enhance stability in Europe? *Journal of Financial Economic Policy, 6*(3), 244–269.

Bengtsson, E. (2016). Investment funds, shadow banking and systemic risk. *Journal of Financial Regulation and Compliance, 24*(1), 60–73.

Beniak, P. (2019). Central bank digital currency and monetary policy: A literature review.

Berg, T., Burg, V., Gombović, A., & Puri, M. (2018). On the rise of the FinTechs–credit scoring using digital footprints. federal deposit insurance corporation. *Center for Financial Research WP, 4*, 2018.

Berg, T., Carletti, E., Claessens, S., Krahnen, J. P., Monasterolo, I., & Pagano, M. (2023). Climate regulation and financial risk: The challenge of policy uncertainty.

Bernanke, B. S. (2013). *The Federal Reserve and the financial crisis*. Princeton University Press.

Bindseil, U. (2004). *Monetary policy implementation: Theory, past, and present*. OUP Oxford.

Bindseil, U. (2014). *Monetary policy operations and the financial system*. OUP Oxford.

Blair, C. E., Carns, F., & Kushmeider, R. M. (2006). Instituting a deposit insurance system: Why? How? *Journal of Banking Regulation, 8*, 4–19.

Blanchard, O., Dell Ariccia, G., & Mauro, P. (2010). Rethinking macroeconomic policy. *Revista de Economía Institucional, 12*(22), 61–82.

BoE. (2019). The bank of England's approach to assessing resolvability.

Boffo, R., & Patalano, R. (2020). *ESG investing: Practices, progress and challenges*. OECD Paris.

Borio, C. E., Farag, M., & Tarashev, N. A. (2020). Post-crisis international financial regulatory reforms: A primer.

Bossone, B. (1999). What makes banks special? A study of banking, finance, and economic development. *A Study of Banking, Finance, and Economic Development*.

Branzoli, N., Rainone, E., & Supino, I. (2023). The role of banks' technology adoption in credit markets during the pandemic. *Bank of Italy Temi di Discussione (Working Paper) No*, 1406.

Brei, M., Gambacorta, L., Lucchetta, M., & Parigi, B. M. (2020). Bad bank resolutions and bank lending.

Brewer III, E., Genay, H., Hunter, W. C., & Kaufman, G. G. (2003). The value of banking relationships during a financial crisis: Evidence from failures of Japanese banks. *Journal of the Japanese and International Economies, 17*(3), 233–262.

Brierley, P. G. (2017). Ending too-big-to-fail: Progress since the crisis, the importance of loss-absorbing capacity and the UK approach to resolution. *European Business Organization Law Review, 18*, 457–477.

Brunnermeier, M. K. (2009). Deciphering the liquidity and credit crunch 2007–2008. *Journal of Economic Perspectives, 23*(1), 77–100.

Brunnermeier, M. K., James, H., & Landau, J.-P. (2019). The digitalization of money. Technical report, National Bureau of Economic Research.

Buchak, G., Matvos, G., Piskorski, T., & Seru, A. (2018). Fintech, regulatory arbitrage, and the rise of shadow banks. *Journal of Financial Economics, 130*(3), 453–483.

Buchetti, B., Miquel-Flores, I., Perdichizzi, S., & Reghezza, A. (2023). Greening the economy: How public-guaranteed loans influence firm-level resource allocation. Available at SSRN 4508502.

Buchetti, B., & Santoni, A. (2022a). Corporate governance (CG) theories and the banking sector. In *Corporate governance in the banking sector: Theory, supervision, ESG and real banking failures* (pp. 19–36). Springer.

Buchetti, B., & Santoni, A. (2022b). Corporate governance in the banking sector (CGBS): A literature review. In *Corporate governance in the banking sector: Theory, supervision, ESG and real banking failures* (pp. 37–91).

Buchetti, B., & Santoni, A. (2022c). *Corporate governance in the banking sector: Theory, supervision, ESG and real banking failures*. Springer Nature.

Buchetti, B., & Santoni, A. (2022d). The meaning of corporate governance and its role in the banking sector. In *Corporate governance in the banking sector: Theory, supervision, ESG and real banking failures* (pp. 1–18). Springer.

Buera, F. J., & Moll, B. (2012). Aggregate implications of a credit crunch. Technical report, National Bureau of Economic Research.

Calello, P., & Ervin, W. (2010). From bail-out to bail-in. *The Economist, 28*(1).

Cappiello, L., Holm-Hadulla, F., Maddaloni, A., Arts, L., Meme, N., Migiakis, P., Behrens, C., Moura, A., Corradin, S., Ferrando, A., et al. (2021). Non-bank financial intermediation in the euro area: Implications for monetary policy transmission and key vulnerabilities.

Carlstrom, C. T. (1988). Bank runs, deposit insurance, and bank regulation, part I. *Economic Commentary*.

Carmassi, J., Herring, R. J., et al. (2015). Corporate structures, transparency and resolvability of global systemically important banks. Technical report.

Chakrabarty, B., & Zhang, G. (2012). Credit contagion channels: Market microstructure evidence from Lehman Brothers' Bankruptcy. *Financial Management, 41*(2), 320–343.

Chava, S., & Purnanandam, A. (2011). The effect of banking crisis on bank-dependent borrowers. *Journal of Financial Economics, 99*(1), 116–135.

Cingano, F., Manaresi, F., & Sette, E. (2016). Does credit crunch investment down? New evidence on the real effects of the bank-lending channel. *The Review of Financial Studies, 29*(10), 2737–2773.

Clerc, L., Giovannini, A., Langfield, S., Peltonen, T., Portes, R., & Scheicher, M. (2016). Indirect contagion: The policy problem. *ESRB: Occasional Paper Series*.

Constâncio, V. (2012). Contagion and the European debt crisis financial stability review no. 16 April.

Cont, R., & Schaanning, E. (2019). Monitoring indirect contagion. *Journal of Banking & Finance, 104*, 85–102.

Cowan, A. R., & Salotti, V. (2015). The resolution of failed banks during the crisis: Acquirer performance and fdic guarantees, 2008–2013. *Journal of Banking & Finance, 54*, 222–238.

Crosetti, S. (2018). Towards the BRRD2: The proposals to harmonise the MREL requirement with the TLAC principles. *Amministrazione in cammino, 13*(1), 1–25.

Crosetti, S., & Di Gaspare, G. (2020). Covid-19: How to channel liquidity to real economy. *Amministrazione in cammino, 15*(1), 1–11.

Crosetti, S., Garonna, P., & Marcelletti, A. (2021). Deposit insurance in the European union: In search of a third way. *LUISS School of Government Working Paper Series* (SOG-WP64/2021):1–65.

Dabrowski, M. (2017). Potential impact of financial innovation on financial services and monetary policy. *CASE Research Paper* (488).

De Bruyckere, V., Gerhardt, M., Schepens, G., & Vander Vennet, R. (2013). Bank/sovereign risk spillovers in the European debt crisis. *Journal of Banking & Finance, 37*(12), 4793–4809.

Demekas, M. D. G., & Grippa, P. (2021). *Financial regulation, climate change, and the transition to a low-carbon economy: A survey of the issues*. International Monetary Fund.

Demirgüç-Kunt, A., Kane, E., & Laeven, L. (2015). Deposit insurance around the world: A comprehensive analysis and database. *Journal of Financial Stability, 20*, 155–183.

Dewatripont, M. (2014). European banking: Bailout, bail-in and state aid control. *International Journal of Industrial Organization, 34*, 37–43.

Dewatripont, M., Praet, P., & Sapir, A. (2023). The silicon valley bank collapse: Prudential regulation lessons for Europe and the world. VoxEU.org 20.

Diamond, D. W., & Dybvig, P. H. (1983). Bank runs, deposit insurance, and liquidity. *Journal of Political Economy, 91*(3), 401–419.

Diamond, D. W., & Dybvig, P. H. (1986). Banking theory, deposit insurance, and bank regulation. *The Journal of Business, 59*(1), 55–68.

Dinica, V. (2004). The evolution of national policy implementation structures under the Europeanization of policy-making. *CSTM Studies and Reports, 217*(1381-6357), 1–12.

Do, C. T., Tran, N. H., Hong, C., Kamhoua, C. A., Kwiat, K. A., Blasch, E., Ren, S., Pissinou, N., & Iyengar, S. S. (2017). Game theory for cyber security and privacy. *ACM Computing Surveys (CSUR), 50*(2), 1–37.

Dobler, M., Moretti, M., & Piris, A. (2021). Confronting banking crises: Lessons from the field. *Annual Review of Financial Economics, 13*, 179–199.

Driscoll, J. C., & Judson, R. (2013). Sticky deposit rates. Available at SSRN 2241531.

Duffie, D., & Younger, J. (2019). *Cyber runs*. Brookings.

Dumontaux, N., & Pop, A. (2013). Understanding the market reaction to shockwaves: Evidence from the failure of Lehman Brothers. *Journal of Financial Stability, 9*(3), 269–286.

Dunn, K., Kohlbeck, M., & Smith, T. (2016). Bargain purchase gains in the acquisitions of failed banks. *Journal of Accounting, Auditing & Finance, 31*(3), 388–412.

Dupont, B. (2019). The cyber-resilience of financial institutions: Significance and applicability. *Journal of Cybersecurity, 5*(1), tyz013.

Duquerroy, A., Matray, A., & Saidi, F. (2020). Sticky deposit rates and allocative effects of monetary policy.

EBA. (2020). Application of early intervention measures in the European union according to articles 27–29 of the BRRD.

EBA. (2021). Report on the application of early intervention measures in the eu.

EBA. (2022). Other systemically important institutions (O-SIIs).

Edwards, J., & Ogilvie, S. (1996). Universal banks and German industrialization: A reappraisal. *Economic History Review* 427–446.

Eisenbach, T. M., Kovner, A., & Lee, M. J. (2022). Cyber risk and the us financial system: A pre-mortem analysis. *Journal of Financial Economics, 145*(3), 802–826.

El-Erian, M. A. (2017). *The only game in town: Central banks, instability, and recovering from another collapse*. Random House Trade Paperbacks.

Fama, E. F., & Jensen, M. C. (1983). Separation of ownership and control. *The Journal of Law and Economics, 26*(2), 301–325.

Farhi, E., & Tirole, J. (2018). Deadly embrace: Sovereign and financial balance sheets doom loops. *The Review of Economic Studies, 85*(3), 1781–1823.

FDIC. (2019). *Resolution handbooks*.

Fell, J., Grodzicki, M., Martin, R., O'Brien, E., et al. (2016). Addressing market failures in the resolution of non-performing loans in the euro area. *Financial Stability Review*, 2.

Fell, J., Moldovan, C., & O'Brien, E. (2017). C resolving non-performing loans: A role for securitisation and other financial structures? *Chart, 100*, 2.

Fender, I., & Mitchell, J. (2009). The future of securitisation: How to align incentives? *BIS Quarterly Review*.

Ferguson, N. (2008). *The ascent of money: A financial history of the world*. Penguin.

Florackis, C., Louca, C., Michaely, R., & Weber, M. (2023). Cybersecurity risk. *The Review of Financial Studies, 36*(1), 351–407.

Foglia, M., Ortolano, A., Di Febo, E., & Angelini, E. (2020). Bad or good neighbours: A spatial financial contagion study. *Studies in Economics and Finance, 37*(4), 753–776.

Freixas, X. (1999). Optimal bail out policy, conditionality and creative ambiguity.

Friedman, M. (2007). The social responsibility of business is to increase its profits. In *Corporate ethics and corporate governance* (pp. 173–178). Springer.

Friedman, M., & Schwartz, A. J. (1963). *A Monetary history of the US 1867–1960*. Princeton University Press.

FSB. (2011). Key attributes of effective resolution regimes for financial institutions.

FSB. (2013). Guidance on identification of critical functions and critical shared services.

FSB. (2015). Principles on loss-absorbing and recapitalisation capacity of G-SIBs in resolution, total loss-absorbing capacity (TLAC) term sheet.

FSB. (2016). Guidance on arrangements to support operational continuity in resolution.

FSB. (2017a). Guiding principles on the internal total loss-absorbing capacity of G-SIBs ('internal TLAC').

FSB. (2017b). List of global systemically important banks (G-SIBs). http://www.fsb.org/wp-content/uploads/P211117-1.pdf

FSB. (2018a). Funding strategy elements of an implementable resolution plan.

FSB. (2018b). Principles on bail-in execution.

FSB. (2019). Review of the technical implementation of the total loss-absorbing capacity (TLAC) standard.

Fulford, S. L. (2015). How important are banks for development? National banks in the united states, 1870–1900. *Review of Economics and Statistics, 97*(5), 921–938.

Furukawa, K., Ichiue, H., Kimura, Y., & Shiraki, N. (2021). *Too-big-to-fail reforms and systemic risk*. Bank of Japan.

Gandhi, P., & Lustig, H. (2015). Size anomalies in U.S. bank stock returns. *The Journal of Finance, 70*, 733–768.

Galparsoro, I., Korta, M., Subirana, I., Borja, Á., Menchaca, I., Solaun, O., ... & Bald, J. (2021a). A new framework and tool for ecological risk assessment of wave energy converters projects. *Renewable and Sustainable Energy Reviews, 151*, 111539.

Galparsoro, I., Pinarbaşi, K., Gissi, E., Culhane, F., Gacutan, J., Kotta, J., Cabana, D., Wanke, S., Aps, R., Bazzucchi, D., Cozzolino, G., Custodio, M., Fetissov, M., Inácio, M., Jernberg, S., Piazzi, A., Paudel, K. P., Ziemba, A. & Depellegrin, D. (2021b). Operationalisation of ecosystem services in support of ecosystem-based marine spatial planning: insights into needs and recommendations. *Marine Policy, 131*, 104609.

Gerschenkron, A. (2015). *Economic backwardness in historical perspective (1962)*. Cambridge MA.

Gibbons, J. S. (1859). *The Banks of New York, their dealers, the clearing house and the panic of 1857.... Thirty illustrations by Herrick*. Appleton.

Gilbart, J. W. (1866). *The history and principles of banking: The laws of the currency, etc.* (Vol. 4). Bell & Daldy.

Giliberto, S. M., & Varaiya, N. P. (1989). The winner's curse and bidder competition in acquisitions: Evidence from failed bank auctions. *The Journal of Finance, 44*(1), 59–75.

Gogolin, F., Lim, I., & Vallascas, F. (2021). Cyberattacks on small banks and the impact on local banking markets. Available at SSRN 3823296.

Goldsmith-Pinkham, P., & Yorulmazer, T. (2010). Liquidity, bank runs, and bailouts: Spillover effects during the northern rock episode. *Journal of Financial Services Research, 37*, 83–98.

Goldstein, M., & Véron, N. (2011). Too big to fail: The transatlantic debate. Peterson Institute for International Economics Working Paper, (11–2).

Gordon, L. A., & Loeb, M. P. (2002). The economics of information security investment. *ACM Transactions on Information and System Security (TISSEC), 5*(4), 438–457.

Gordon, L. A., Loeb, M. P., & Zhou, L. (2020). Integrating cost–benefit analysis into the NIST cybersecurity framework via the Gordon–Loeb model. *Journal of Cybersecurity, 6*(1), tyaa005.

Gorton, G. B. (2010). *Slapped by the invisible hand: The panic of 2007*. Oxford University Press.

Granja, J., Matvos, G., & Seru, A. (2017). Selling failed banks. *The Journal of Finance, 72*(4), 1723–1784.

Greenwood, J., & Jovanovic, B. (1990). Financial development, growth, and the distribution of income. *Journal of Political Economy, 98*(5, Part 1), 1076–1107.

Griffin, P., & Jaffe, A. M. (2022). Challenges for a climate risk disclosure mandate. *Nature Energy, 7*(1), 2–4.

Gropp, R., & Vesala, J. (2004). Deposit insurance, moral hazard and market monitoring. *Review of Finance, 8*(4), 571–602.

Gurley, J. G., Shaw, E. S., & Enthoven, A. C. (1960). Money in a theory of finance. (No Title).

Hadjiemmanuil, C. (2015). Bank stakeholders' mandatory contribution to resolution financing: Principle and ambiguities of bail-in. In *ECB Legal Conference* (pp. 225–248).

Hahn, R., Reimsbach, D., & Schiemann, F. (2015). Organizations, climate change, and transparency: Reviewing the literature on carbon disclosure. *Organization & Environment, 28*(1), 80–102.

Harris, R. V. (2013). Operationalisation of the construct of access to dental care: a position paper and proposed conceptual definitions. *Community Dent Health, 30*(2), 94–101.

Haselmann, R., Krahnen, J. P., Tröger, T., & Wahrenburg, M. (2022). *Institutional protection schemes: What are their differences, strengths, weaknesses, and track records?* Number 88. SAFE White Paper.

Hein, S. E. (1992). A reexamination of the costs and benefits of federal deposit insurance. *Business Economics, 27*, Fasc. 3, 26–31. https://www.proquest.com/scholarly-journals/reexamination-costs-benefits-federal-deposit/docview/199791025/se-2.

Hellwig, M. (1990). *Banking, financial intermediation and corporate finance*. Wirtschaftswissenschaftliches Zentrum der Universität.

Hicks, J. (1935). "a suggestion for simplifying the theory of money", econometrica; as repr. in id. *Critical Essays in Monetary Theory*.

Hirtle, B., Kovner, A., & Plosser, M. (2020). The impact of supervision on bank performance. *The Journal of Finance, 75*(5), 2765–2808.

Hoggson, N. F. (1926). *Banking through the ages*. Dodd, Mead.

Holmstrom, B., & Tirole, J. (1997). Financial intermediation, loanable funds, and the real sector. *The Quarterly Journal of Economics, 112*(3), 663–691.

Huang, M. H., & Goodhart, M. C. (1999). *A model of the lender of last resort*. International Monetary Fund.

Huber, M., van Vliet, M., Giezenberg, M., Winkens, B., Heerkens, Y., Dagnelie, P. C., & Knottnerus, J. A. (2016). Towards a 'patient-centred' operationalisation of the new dynamic concept of health: a mixed methods study. *BMJ Open, 6*(1), e010091.

Huizinga, H. (2022). *Institutional protection schemes: What are their differences, strengths, weaknesses, and track records?* Number 22. ECOFIN In-depth analysis.

Hull, J. C. (2009). The credit crunch of 2007: What went wrong? Why? What lessons can be learned? In *The first credit market turmoil of the 21st century: Implications for public policy* (pp. 161–174). World Scientific.

Hüpkes, E. H. et al. (2016). *Towards a global solution to a global problem*. World Scientific Publishing Singapore.

Ihrig, J. E., Weinbach, G. C., Wolla, S. A., et al. (2021). Teaching the linkage between banks and the fed: Rip money multiplier. *Page One Economics Newsletter*.

Iyer, R., Peydró, J.-L., da Rocha-Lopes, S., & Schoar, A. (2014). Interbank liquidity crunch and the firm credit crunch: Evidence from the 2007–2009 crisis. *The Review of Financial Studies, 27*(1), 347–372.

Jackson, M. O., & Pernoud, A. (2021). Systemic risk in financial networks: A survey. *Annual Review of Economics, 13*, 171–202.

James, S., & Quaglia, L. (2020). *The UK and multi-level financial regulation: From post-crisis reform to Brexit*. Oxford University Press.

Jamilov, R., Rey, H., & Tahoun, A. (2021). The anatomy of cyber risk. Technical report, National Bureau of Economic Research.

Jensen, M. C., & Meckling, W. H. (1979). Rights and production functions: An application to labor-managed firms and codetermination. *The Journal of Business, 52*(4), 469–506. https://www.jstor.org/stable/2352442.

Jiang, E. X., Matvos, G., Piskorski, T., & Seru, A. (2023). Monetary tightening and us bank fragility in 2023: Mark-to-market losses and uninsured depositor runs? Technical report, National Bureau of Economic Research.

Kacperczyk, M., & Peydró, J.-L. (2021). Carbon emissions and the bank-lending channel. Technical report, Centre for Economic Policy Research.

Kandrac, J., & Schlusche, B. (2021). The effect of bank supervision and examination on risk taking: Evidence from a natural experiment. *The Review of Financial Studies, 34*(6), 3181–3212.

Kashyap, A. K., & Wetherilt, A. (2019). Some principles for regulating cyber risk. In *AEA Papers and Proceedings* (Vol. 109, pp. 482–487). American Economic Association.

Kaufman, G. G. (2014). Too big to fail in banking: What does it mean? *Journal of Financial Stability, 13*, 214–223.

Kazandjieva-Yordanova, I. P. (2017). Does the too big to fail doctrine have a future. *Economic Alternatives, 1*, 51–78.

Keynes, J. M., Moggridge, D. E., Johnson, E. S., et al. (1971). *The collected writings of John Maynard Keynes* (Vol. 30). Macmillan London.

Kindleberger, C. (1993). *A financial history of Western Europe*. Oxford University Press.

Kindleberger, C. P., Aliber, R. Z., & Solow, R. M. (2005). *Manias, panics, and crashes: A history of financial crises* (Vol. 7). Palgrave Macmillan London.

King, P., & Tarbert, H. (2011). Basel III: An overview. *Banking & Financial Services Policy Report, 30*(5), 1–18.

Klimek, P., Poledna, S., Farmer, J. D., & Thurner, S. (2015). To bail-out or to bail-in? Answers from an agent-based model. *Journal of Economic Dynamics and Control, 50*, 144–154.

König, E. (2021). Single point of entry—a resolution strategy addressing the home—host issue in Europe's banking union.

Kumar, P., Debele, S. E., Sahani, J., Aragão, L., Barisani, F., Basu, B., Bucchignani, E., Charizopoulos, N., Di Sabatino, S., Domeneghetti, D., Sorolla-Edo, A., Finer, L., Gallotti, G., Juch, S., Leo, L. S., Loupis, M., Mickovski, B., Rutzinger, M., Basu, A. S., Shah, M. A. R., Soini, K., Stefanopoulou, M., Toth, E., Ukonmaanaho, L., Vranic, S., & Zieher, T. (2020). Towards an operationalisation of nature-based solutions for natural hazards. *Science of the Total Environment, 731*, 138855.

Laboureix, D., & Decroocq, V. (2016). Enhancing the capacity to apply a bail-in through the MREL setting. *European Economy*, (2), 117.

Laeven, L. (2011). Banking crises: A review. *Annual Review of Financial Economics, 3*(1), 17–40.

Lawson, E., Farmani, R., Woodley, E., & Butler, D. (2020). A resilient and sustainable water sector: barriers to the operationalisation of resilience. *Sustainability, 12*(5), 1797.

Leiss, W. (2011). *The doom loop in the financial sector: And other black holes of risk*. University of Ottawa Press.

Levine, M. R. (2021). *Finance, growth, and inequality*. International Monetary Fund.

Levine, R. (1998). The legal environment, banks, and long-run economic growth. *Journal of Money, Credit and Banking, 30*(3), Part 2, 596–613. https://doi.org/10.2307/2601259.

Levine, R. (1999). Law, finance, and economic growth. *Journal of Financial Intermediation, 8*(1–2), 8–35.

Levine, R., & Zervos, S. (1998). Stock markets, banks, and economic growth. *American Economic Review, 88*(3), 537–558. http://www.jstor.org/stable/116848.

Li, L., Strahan, P. E., & Zhang, S. (2020). Banks as lenders of first resort: Evidence from the covid-19 crisis. *The Review of Corporate Finance Studies, 9*(3), 472–500.

Liang, H.-Y., & Reichert, A. K. (2012). The impact of banks and non-bank financial institutions on economic growth. *The Service Industries Journal, 32*(5), 699–717.

Lindgren, C. J. (1999). Financial sector crisis and restructuring: Lessons from Asia.

Lo, A. W. (2012). Reading about the financial crisis: A twenty-one-book review. *Journal of Economic Literature, 50*(1), 151–178.

Locatelli, R., Schena, C., Coletti, E., & Dabbene, F. (2018). Gestione e costi delle crisi bancarie dopo la brrd. *Banca Impresa Società, 37*(1), 27–78.

Lucchetti, R., Papi, L., & Zazzaro, A. (2001). Banks' inefficiency and economic growth: A micro-macro approach. *Scottish Journal of Political Economy, 48*(4), 400–424.

Machado, P. (2016). Bail-in as new paradigm for bank resolution: Discretion and the duty of care. *e-Pública, 3*(1), 29–49.

Mariathasan, M., Merrouche, O., & Werger, C. (2014). Bailouts and moral hazard: How implicit government guarantees affect financial stability. Available at SSRN 2481861.

Martin, C., Puri, M., & Ufier, A. (2016). On deposit stability in failing banks. Available at SSRN 2898425.

Mayer, C. (1988). New issues in corporate finance. *European Economic Review, 32*(5), 1167–1183.

McGuire, C. L. (2012). Simple tools to assist in the resolution of troubled banks.

Merler, S., Pisani-Ferry, J., et al. (2012). Hazardous tango: Sovereign-bank interdependence and financial stability in the euro area. *Financial Stability Review, 16*, 201–210.

Merton, R. C. (1977). An analytic derivation of the cost of deposit insurance and loan guarantees an application of modern option pricing theory. *Journal of Banking & Finance, 1*, 3–11.

Merton, R. (1993). Operation and regulation in financial intermediation: A functional perspective [w:] operation and regulation of financial markets, red. *Englund. Stockholm: The Economic Council.*

Merton, R. C. (1990). The financial system and economic performance. *Journal of Financial Services Research, 4*(4), 263–300.

Mesnard, B., Margerit, A., Power, C., & Magnus, M. (2016). Non-performing loans in the banking union: Stocktaking and challenges. *Briefing EU Commission.*

Miglionico, A. (2019). Restructuring non-performing loans for bank recovery: Private workouts and securitisation mechanisms. *European Company and Financial Law Review, 16*(6), 746–770.

Milic, D. (2021). The impact of non-banking financial institutions on monetary policy transmission in euro area. *Empirical Economics, 61*(4), 1779–1817.

Milne, D., Niskanen, E., & Verhoef, E. (2000). Operationalisation of marginal cost pricing within urban transport. Research Reports 63, VATT Institute for Economic Research.

Mishkin, F. S. (2007). *Monetary policy strategy*. MIT Press.

Mishkin, F. S., & Eakins, S. G. (2006). *Financial markets and institutions*. Pearson Education India.

Mitchener, K. J., & Trebesch, C. (2021). Sovereign debt in the 21st century. Technical report, National Bureau of Economic Research.

Miwa, Y., & Ramseyer, J. M. (2002). Banks and economic growth: Implications from Japanese history. *The Journal of Law and Economics, 45*(1), 127–164.

Mizen, P. (2008). The credit crunch of 2007–2008: A discussion of the background, market reactions, and policy responses. *Federal Reserve Bank of St. Louis Review, 90*(September/October 2008).

Monasterolo, I. (2020). Climate change and the financial system. *Annual Review of Resource Economics, 12*, 299–320.

Monasterolo, I., Mandel, A., Battiston, S., Mazzocchetti, A., Oppermann, K., Coony, J., Stretton, S., Stewart, F., Dunz, N., & Max, F. (2022). The role of green financial sector initiatives in the low-carbon transition: A theory of change. Technical report, World Bank.

Morgan, D. P. (2002). Rating banks: risk and uncertainty in an opaque industry *American Economic Review, 92*(4), 874–888.

Mortágua, M., & Solipa, I. (2022). Reviving financial markets—a critical assessment of the single resolution mechanism. *International Review of Applied Economics, 36*(3), 403–423.

Müller, J. (2006). Interbank credit lines as a channel of contagion. *Journal of Financial Services Research, 29*, 37–60.

Murphy, C. C. (2014). Counter-Terrorism Law and Policy: Operationalisation and Normalisation of Exceptional Law after the "War on Terror". In Arcarazo, D. A., & Murphy, C. C., (Eds). EU Security and Justice Law: After Lisbon and Stockholm, Hart Publishing.

O'hara, M., & Shaw, W. (1990). Deposit insurance and wealth effects: The value of being "too big to fail". *The Journal of Finance, 45*(5), 1587–1600.

Osmundsen, T. C., Amundsen, V. S., Alexander, K. A., Asche, F., Bailey, J., Finstad, B., Olsen, M. S., Hernández, K., & Salgado, H. (2020). The operationalisation of sustainability: Sustainable aquaculture production as defined by certification schemes. *Global Environmental Change, 60*, 102025.

Petitjean, M. (2013). Bank failures and regulation: A critical review. *Journal of Financial Regulation and Compliance, 21*(1), 16–38.

Pierri, N., & Timmer, Y. (2022). The importance of technology in banking during a crisis. *Journal of Monetary Economics, 128*, 88–104.

Prasad, E. (2017). *Gaining currency: The rise of the renminbi*. Oxford University Press.

Qian, Y. (2023). Evaluating the potential of asset management companies to relieve global debt distress. *Global Development Policy Center* (Global China Initiative Working Paper N.28):1–30.

Quaglia, L., & Spendzharova, A. (2019). Regulators and the quest for coherence in finance: The case of loss absorbing capacity for banks. *Public Administration, 97*(3), 499–512.

Raimondo, C., & Tubi, A. (2016). Band banks out, GACS in. *International Financial Law Review, 35*, 62.

Rajan, R. G. (2006). Has finance made the world riskier? *European Financial Management, 12*(4), 499–533.

Ramakrishna, S. P. (2023). Climate change risk management in banks: The next paradigm. In *Climate change risk management in banks*. De Gruyter.

Roncoroni, A., Battiston, S., D'Errico, M., Hałaj, G., & Kok, C. (2021). Interconnected banks and systemically important exposures. *Journal of Economic Dynamics and Control, 133*, 104266.

Rostagno, M., Altavilla, C., Carboni, G., Lemke, W., Motto, R., Saint Guilhem, A., & Yiangou, J. (2021). *Monetary policy in times of crisis: A tale of two decades of the European Central Bank*. Oxford University Press.

Rousseau, P. L., & Sylla, R. (2003). Financial systems, economic growth, and globalization. In *Globalization in historical perspective* (pp. 373–416). University of Chicago Press.

Salleo, C. (2015). Loss absorbing capital and bank asset allocation. *European Economy*, (1), 95.

Sandberg, L. G. (1978). Banking and economic growth in Sweden before world war I. *The Journal of Economic History, 38*(3), 650–680.

Schiavo, G. L. (2016). *The role of financial stability in EU law and policy*. Kluwer Law International BV.

Schich, S. (2009). Financial crisis: Deposit insurance and related financial safety net aspects. *OECD Journal: Financial Market Trends, 2008*(2), 1–39.

Schoenmaker, D. (2016). *The banking union: An overview and open issues*. Springer.

SRB. (2016). Introduction to resolution planning. https://www.srb.europa.eu/system/files/media/document/intro_resplanning.pdf

SRB. (2019a). Framework for valuation: February 2019.

SRB. (2019b). Public interest assessment: SRB approach. *Paper presented by the Single Resolution Board*, 28.

SRB. (2020). SRB expectations for banks.

SRB. (2021a). Operational guidance for banks on separability for transfer tools.

SRB. (2021b). Work programme. https://www.srb.europa.eu/system/files/media/document/2021-11-26_Work-Programme-2022.pdf
SRB. (2023). Work programme.
Stern, G., & Feldman, R. (2004). Too big to fail: The hazard of bank Bailouts–Brookings Institution Press. Washington DC.
Stern, T. (2014). Regulating liquidity risks within "institutional protection schemes". *Beijing Law Review, 5*, 210.
Stiglitz, J. E., Stern, N., Duan, M., Edenhofer, O., Giraud, G., Heal, G. M., La Rovere, E. L., Morris, A., Moyer, E., Pangestu, M., et al. (2017). Report of the high-level commission on carbon prices.
Stucki, G., Rubinelli, S., & Bickenbach, J. (2020). We need an operationalisation, not a definition of health. *Disability and Rehabilitation, 42*(3), 442–444.
Thakor, A. V. (2014). Bank capital and financial stability: an economic tradeoff or a faustian bargain? *Annual Review of Financial Economics, 6*, 185–223.
Toader, O. (2015). Quantifying and explaining implicit public guarantees for European banks. *International Review of Financial Analysis, 41*, 136–147.
Triner, G. D. (2000). *Banking and economic development: Brazil, 1889–1930*. Springer.
Varian, H. R. (2014). Beyond big data. *Business Economics, 49*(1), 27–31.
Verschuere, B., & Vancoppenolle, D. (2012). Policy-making in an era of agencification: An exploration of task divisions between politicians, core departments and public agencies. *Policy and Society, 31*(3), 249–258.
Vives, X. (2019). Digital disruption in banking. *Annual Review of Financial Economics, 11*, 243–272.
von Hayek, F. A. (1951). Prices and production. (No Title).
Walsh, C. E. (2017). *Monetary theory and policy*. MIT Press.
Watanabe, W. (2007). Prudential regulation and the "credit crunch": Evidence from Japan. *Journal of Money, Credit and Banking, 39*(2–3), 639–665.
Welburn, J. W., & Strong, A. M. (2022). Systemic cyber risk and aggregate impacts. *Risk Analysis, 42*(8), 1606–1622.
Werner, R. A. (2005). *New paradign in macroeconomics* (Vol. 213). Springer.
Werner, R. A. (2014). How do banks create money, and why can other firms not do the same? An explanation for the coexistence of lending and deposit-taking. *International Review of Financial Analysis, 36*, 71–77.
Wiggins, R., & Metrick, A. (2014). The Lehman Brothers Bankruptcy H: The global contagion. *Yale Program on Financial Stability Case Study*.
Wojcik, K.-P. (2016). Bail-in in the banking union. *Common Market Law Review*, 53(1).
Zagorsky, J. (2018). The curse of cash, by Kenneth S. Rogoff (Princeton University Press, Princeton, NJ, 2016). Economic Record.

GPSR Compliance

The European Union's (EU) General Product Safety Regulation (GPSR) is a set of rules that requires consumer products to be safe and our obligations to ensure this.

If you have any concerns about our products, you can contact us on ProductSafety@springernature.com

In case Publisher is established outside the EU, the EU authorized representative is:

Springer Nature Customer Service Center GmbH
Europaplatz 3
69115 Heidelberg, Germany

Batch number: 08246518

Printed by Printforce, the Netherlands